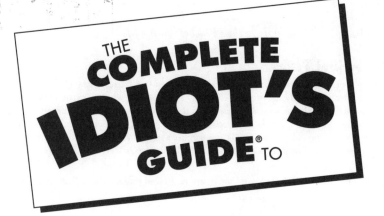

Sharks

by Mary L. Peachin

ALPHA

A Pearson Education Company

Lovingly to the "Peaches" in my life.

Copyright © 2003 by Mary L. Peachin

International Standard Book Number: 0-02-864438-7
Library of Congress Catalog Card Number: 2002115298

05   04   03   8   7   6   5   4   3   2   1

Interpretation of the printing code: The rightmost number of the first series of numbers is the year of the book's printing; the rightmost number of the second series of numbers is the number of the book's printing. For example, a printing code of 03-1 shows that the first printing occurred in 2003.

Printed in the United States of America

Note: This publication contains the opinions and ideas of its author. It is intended to provide helpful and informative material on the subject matter covered. It is sold with the understanding that the author and publisher are not engaged in rendering professional services in the book. If the reader requires personal assistance or advice, a competent professional should be consulted.

The author and publisher specifically disclaim any responsibility for any liability, loss, or risk, personal or otherwise, which is incurred as a consequence, directly or indirectly, of the use and application of any of the contents of this book.

For marketing and publicity, please call: 317-581-3722

The publisher offers discounts on this book when ordered in quantity for bulk purchases and special sales.

For sales within the United States, please contact: Corporate and Government Sales, 1-800-382-3419 or corpsales@pearsontechgroup.com

Outside the United States, please contact: International Sales, 317-581-3793 or international@pearsontechgroup.com

Publisher: *Marie Butler-Knight*
Product Manager: *Phil Kitchel*
Managing Editor: *Jennifer Chisholm*
Senior Acquisitions Editor: *Renee Wilmeth*
Development Editor: *Michael Koch*
Copy Editor: *Heather Stith*
Illustrator: *Chris Eliopoulos*
Cover/Book Designer: *Trina Wurst*
Indexer: *Tonya Heard*
Layout/Proofreading: *Angela Calvert, Megan Douglass*

Contents at a Glance

Contents

Foreword

Few animals generate as intense emotion and interest from humans as sharks. Sure, many domesticated animals, such as fowl, swine, goats, and cattle, have played important and continuous roles in human cultures for centuries. Working animals and pets—dogs and cats in particular—clearly are respected and even revered by segments of humanity. Still, when it comes down to how humans perceive and react to animals, something separates sharks from the rest of the world's biota.

The fear of getting eaten is mostly responsible for people's attitude toward sharks. Although numerous animals bite and occasionally kill humans, only a few actually attack humans as an act of predation. The large cats (lions and tigers in particular) probably are more dangerous than the handful of shark species most commonly implicated in feeding attacks on humans, but these felines are more limited in geographical distribution and, of course, are more visible to humans, who generally can avoid confronting them. Or, if need be, people can even eliminate the threat with a high-powered rifle. Sharks, by contrast, are found in all of the world's seas and are largely unseen by humans visiting a foreign environment.

Hence sharks historically have drawn more attention than most land-based predators. The only other aquatic animals who consider us worthy as a meal are the crocodilians, especially crocodiles and alligators. But these crooked-grinned relics of evolution are prone to sunning themselves on banks, which ruins their image and some of the surprise factor and makes them vulnerable to preemptive strikes by humans. Sharks do not extend us that courtesy.

We fear and hyperbolize what we cannot see or understand. Theories are accepted without proof, stories are embellished, and speculation becomes truth. In an age when mass communication (newspapers and magazines, radio and television, e-mail and the Internet) has facilitated and even promoted the passing of rumors masquerading as fact, an entire generation has grown up with a distorted view of sharks. And so sharks have come to represent what is cutthroat or seamy in our culture: to wit, card shark, pool shark, and loan shark. Similarly, sharks do not inhabit the ocean; they "infest" its waters.

But scientific studies of sharks reveal a very different view of these fish. For instance, sharks have a lot more to fear from humans than humans do from sharks. Each year about 100 million sharks and their relatives, the skates and rays, fall prey to human fishing activities. When one considers that fewer than 10 humans die from shark attack throughout the world annually, the fatality ratio works out to about 10 million to 1! Sharks, the great killing machines of lore, are no match for a baited hook or a well-placed net.

Interestingly, sharks are more like humans in their population dynamics than they are like the fishes they eat. Sharks are slow growers who live a long time. Sexual maturity is achieved relatively late in life, fertilization is internal, young are nurtured in the mother during a prolonged gestation period in most species, and females generally wait a year between pregnancies. So once a population "crashes," recovery is exceedingly slow and is generally measured in decades.

Sharks have been evolving for millions of years, and they are blessed with an amazing array of adaptations that befit their position as apex predators of the sea. More worthy of awe than hatred, respect than fear, sharks are finally being viewed in a rational manner. Mary L. Peachin has done a wonderful job introducing these magnificent creatures to the nonscientist—read on and learn all about them!

George H. Burgess
Gainesville, Florida
August 7, 2002

George H. Burgess is an ichthyologist, shark biologist, and Coordinator of Museum Operations of the Florida Museum of Natural History at the University of Florida in Gainesville. He is also director of the International Shark Attack File (ISAF) that is administered jointly by the Florida Museum and the American Elasmobranch Society.

Introduction

During the late 1970s, my husband David and I spent a fall weekend in San Carlos, Mexico. Too active to lounge on a beach, I borrowed a mask, snorkel, and fins and spent two days totally waterlogged, becoming fascinated by the underwater world. That Christmas holiday, David presented me with dive gear and scuba lessons. It would be 100 dives before I encountered my first shark, and my feelings of fear gave way to curiosity. Then curiosity turned into a quest and passion that lead to a 23-year worldwide search for whale sharks.

Afraid of sharks? Me? Well, let me say that I have a healthy respect for them. I'll confess to being probably the only person over 30 who never saw the movie *Jaws*. I simply was afraid that the vision would scare me from the enjoyment of my new passion: scuba diving.

I kept my eyes glued to the reef for first 100 dives. I was afraid I might have a shark encounter. I didn't know how I would react when the inevitabe was bound to happen.

When I did see my first shark, I glued my back to the reef and anxiously watched a reef shark gracefully glide by. Suddenly, the anticipation of shark anxiety dissolved, and like other passionate divers, I wanted more, bigger critters like the hammerhead, and ultimately, the whale shark.

Through countless time zones and across the international date line, for more than 20 years, I searched for more and bigger. I wanted to see sharks on my terms: being at depth and not snorkeling.

The adrenaline still rushes through my body, and at times my heart is in my throat. I've bopped a couple blue sharks on the nose to keep them out of my cage, but throughout the years, although I got out of the water several times (out of due respect), I was never threatened by a shark attack.

No one meeting me in those first years would associate me with shark diving. During the early days, I didn't even share my shark encounters with my family because I didn't want to create any undue anxiety. The closest I came to being exposed as a shark-diving enthusiast was in an article by a San Diego sportswriter. In a story about scuba diving with blue sharks, he described me as a "smiley-face grandmother with silvery hair from Tucson." The latter is true, but I am still waiting for those grandkids. Although I had not been identified by name, Tucsonians who happened to read the article and knew me called to ask if I had been recently diving with sharks in San Diego. My secret was out.

I wear lots of hats: I'm a wife and mother, a community leader, a businesswoman, an adventure travel writer and photographer, and an electronic publisher. But scuba diving continues to be my passion. Living and enjoying each day to its fullest is my goal—may it continue indefinitely.

How This Book Is Organized

This book is divided into five parts:

Part 1, "Introducing Sharks," explains what makes a shark a shark.

Part 2, "Categorizing Sharks," looks at different types of sharks, including the celebrities of the shark world such as the great white (star—or rather villain—of the movie *Jaws*) and the mako.

Part 3, "The Evolution and Life Cycle of Sharks," takes you back in time—about 400 million years to be less than exact—to trace the origins of the shark.

Part 4, "Researching Sharks," describes how scientists are learning to track sharks across vast distances by using tagging and telemetry and what scientists learn from sharks in labs.

Part 5, "Humans and Sharks," takes a look at the actual danger sharks pose to humans and why sharks are not necessarily the most dangerous forms of marine life. If anything, humans are more of a threat to sharks than the other way around.

Extras

Along the way in this book, I throw in extra bits and miscellaneous tasty morsels in the form of four different sidebars:

Taste of the Bizarre

I couldn't resist putting in the oddities and unusual stories about sharks that you'll find in these sidebars.

Shark Lore

Here you'll find anecdotes, legends, and stories that bear on sharks and how humans interact with them.

Shark Facts and Stats

These sidebars offer relevant information and statistics that elaborate on the subject matter presented in the chapter.

What Does It Mean?

Here you'll find definitions of unfamiliar terms used in the text.

Acknowledgments

Without the support of my husband David and my children Suzie and Jeffrey, I could never have been a free spirit, one who searched the oceans of the world chasing whale sharks and getting an adrenaline rush from other species of sharks.

I also would like to thank the late Dick Vonier, then publisher of *Phoenix Magazine*, who inspired my career as a writer/photographer. During a chance encounter in a parking lot during Tucson's summer heat, he asked what I had been up to. When I told him that I had just returned from a shark diving trip, he thought that it was a story he should share with his many readers. That launched my writing career. I also wish to express my appreciation to Beth Deveny, now an editor at *Arizona Highways*, who taught me how to put a sentence together. Other editors along the way who taught me the nuances of travel writing include Sue Giles, editor in chief of *Tucson Lifestyle* along with executive editor Scott Barker. Newspaper travel editors such as Howie Shapiro of the *Philadelphia Inquirer*, Larry Bleiberg of the *Dallas Morning News*, and Randy Curwen of the *Chicago Tribune* also helped me a great deal. Lynn Ferrin, former editor in chief of *VIA* magazine, encouraged me to find a photography agent. I still miss the mentoring of Ted Streshinsky of Photo 20-20 (now Lonely Planet Images).

My friend Mark Kimble, now a big shot at the *Tucson Citizen*, taught me to type and recalls when I couldn't put a sentence together. Recently, while sharing breakfast with friends, he accused me of "attacking" a cinnamon bun like "a shark in chum". Photo editor of the *Tucson Citizen*, P. K. Weis, has always been supportive, and I've always shared a mutual writing admiration with sports columnist Corky Simpson. Thanks to Lisa Gluskin for her editing skills and advice, which have helped me become a better writer. My webmaster, Bruce Nevins, gave me a leg up technically.

I have a wonderful e-mail relationship (we haven't met) with my agent Gene Brissie, who responded to my query and believed in me, and Leslie Horvitz, whose writing and research expertise made this book possible. I can't wait to meet the New York members of my team. Other Alpha teammates include Michael Koch, an editor from Richmond, California, copy editor Heather Stith, and senior acquisitions editor Renee Wilmeth.

Technical support was provided by many, some of them responding with a day's notice. Dr. Don Hunsaker II head of The Environmental Trust, Inc., in San Diego and George Burgess and Alexia Morgan of the Florida Museum of Natural History verified the accuracy of chapter information. Immunologist John Marchalonis, Ph.D., was able to provide expertise on his shark research and suggest other areas where researchers were involved in the study of sharks. Hank Armstrong, Bruce Upton, and Ken Peterson of the Monterrey Bay Aquarium and Angela Nielsen and Takuji Oyama of the Vancouver Aquarium also lent their expertise.

An old dive buddy, Carl Roessler, resurfaced. Carl has encountered and photographed much of the underwater world and shared some of his experiences with incredible photographs for the book. Thanks also to Marc Bernardi of Aquatic Encounters for his help, photographs, enthusiasm, and getting me to the Galapagos in time to finally see the whale shark, Paul Anes of San Diego Shark Diving for reintroducing me to the blue and mako sharks. Finally, photographers Dana Africa, C. S. "Nick" Ferris, friends of Bill Kimball, who sent out a bulletin to his shark diving photographer buddies, and *Sport Fishing* editor in chief, Doug Olander for adding species of their close up encounters for the color photograph insert.

Special Thanks to the Technical Reviewers

The Complete Idiot's Guide to Sharks was reviewed by experts who double-checked the accuracy of what you'll learn here, to help us ensure that this book gives you everything you need to know about sharks. We extend our special thanks to George H. Burgess, Alexia Morgan, Dr. Don Hunsaker II, John Marchalonis, Ph.D., and aquarist Takuji Oyama.

Trademarks

Part 1

Introducing Sharks

Beautiful, elegant, sleek, streamlined—these are not the kind of words that spring readily to mind when you think of sharks, yet they all apply. Sharks are marvels of evolutionary engineering. Feared as man-eaters, dismissed as "trash fish," hunted mercilessly for their fins and cartilage, sharks nonetheless continue to be a subject of mystery and fascination. You're about to discover why.

Tracing Sharks Between Myth and Reality

In This Chapter

- ◆ Why sharks inspire both fascination and fear
- ◆ Shark myths and legends
- ◆ The curious history of human-shark relations
- ◆ Common misconceptions about sharks

Sharks hold a tremendous fascination for people all over the world. Some react with terror; others react with astonishment and curiosity. Children chewing Sharkie candies are as enthralled as seniors when viewing sharks on the Discovery Channel. Sharks have exerted such a hold on people's imagination for millennia that it's no wonder that they have figured in legends and mythical tales of coastal and seafaring peoples, usually in the familiar role as harbingers of disaster or embodiments of evil. Sharks are seen as menacing creatures who stealthily shadow their prey (fish or human), slowly circling in anticipation of a quick kill. For writers as diverse as Edgar Allen Poe and Ernest Hemingway, sharks represented malevolent, even supernatural forces. In some societies, though, sharks have been venerated and regarded as protective spirits. This same ambivalence persists today.

Sharks are not lovable creatures. If unborn pups aren't devoured in the womb, their mom will probably eat them after birth. But at the same time we need to recognize their role as an apex predator; they are at the top of the marine food chain, and as a result they play a pivotal role in maintaining the health of the ocean environment. All the same, humans have been methodically, if not always intentionally, eliminating sharks from the seas for years, putting many species in danger of extinction.

Americans, no less than ancient Pacific tribes whose survival depended on the sea, are still susceptible to myths and misconceptions about sharks and the nature of the threat they pose to human beings. In this chapter, you will learn about the tumultuous, often bloody relationship between sharks and humans and why, after having gotten off on the wrong foot, things may be changing for the better—for both species.

Sharks in Mythology

It's no wonder that humans regarded sharks as alien, predatory beings for so long since until recently very few people ever saw one up close or had any idea how they lived or reproduced. There were, however, some exceptions—people who lived close to the sea and depended on fishing for their survival, especially indigenous peoples of the Pacific islands and Southeast Asia. For centuries they had direct encounters with sharks, hunting them—and occasionally being hunted by them. Sharks were revered—and feared—for their power, grace, agility, and speed.

Not surprisingly then, sharks figure prominently in the myths of these peoples. One of the most common legends in the Hawaiian Islands, for instance, involves a creature called Shark Man. The legend varies slightly from island to island. Shark Man is a mutable being, capable of changing from a human to a shark and back again at whim. He can be identified by the shark's mouth on his back. In most of the stories Shark Man accosts people on their way to the beach and warns them that they are in danger from sharks if they go swimming. The beach goers proceed on to the beach anyway. At that point Shark Man changes into a shark and proceeds to devour the people who refused to heed his advice.

> **Shark Lore**
>
> The Australian Aborigines hold that before creation there was a time when ancestor spirits came down to Earth in human and other forms. This time is known as dream time and alternatively as kangaroo, honey bee, or shark dreaming.

In Hana (a district of Maui), Shark Man is called Kamaikaahui. Kamaikaahui would conceal his true identity by wearing a cloth to cover up the shark mouth on his back. When beach goers failed to heed his warnings, he would take a shortcut to the ocean and eat the people. After a while his fellow villagers got wind of his scheme and plotted his capture. Kamaikaahui fled to Oahu where he resumed his custom of eating people until he was slain by a warrior who sought his daughter in marriage.

Kawelo of Kauai

The Shark Man of Kauai, Kawelo, is a bit different from the usual run-of-the-mill Shark Man because he boasts both a shark mouth on his back *and* a tail (plus other shark-like appendages). Kawelo also has a greater repertoire of identities, being able to transform himself into a worm, a moth, a butterfly, and a caterpillar as well as a human and a shark. As a shark, he lives in the Wailua River, and as a human, he dwells below a cave. If he caught children swimming in the water between these two locations he would eat them. His murderous career came to an end when outraged villagers stoned him to death.

Pauwalu of Maui

Pauwalu, the Shark Man who lived in Wailua on the island of Maui, was more specific in his warnings, saying that there would be eight fatal attacks. When his predictions turned out to be accurate, villagers began to suspect that he must be a Shark Man in disguise. A little boy named Akeake was the one to finally confront him. Akeake was known to be a tough fighter for someone his age. Pauwalu brushed the boy off, laughing at his accusation. But the boy surprised him, and after subduing Pauwalu and tying him up, Akeake tore off Pauwalu's shirt, exposing the telltale shark's mouth on his back. Pauwalu was then fed to the flames.

The Poisonous Limu

Long ago children used to swim in a bay at the northern end of Haleakala. To reach the shore they had to pass the house of a strange man named Nanaue who wore a mysterious cloak. The man would accost the children and ask where they were headed. Frightened, the children would reply only that they were going swimming. He would tell them to be on alert for a mutilated body floating in the bay. Sure enough, once they reached the bay they'd discover a torso or a limb in the water.

Eventually these ominous predictions aroused the suspicion of the villagers who went in search of Nanaue. They were directed to a dark lava tube that opened up into the ocean. The villagers waited in the tube until a figure was swept up into the tube by a wave, and there was Nanaue with the jaws of a shark protruding from his back. They captured him and were ready to burn him over a fire, but he slipped away and ran to the water, ready to turn himself into a shark. At the very last moment, a man grabbed him by his leg. The incensed villagers clubbed Nanaue and flung him into the blazing fire pit. But the story doesn't end there; shortly after Nanaue's fiery end a strange silvery sea moss appeared on the bay floor. No one had ever seen anything like it. A villager fed some of the moss to his pig, and the pig died. The people decided that the moss must be Nanaue in another incarnation. To this day, any silvery limu (sea moss) found at the bottom of the bay is considered poisonous.

The Shark Man in the Solomon Islands

Shark men of a somewhat different sort play an important role in myths of the Solomon Islands in the southwest Pacific Ocean. According to local tradition, if a man had great power in his lifetime that power would carry over after his death. The man would become a *tindalo,* or powerful spirit. The tindalo would be venerated almost as if he were a minor deity, and his image would be displayed at some sacred spot that was associated with him in his lifetime, perhaps a garden or a place by the shore. According to the legend, though, once dead, a tindalo didn't always stay dead; he might decide to inhabit another living creature, such as a snake, a crocodile, or, of course, a shark.

> **Shark Facts and Stats**
>
> The Solomon Islands are an independent country made up of a group of islands and atolls in the southwestern Pacific, extending for about 900 miles.

The Shark as Protective Spirit

Sharks aren't feared everywhere. In some religions, they were revered as gods or protectors. It is not surprising that so many cultures in lands bordering the Pacific should make the shark a prominent figure in their myths. Sharks, after all, played such a significant part in the life of these Pacific tribes. Shark skins were used for drums, and shark teeth were used for weapons and tools. In some cultures the men were permitted to eat the meat of a few species, but for women shark meat was taboo because of religious reasons. Sharks were considered protectors. For other early inhabitants of Pacific lands, the shark was a merciless ruler of the sea, a feared demon who people could only appease by sacrificing human flesh.

In the Solomon Islands, for instance, the shark god was known as "takw manacca." This god was worshipped in caves, and shamans would engage in a practice called "shark calling" intended to bring sharks to them. Evidently the sharks obliged. Once the shamans succeeded in attracting sharks, according to legend, they would go swimming with them. The worship of sharks seems to have been taken to extremes; as recently as the 1900s, some tribes on the Solomon Islands continued to make human sacrifices to their shark god.

In Vietnam, too, the shark was held in high esteem. The whale shark was known as Lord Fish, and its bones were taken to selected temples and given sacred burials. In the Fiji Islands, the shark god was known as Dakuwaqa; the high chiefs of the tribe were believed to be its direct descendants. In Japan, people used to pay homage to Shark Man, or Same-Hito, considered a god of the storms.

In parts of South America, the constellation of Orion was interpreted as representing a shark biting off the leg of a man.

Some early Hawaiians believed that the shark was their protector (or *aumakua*). The shark god was called Moho, and there is some evidence that human sacrifice was practiced in veneration of this god. Generally, sharks were supposed to save people from drowning, help fishermen with their catch, and chase away enemies. For some Hawaiian tribes, it was considered a great honor if a dead person returned to life as a shark.

The Modern World Discovers Sharks

While Solomon Islanders and Hawaiians were familiar with sharks from personal experience and the accounts of relatives and friends, the rest of the world lived in complacent ignorance. What they knew about sharks came from fishermen—and that wasn't very much.

Today, of course, you can drop into an aquarium for a visit with sharks and observe them in exhibits designed to simulate their watery habitats. But for hundreds of years only commercial fishermen had seen sharks close up, and for the most part these encounters did not leave a favorable impression on humans. Sharks were considered either as a source of oil (from their liver) or occasionally as food. Mostly, though, they were a menace to humans luckless enough to fall into their midst as a result of a shipwreck. As far as fishermen were concerned, the only good shark was a dead one.

Sharks remained a mystery to most people on land until the summer of 1916 when a rogue shark struck the New Jersey shoreline, killing several swimmers. The shark was originally thought to be a great white (but it was never identified and was more likely a bull shark). The attacks caused such a sensation that they even prompted President Woodrow Wilson to call an emergency cabinet meeting to discuss ways of dealing with the "crisis." The image of the shark as a marauding beast, capable of ambushing unwary humans, seared itself on the collective mind.

The very word *shark* continues to carry a distinctly negative connotation. News of any shark attack on a swimmer is usually sufficient to throw people into a panic. In the summer of 2001, a spate of attacks on the eastern seaboard caused such a hysterical reaction, fueled by sensational media reports, that one supermarket tabloid accused Cuban dictator Fidel Castro of launching sharks against unwary American waders.

A recent movie, *Swimming with the Sharks*, had nothing to do with the sharks found in the sea but instead focused on the human kind, the ones who produce movies. We all know about loan sharks and not a few members of the legal profession have been derisively labeled sharks as well. In a somewhat more flattering sense, high-energy, highly motivated people are called "land sharks."

Hollywood Discovers Sharks

In 1974, a freelance journalist named Peter Benchley published his first novel, *Jaws*, which subsequently was made into one of the most successful movies of all by Steven Spielberg. It has been suggested that the inspiration for the book came from that rogue shark that killed New Jersey swimmers in 1916. The book (and movie) certainly caused as much of a sensation as the 1916 attack, further perpetuating the image of sharks as sea monsters. In his 2002 book *Shark Trouble*, Benchley offered an apology for the damage his earlier work had done to the shark's reputation. "We knew so little back then, and have learned so much since, that I couldn't possibly write the same story today," he wrote. "I know now that the mythic monster I created was largely a fiction. I also know now, however, that the genuine animal is just as—if not even more—fascinating."

Jaws, Jaws, and More Jaws

The success of the movie *Jaws* didn't escape the notice of Hollywood movie studios; one of the first movies to gross more than $100 million, it ranks as number 15 in box office receipts (as of 2002). Sequels were inevitable, and not one of them featured a rehabilitated great white as its hero—and neither Benchley nor Spielberg were involved in these sequels. *Jaws 2* (1978) made little effort to be anything but a rerun of its predecessor. In this sequel, Roy Scheider again plays the sheriff of the Amity, the coastal town in Martha's Vineyard bedeviled by the great white in the original movie, and again his words of caution go unheeded by the local authorities who are hell-bent on promoting a sailing regatta in the shark-infested waters. Disaster, of course, follows swiftly. Viewers were not entranced. The movie, wrote one reviewer, "manages to be both stylistically flat and openly cynical about its commercial intentions."

In spite of the relatively tepid performance of *Jaws 2* at the box office, especially compared to *Jaws*, moviemakers were not discouraged from attempting a third outing. The result was the 1983 film *Jaws 3D*. This time the setting is Sea World in Florida where Dennis Quaid plays an engineer who is involved with a marine biologist and dolphin trainer played by Bess Armstrong. The story, such as it is, is set in motion when a female great white and her pup become trapped inside the park; the pup dies, and the mother takes revenge, wreaking havoc on the park. (In reality, shark mothers are more apt to eat their young than take umbrage at their loss.) In the end, the heroes blow the great white to smithereens.

Viewers even complained about the special effects in *Jaws 3D*, which presumably was one of the chief selling points of the film. The shark looked fake, viewers said, and swam slower than the people she was chasing. The shark even swam backwards, which sharks cannot do in real life. What's more, when one of the victims was caught in the shark's mouth, the shark "gummed" him to death when one would have thought that a single bite with her formidable incisors would have done the trick just fine. Apparently the film's budget didn't allow for a technical advisor.

Even after this fiasco, Hollywood producers felt that there was still more blood (however fake) to be squeezed out of the poor great white. And so, even if audiences weren't clamoring for another *Jaws*, they got one anyway in the form of *Jaws: The Revenge* (1987). In this version, which begins on Martha's Vineyard, where the first two films were set, a great white kills a police deputy on Christmas Eve. The bereft mother, played by Lorraine Gary, flies to the Bahamas to take refuge with her eldest son, a marine biologist. The great white somehow follows her (making the trip in three days!) to visit further destruction on the poor woman who by this time has taken a romantic interest in a carefree pilot played by Michael Caine. (There is some dispute among the few people who actually saw this movie as to whether the evil shark is the same one from Martha's Vineyard or whether it is another vengeful shark altogether. How the shark could swim so fast to reach the Bahamas in three days or how it managed to trace its victim are questions the makers of this concoction never answer.) One viewer said that the shark looked as "frightening as a rubber duckie." *Jaws: The Revenge* marked the end of the *Jaws* franchise but not the end of movies in which lethal sharks go on a rampage.

In 1999, 24 years after *Jaws*, a movie called *Deep Blue* was released that featured sharks who were "bigger, smarter, faster, meaner," as the posters for the movie boasted. *Deep Blue* takes place inside a cutting-edge oceanographic research center called Aquatica where a marine biologist (yet again) played by Australian actress Saffron Burrows is breeding a new generation of sharks with genetically enlarged brains. Tissue from these brains, it seems, has a therapeutic property that makes it a miracle cure for Alzheimer's disease. Naturally, the sharks do not share the idealistic goal of the scientists responsible for creating them and now they are endowed with high intelligence that makes them even more dangerous. Several characters have to die a grisly death before the scientists learn that tampering with nature can have disastrous consequences. The lesson that Hollywood seems to have learned, however, is that sharks can still sell movies so long as they are depicted as thugs of the high seas.

Separating Fact from Fantasy: The Science of Sharks

Needless to say, *Deep Blue* is nonsense, but obviously the movie's producers were playing on deep-rooted fears that people harbor about sharks. However, ever so gradually, the image of sharks is undergoing rehabilitation. This is largely due to the efforts of scientists and divers who have studied sharks and discovered a much more interesting and complicated marine predator than any that Hollywood ever dreamed up. How humans discovered sharks—not the myth but the reality—makes for an intriguing tale.

For centuries sharks remained shrouded in mystery. How many species were there? How did they reproduce? Where did they live? The only way that these puzzles could be solved was by observing sharks in their natural habitat. Until the 1940s, however, the available technology prevented divers from descending to depths where many species of sharks swam or remaining underwater for very long. That situation was soon to change.

During World War II, an enterprising French naval officer named Jacques-Yves Cousteau designed and tested the Aqua-Lung, a predecessor to the scuba systems used today by divers worldwide, in collaboration with engineer Emile Gagnon. Used by the Allies to remove enemy mines from international waters, the device was a cylinder containing compressed air connected via a pressure-regulated valve to a face mask. Its great advantage was that it allowed divers to remain underwater for hours.

By the late 1940s, Cousteau set out to explore the oceans of the world on his boat *Calypso*. In the process, he filmed 120 documentaries that became synonymous with underwater adventures. Through these documentaries, which were shown in movie theaters and on television, he introduced sharks to a larger public. Through these efforts, the image of the shark as a marauding trash fish began to undergo a change. Sharks were shown to be remarkable creatures who, for the most part, had no interest in harming humans.

Shark Facts and Stats

Jacques-Yves Cousteau (1910–1997) is one of the most famous oceanographers and marine explorers of all time. He began his underwater research while in the French navy during World War II. After the war he made several documentary films including *The Silent World* and *World Without Sun,* both of which won the Academy Award for documentaries. He was also the author of several books aimed at popularizing the ocean world. In addition, he was instrumental in establishing a world-renowned aquarium and oceanography center in Monaco.

The Beginnings of the Scientific Study of Sharks

In the early 1970s, the world began to learn a great deal more about these mysterious creatures thanks to the efforts of ichthyologist Dr. Eugenie Clark. One of the first to don a chain mail suit to work with sharks, she attempted to condition sharks to respond to stimuli for food, making her one of the first human "shark feeders." She also studied how sharks perceive the world, devising experiments to study the sharks' ability to visually discriminate between targets of different shapes and color. Today she continues to study shark behavior in the deep sea, relying on submersibles capable of descending to depths up to 12,000 feet.

The Contributions of Recreational Divers

Vanquishing the image of the "mythical monster" became easier with the increasing popularity of recreational diving beginning in the late 1970s as divers encountered sharks on their home turf. These experiences proved so exciting and such an adrenaline rush that any apprehensions divers might have had about being with sharks quickly vanished. Ironically, these favorable encounters underwater were occurring even as swimmers and surfers, scared witless by Benchley's novel, *Jaws,* and Steven Spielberg's hit film of the same name, were staying far from shore. Now sharks represent a challenge for divers. They are so eager to see sharks in their homes that they seek them out in remote parts of the world and spend thousands of dollars apiece for shark diving tours.

Underwater photographers such as Al Giddings, Howard Hall, Stan Waterman, Bob Cranston, Stephen Frink, and Marty Snyderman have set aside any concerns for their personal safety and have filmed close-up features of sharks for magazines such as *Nature* and *National Geographic* and for PBS and the Discovery Channel. TV producers realized that sharks could be a great draw. The Discovery Channel began devoting an entire week to shark stories—Celebrity Shark Week.

Modern Myths and Reality: How Dangerous Are Sharks?

The number of shark attacks has remained fairly consistent over the last several years. And there is good evidence that great whites—the most feared of all shark species—do not as a rule seek out humans as prey but bite them only because they mistake humans for sea lions. People share some of the blame, too: Swimmers in Florida, for instance, continued to venture into waters inhabited by sharks even after an attack had taken place nearby. More people in the water tend to lead to more attacks. I certainly wouldn't walk into the surf in shark-infested waters where the view was one-way (the shark could see me and not vice versa).

Ironically, many divers who spend a good deal of their time in the company of sharks have sustained injuries, not from sharks, but from other treacherous creatures in the deep. One shark expert, Dr. Sylvia Earle (known as "Her Deepness"), who has spent more than 6,000 hours underwater in her career, was badly stung by a lionfish in the South Pacific. In intense pain and close to death, she was rescued by underwater photographer Al Giddings. A brief swipe by an unseen jellyfish in swift currents in Palau left me suffering for six weeks. So why do sharks inspire such fear, especially when several other creatures in the sea pose an equal or greater threat to humans?

Take, for example, the broadbill fish, also known as billfish. Billfish can pierce wood as deep as 22 inches and even penetrate steel to a depth of 4 inches. The broadbill swordfish, described by *Sport Fishing Magazine* as a "Prince of Darkness," has been known to sink boats with astonishing frequency. Black marlins, another billfish, have leapt on the decks of fishing vessels and impaled deckhands.

Disbanding Popular Misconceptions

Thanks to the combined efforts of marine biologists and diving enthusiasts, we are able to clarify some common misconceptions about sharks:

- **Myth:** Most sharks are man-eaters.

  Fact: Of the nearly 400 species of sharks, only about 11 of them have ever been known to attack humans. In the first place, most sharks are too small to threaten humans. Even great whites do not like humans, although they sometimes mistake humans for the sea lions or seals whom they prefer. Moreover, they live in deep waters where encounters with humans are rare. Although about 100 shark attacks occur each year (a subject we discuss in more detail in Chapter 18), the fact is that elephants kill twice as many people each year (about 200). Dogs kill thousands each year.

♦ **Myth:** Sharks are stupid with tiny, primitive brains.

Fact: Sharks (as well as rays) have a brain/ body ratio that is comparable to that of birds and mammals. Researchers have done studies that demonstrate that lemon sharks learn faster and retain a condi- tioned response longer than a cat or rab- bit. However, sharks are not necessarily as intelligent as birds or mammals.

> ### Shark Facts and Stats
>
> Of the 11 shark species that have attacked humans, only 4 of those are actually man-eaters: great whites (possibly by mis- take), bull sharks, tiger sharks, and oceanic white tip sharks.

♦ **Myth:** Sharks have to roll over to bite.

Fact: Because sharks have loose, hinge- like jaws, they can thrust them forward to grip their prey without having to maneuver. Most species of sharks do not chew their food; they simply swal- low their prey whole.

> ### Taste of the Bizarre
>
> Some victims of bites by great whites insist that they never felt any pain.

♦ **Myth:** Sharks eat continuously.

Fact: Sharks eat periodically; exactly when they eat depends on their metabo- lism, the availability of food, and the expenditure of energy required to capture prey. Juvenile lemon sharks eat less than 2 percent of their body weight per day. Some sharks have been known to go a year without eating!

♦ **Myth:** Most sharks are scavengers.

Fact: Some sharks are omnivorous and eat anything that strikes their fancy. However, most sharks have relatively conservative diets; some species consume only plankton and small fish, others prefer mollusks and octopuses, and still oth- ers hunt for larger fish and even other sharks.

♦ **Myth:** Most sharks are fast swimmers.

Fact: In spite of the high speeds (often in excess of 20 miles an hour) achieved by pelagic sharks such as the mako and great whites, most sharks, especially bot- tom feeders, swim very slowly at cruising speeds of little more than 5 miles an hour.

◆ **Myth:** Sharks can't see in the dark.

Fact: Sharks' eyes may be very good or not, depending on their habitat and the nature of their prey. Sharks can distinguish colors, and some species can detect light 10 times dimmer than that which humans can perceive.

◆ **Myth:** Sharks are hard to kill.

Fact: Unfortunately, sharks are relatively easy to kill; they weaken and succumb to captivity and often die when they are caught by nets or by hook and line.

◆ **Myth:** Sharks are trash fish.

Fact: Sharks occupy the apex of the marine food chain and keep populations of other marine life in check. Sharks are vitally important to the health of the ocean ecosystem.

◆ **Myth:** Shark behavior is completely unpredictable.

Fact: Some shark behavior can be predicted, and most patterns of shark behavior are logical and consistent (which is more than can be said about much human behavior).

Shark Lore

One of the most widely circulated photos on the Internet in 2002 (which was falsely labeled as *National Geographic*'s "Photo of the Year") showed a great white shark leaping out of the water to attack a helicopter. The image undoubtedly confirmed in many people's minds that sharks are capable of remarkable acrobatic feats (as indeed several species are) and that they will attack anything that moves in the belief that it might make a good meal. There was only one problem: the photo was a fake, a composite spliced together from a U.S. Air Force photo taken near San Francisco's Golden Gate Bridge and a photo of a shark from South Africa. Who was responsible for the fake has not been determined.

What Remains to Be Learned

In spite of the combined efforts by marine biologists, conservationists, underwater photographers, and diving enthusiasts, we still know astonishingly little about sharks. And there is often heated debate among scientists about what we do know. That's because sharks are difficult to maintain and study in aquariums. And as noted above, divers have been able to observe and photograph sharks in their habitats only in recent years. New technologies have played a role in illuminating the natural history of the shark, too—the use of satellites, for instance, has allowed researchers to track sharks across thousands of miles (some sharks are nomads, some homebodies) and follow them into the deepest regions of the ocean untouched by sunlight. We now have a much better idea how they are able to navigate and find prey even from a great distance away. Sharks (and their close cousins, the rays), it turns out, possess a unique arsenal of special detection devices that one shark expert compared to the array of sensors on the Starship Enterprise.

In the chapters that follow you will learn about the latest discoveries of scientists—whether sharks sleep, for instance, or whether shark cartilage has any use as a cancer fighting agent—but you will also get to know the real shark, not the shark of myth and movies.

The Least You Need to Know

- For centuries people have regarded sharks with ambivalence, often with fear, but always with fascination.

- Sharks have figured prominently in the myths of many cultures, especially in the Pacific islands.

- People still harbor many misconceptions about sharks, perceiving them to be much more of a threat to humans than they actually are.

- In spite of scientific research, we still have a great deal to learn about shark behavior, reproduction, and habitats.

Chapter 2

What Is a Shark?

In This Chapter

- What makes a shark so flexible
- What makes sharkskin so tough
- How sharks stay afloat
- How sharks breathe
- Why a shark would drive a dentist crazy

Although sharks are formally classified as fish, they are not your average, ordinary fish. Sharks have several characteristics that set them apart from, say, salmon or tuna. In this chapter, you'll learn how everything from the structure of their bodies to the surface of their skin sets sharks apart. You'll also discover how sharks have their own way of doing the normal fishy tasks of breathing, eating, procreating, and moving.

Sharks are endowed with special senses lacking in the "bony" fish. Sharks, for instance, can detect minute electric impulses and vibrations as they swim silently through the ocean. These unique senses help them find prey that they can't see and allow them to navigate along the ocean floor even in the absence of any landmarks to guide them. Sharks also happen to be one of evolution's triumphs—in one form or another, they have inhabited the Earth's waters for close to 400 million years. In comparison, we humans are mere babes in the woods. And one other thing: The vast majority of sharks pose no danger to humans—some of them have such small teeth you can barely make them out! So forget everything you've read or heard about sharks—put aside your preconceptions. This is your opportunity to find out what sharks are truly like.

Sharks and Fish—What's the Difference?

Sharks are fish—but they differ from other fish (think salmon, tuna, and mackerel) in several respects. The most important difference is *structure*. Sharks are made up of cartilage (the same flexible material that's in your nose, ears, and joints); they do not have bones like other fish. Sharks also have certain limitations—their breathing depends (in most species anyway) on movement—and when they move they do not have the same mobility as bony fish do. They cannot, for instance, stop on a dime or swim backward. On the other hand, they are endowed with some unique capacities evolution has denied to other types of fish.

Sharks dominate the seas in which they swim—they occupy the top rung of the marine food chain. Sharks have no predators apart from one another (bigger sharks will prey on smaller ones) and humans. Evolution has endowed them with some special capacities that have allowed them to maintain their dominance for eons. In this section, you'll find out what makes sharks so extraordinary and what makes them different from other fish.

Taste of the Bizarre

In the early stages of development, vertebrates, including humans, have cartilage instead of bones. As fetuses grow, most of the cartilage is replaced by bone.

Shark Facts and Stats

Naturalists classify about 350 to 400 species of sharks as belonging to the class *Chondrichthyes* and the subclass *elasmobranchii*. They are further divided into 8 orders and 30 families. Each subcategory is defined by narrower criteria.

Different on the Inside: Cartilage vs. Bone

Sharks belong to a group of fish known as *elasmobranchs*. That's a fancy way of saying that they are composed of cartilage. Essentially, cartilage is gristle—a fibrous, connective material that is found in the human nose, ears, trachea, larynx, and joints and whose principal role is to provide support to bony skeletons in vertebrates. Sharks, however, have no bones; they just have cartilage. By contrast, bony fish have bones composed of calcium just like mammals, reptiles, amphibians, and birds.

Cartilage has a few special attributes that are of particular value to sharks. First, cartilage has a much lower density than bone, which is why sharks are relatively lightweight and don't sink. Aside from making a shark more lightweight, cartilage is flexible, which allows a shark to turn around in a smaller space than a bony fish. However, just because cartilage is more flexible than bone doesn't mean it isn't tough. In addition, sharks don't move with quite the same grace or mobility as bony fish because sharks don't have as many movable parts.

Humans might begin to experience bone loss as they grow older, but sharks have no similar complaint. They can keep growing cartilage as long as they live.

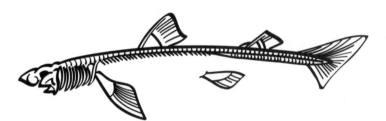

The bodies of many shark species, which are often described as "streamlined," are uniquely designed to move swiftly through water.

Meet the Shark's Closest Relations

Like sharks, rays and chimaeras consist of cartilage and therefore also belong to the *elasmobranchs*. The nearly 400 species of rays include skates, stingrays, electric rays, devilfish, mantas, and guitarfish. Rays come in all shapes and sizes, with the smallest barely a few centimeters in length and the largest (mantas and devilfish) measuring up to 20 feet and weighing in at a staggering 3,000 pounds! Although some species are hatched from eggs, most are born fully developed, which is also true of most sharks.

Rays are distinguished by large pectoral fins (fins in the chest region) that move them through water at a slow pace. In contrast, some species of sharks are capable of breathtaking speeds. Rays also have slender, whiplike tails that act as rudders.

Rays remain resting or buried in the sand on the sea bottom, feeding on shellfish and mollusks. Some species can even camouflage themselves as they lurk at the ocean bottom. They have small mouths (unlike most sharks, whose mouths are often gaping cavities) with blunt teeth that prove useful in crushing shellfish and crustaceans. To punish predators who stray too close, some rays, such as stingrays and electric rays, have refined special defensive mechanisms, as no doubt many hapless swimmers and divers can attest.

Chimaeras can grow up to six feet and feed on smaller creatures in temperate waters. They are distinguished by large eyes and scaleless skin with coloration that ranges from black to brown. Chapter 11 discusses rays and chimaeras in more detail.

Different on the Outside: Denticles vs. Scales

You have seen how the interior structure of the shark differs from the skeletal structure of a bony fish. The shark's exterior also differs from that of most other fish.

Most fish have scales, which are essentially overlapping bony plates that cover all or most of the fish's body. There are four types of scales:

- Cycloid scales are smooth and rounded. Herring, salmon, bluefish, tuna, and most other fish have this type of scales.

- Ctenoid scales have small points on the surface of the skin and are rough to the touch.

- Ganoid scales are interlocking, diamond-shaped scales that are rough to the touch and are found in some primitive fish such as the gar.

- Placoid scales are sharp and shaped like small teeth, which is why they are also called *denticles*. Sharks have this type of scales.

Shark Facts and Stats

Sharks are some of the most diverse creatures of any species and have been on the planet for a very long time. Some paleontological evidence indicates that the earliest ancestors of modern-day sharks lived as long as 480 million years ago.

The scales of bony fish grow larger as the fish grows. This is not true with sharks. Their placoid scales stay the same size throughout the shark's life. However, as the shark gets larger, more placoid scales are added. Chapter 3 explains how sharks benefit from having placoid scales.

Staying Afloat: Swim Bladders vs. Livers

Yet another distinction between bony fish and sharks is the way in which they stay afloat. Bony fish have a swim bladder (sometimes called an air bladder) that contains gas. The bladder works this way: When the fish takes in oxygen, some of the gas is released into the bladder, which in turn increases the fish's buoyancy, allowing it to rise through the water. If the fish wants to descend, it squeezes oxygen out of the bladder and decreases its buoyancy. This process operates much like a blimp or hot air balloon by compressing and decompressing gas to raise or lower altitude. Or you can think of these swim bladders as ballast tanks; by varying the amount of gas in the swim bladder, the fish can rise or descend in the water or remain stationary. An angler who quickly pulls in a bottom fish to the water surface can witness the "explosion" of the fish bladder by the fish's bulging eyeballs.

Sharks lack swim bladders and must rely on oil-filled livers for their buoyancy. A shark's liver can occupy up to 25 percent of the shark's body weight. Because oil is lighter than water, the liver gives the shark a certain amount of buoyancy. To attain adequate lift, however, most sharks also rely on their large caudal fins. Forward motion comes from the caudal fin; the up, down, and turning motions come from pectoral fins like bow planes. Dorsal fins keep the roll rate down. For this reason, sharks must remain in constant motion in order not to sink to the bottom. A shark won't necessarily die if it sinks, but it won't last long if it can't swiftly recover and resume swimming at a depth to which it is accustomed.

Because of their swim bladders, bony fish are much more dependent on water pressure than sharks are. For instance, fish who are used to inhabiting great depths will die—sometimes by exploding or melting—if they are raised to water levels with less pressure.

Breathing—Same Process, Different Look

Both bony fish and sharks breathe by extracting dissolved oxygen from water. Water enters the mouth, passes through the *gills* and is expelled through *gill slits* that are located behind the head. The difference is that the gill slits are covered in bony fish whereas the slits are clearly visible in most sharks. Sharks also have an alternative source of absorbing oxygen that bony fish lack: two holes above their eyes. Water flows into these holes and passes over the gills.

What Does It Mean?

Gills are a series of thin sheets or filaments through which blood circulates. Fish use gills to take in oxygen and expel carbon dioxide.

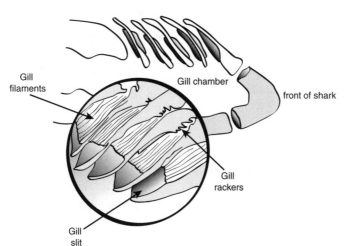

Gill
filaments

Gill chamber

front of shark

Gill
rackers

Gill
slit

The gill slits are the shark's "lungs." As the water flows over and through the gill slits, oxygen is filtered out and carried by blood to the shark's organs and tissues.

Surviving in a Fishy World

Sharks are the apex of the marine food chain. Their behavior and choice of habitats are governed by the availability of food sources. With so few predators, they can concentrate on finding prey, but this isn't always easy. Sharks may have to hunt far and wide to find sustenance, especially the big pelagic sharks such as great whites and makos that feed on marine mammals. Even bottom feeders that consume plankton and small fish need to invest energy to get their meals—it's more work than you'd think simply cruising the ocean floor with your mouth wide open.

Gourmands vs. Gourmets

Here's a fact that may come as a surprise. Sharks usually don't eat as often as we do (or other mammals for that matter)—that's because most sharks are cold-blooded and don't need so many calories to heat their bodies. And some sharks turn out to be picky eaters, dining only on mollusks and plankton, while others won't turn up their nose (eh, snout) at anything they can swallow. Yet for the most part it's safe to say that sharks are gourmands, not gourmets. Trash from boats, car tires, license plates, and tin cans have all been found in the bellies of sharks. Many sharks are not quite so indiscriminate, but they're not likely to live down their reputation as "the garbage cans of the sea" any time soon. Fish cannot begin to match the omnivorous appetites of sharks or demonstrate such a lack of discrimination when it comes to food. Sharks aren't good models for small children, either: Sharks don't chew their food; they simply swallow it whole or else cut it into a few bite-sized pieces.

> **Shark Facts and Stats**
>
> Fish with hinged jaws are known as *Gnathostomata*. This group is divided further into the class *Chondrichthyes*, which includes sharks, rays, and chimaeras, and the class *Osteichthyes*, which includes the bony fishes. Yet not all fish have jaws—the lamprey, for instance. These jawless fish are classified *Agnatha*.

Sharks are able to swallow prey whole because of their short, powerful, hinged jaws and multiple rows of teeth. Shark jaws contain additional mineral deposits that imbue them with extra strength. And thanks to Peter Benchley and Steven Spielberg, jaws have practically become a synonym for the sharks themselves.

Sharks are a dentist's worst nightmare because they possess anywhere from 3 to 15 rows of teeth. Megamouth, for example, has 50 rows of teeth (though only 3 rows are functional at any given time) while Whale sharks have thousands of teeth in 310 rows with 10 to 15 functional at any given time. A shark needs a lot of teeth because they invariably fall out while the shark is devouring his prey. Yet the day after a tooth is lost, a new one grows in to replace it.

Bony fish also have teeth, but their teeth are neither as prominent nor as intimidating as those of sharks and are often located further back in the mouth near the esophagus. Some fish, such as seahorses and piper fish, lack teeth and get their food by drawing their prey with a suctioning action through the mouth.

Shark Facts and Stats
Nurse, leopard, wobbegong, and sand sharks breathe so lightly that it's hardly noticeable. These bottom feeders appear to be sleeping even when they are actually wide awake.

Sensing Prey from Miles Away

As vaunted hunters, sharks have developed a highly sensitized—and unique—detection system. What makes it so unique? For one thing, sharks can detect electricity, even minute voltages. Most other fish cannot. For another, sharks have a special capacity that allows them to register vibrations made by prey. Bony fish, by contrast, lack these specialized organs. Sharks also have acute hearing for low-pitched sounds at a distance of about 100 yards. Some experts believe that great white sharks can be lured up to 100 miles by the clanging of shark cages, signaling the availability of free food. It takes three or four days for them to congregate around the cages. And their sense of smell is legendary; they can pick up the scent of a single drop of blood in a million drops of water (the equivalent of 10 buckets) as far as 2 miles away. Their vision is equally sensitive. Sharks can see in the dark like cats. They also have a special mirrorlike layer in the back of their eyes that doubles the intensity of incoming light.

Shark Lore

When fishermen in the South Seas wanted to attract sharks for food, they would stand on shore and use coconut rattles. The sharks could hear the rattles from great distances and would rush to the shore, believing that the rattles represented tempting prey.

All living creatures emit electrical impulses when their muscles contract, but very few species have the capacity to pick them up. Until Marconi invented the radio no one could pick up radio waves—but radio waves were there all along. Sharks, however, have a gift that few species have in that they are able to register these impulses even though they are usually very weak. Sharks then can trace the impulses to their source—often to the detriment of the source. Some experts believe that this detection system is not to be found in bony fish.

Procreating with Eggs and Claspers

Sharks are essentially loners, rarely swimming or hunting in packs. And while they can't procreate alone they can't be bothered with elaborate courtship rituals; mating is a brief, messy—and brutal—business. Once the female is impregnated she's gone, leaving the male to recover his strength to swim another day. Male sharks have a visually distinctive sexual organ called claspers, which are extensions of the pelvic fins. These claspers are used to hold the female in place until sperm can be transferred to the female and fertilize her eggs—a process that takes only a few minutes. Claspers make male sharks easily identifiable in the water.

Reproduction among sharks is much more complicated than among bony fish and different species of sharks reproduce in different ways. When bony fish reproduce they do so profligately, often hatching thousands of eggs at a time. Most will be food for predators, but enough will survive to keep the species going. Sharks, however, don't reproduce that often—once every two years on average—and their litters are much smaller (a hundred is exceptional and four or six is not unusual)—and what's more, they reach sexual maturity later on. That means they don't reproduce until much later in life than bony fish. If the offspring of sharks—called pups—were as expendable as fish eggs there would hardly be any sharks left in the sea by now. Some sharks do lay eggs, to be sure, but these eggs are protected (by camouflage or other means) to keep them safe from possible predators. Other sharks hatch eggs but nurture them inside the mother's bodies, and still other species give birth to live young which are fully able to fend for themselves as soon as they are born. (And they'd better be since mom isn't about to give them any help.)

Getting Around

A shark's movement in the water is comparable to the flight of an airplane. An airplane can't remain stationary in the air; it has to continue to fly or else it will stall and plummet to the ground. In that respect, sharks, as one observer put it, don't swim so much as they fly through water.

Some sharks can hurtle through the sea at speeds of up to 40 miles an hour. Other species of sharks are less given to feats of athletic prowess, preferring to remain territorial and close to the bottom of the sea. These slower moving sharks feed on shellfish, plants, and tiny sea creatures that they filter out from the water. Because these sharks have no incentive to move very far, they do not need to attain the meteoric speeds of their high-flying cousins closer to the surface. (Some of these bottom-feeding sharks are content to stay in one place because they get all the food they need without moving and end up dying close to where they were born.)

Sharks can be fast, but they are not as agile as bony fish. Sharks cannot, for instance, stop on a dime. Nor can sharks swim backwards. They are limited to a weaving, forward motion.

Hiding in a Sea of Blue and Gray

As a visit to any aquarium will tell you, fish come in many colors, some of which are startlingly iridescent. Many of the more extravagant color schemes that certain species of fish display are probably meant to attract mates. Sharks are among the fish that use their coloration as camouflage to prevent them from being spotted by prey and predators alike. They are dark on top—making them difficult to spot against the water—and light on the bottom, camouflaging them from being recognized by prey below them. This coloration—called countershading—is a distinguishing feature of sharks.

Comparing Sharks and Bony Fish at a Glance

The following table summarizes the differences between bony fish and sharks.

Attribute	Sharks	Bony Fish
Skeleton	Cartilage	Bone and cartilage
Locomotion	Forward motion only	Forward and backward
Buoyancy	Large oily liver	Swim bladder
Gills	Visible externally	Covered
Reproduction	Eggs fertilized in female's body	Eggs usually laid in water
Skin	Rough, sharp placoid scales (denticles)	Smooth, slippery scales
Coloration	Dark on top, light on their bellies	Varied (Many colors)

Shark Extremes

With nearly 400 species of sharks you would naturally expect that some stand out—for their size, their weight, their speed, or other attributes. Here is a sampling of shark species who, because one particular characteristic, are deserving of mention.

◆ **Most frightening shark: great white.** This is the celebrity shark, the real star (in however simulated form) of *Jaws*, with 3,000 teeth, growing to 20 feet or longer and weighing in at 7,000 pounds. It also has the unnerving habit (to humans anyway) of poking its head above the surface of the water, presumably to look for prey.

- **Most dangerous shark: oceanic white tip (runner-up: bull).** Great whites might be the most frightening shark—and the best known thanks to Hollywood—but they are not necessarily the species that poses the most danger to humans. (As you'll discover in Chapter 18, great whites might actually confuse humans with their favored prey, sea lions and elephant seals.) The oceanic white tip is an aggressive deep-sea predator that has attacked and killed many survivors of shipwrecks and plane crashes at sea. The bull shark is also a very treacherous aggressive that has attacked many humans without provocation; because bulls can live in fresh water as well as saltwater they have even more opportunity to attack humans.

- **Biggest shark: whale shark.** The largest shark—and the largest fish—in the waters, the whale can grow to 40 feet (or longer); its dark body with white spots as well as its huge size recall certain types of whales, thus its name. In spite of its intimidating size, the whale shark has small teeth and feeds mainly on small fish and plankton.

- **Smallest shark: dwarf dog shark.** This shark, only discovered in 1985, is only six to seven inches long at maturity. Unlike most species of sharks, who prefer to live and hunt alone, the dog shark, like its name sake, lives and hunts in packs, gaining in numbers what it lacks in strength by himself. The shark can hardly be considered cute; it has a pointy head full of pointy little teeth.

- **Fastest shark: mako.** Mako sharks, who are pelagic (or ocean-going), can reach speeds of 20 miles per hour, but in short bursts can attain speeds two and possibly three times faster. This shark is also capable of acrobatics, leaping out of the water, even turning somersaults.

- **Slowest shark: basking shark.** Although it is difficult to know which of the many filter-feeders that cruise at a leisurely pace, looking for food, is the absolute slowest the basking is certainly in the running (so to speak). This plankton-eating shark can grow to 40 feet in length and swim along at about 1.8 miles an hour, its mouth gaping open for food.

- **Longest tail: thresher.** The thresher shark can grow to about 20 feet, nearly half of which is devoted to its tail (or caudal fin). The tail is used as a weapon, too; in a whiplike motion, the tail can stun prey or corral schools of fish to within easy reach of its mouth. There are even reports of humans being knocked over by its tail when they come between the shark and fish that it's after.

- **Most common shark: piked dogfish.** A small shark, measuring about 63 inches long, the piked dogfish may be the most common shark and is especially abundant in the North Atlantic Ocean.

- **Strangest head: hammerhead.** The name gives it away: the head of this predator, who prefers fish, squid, and other hammerheads and who often hunts in schools, looks like a hammer. The head is flat and wide with eyes spaced far apart (up to 23 inches) and bristles with special organs used to detect prey. They usually grow to about 12 feet in length.

- **Strangest shark: albino zebra.** A mature zebra shark, discovered in 1973 in the Indian Ocean, had a uniformly white body (most sharks are black or grayish). It had no black spots or blotches typically seen in this species although the fins were a grayish. Scientists were surprised that this female had survived as long as it had because its unusual coloring would have caused it to stand out against the dark background of the ocean, making it more vulnerable to predators.

- **Most ornamental: tasseled wobbegong.** This is a bottom-feeder whose bodies are covered with a profusion of spots, bands, and other markings that act as camouflage, causing it to blend into coral reefs and mud while it waits in ambush for passing prey. It gets its name from the fringe of skin that droops over its broad mouth. Growing to eight feet in length as an adult, the wobbegong has a low, flat body.

- **Most unsharklike body: angel shark.** Angel sharks look more like rays than they do other sharks, with their flattened bodies and blunt snout. They derive their name from their broad pectoral fins that give them an angelic appearance, similar to that of a ray. They are also called "monk fish" because their rounded heads recall the hoods on monk cloaks. These bottom feeders are distinguished from rays, however, by certain anatomical features: for one, their pectoral fins are not completely attached to their head as rays' heads are, and for another, their gill slits are on the side of the head whereas the gill slits of rays are located on their underside.

The Least You Need to Know

- Sharks are fish, but unlike bony fish, who have skeletons, sharks have skeletons that are made out of cartilage.

- Sharkskin consists of sharp, rough, toothlike scales called denticles, which are unlike the smooth, slimy scales that typify most bony fish.

- Sharks (and other cartilaginous fish) have a much longer evolutionary history than bony fish, extending back about 400 million years.

- Unlike bony fish, which hatch a great many eggs, sharks typically have small litters and several species give birth to live young.

- Sharks are the most important predators in the ocean.

Looking at Sharks from the Outside

In This Chapter

- ◆ How big sharks can be and how little
- ◆ What the shark's only weapon is
- ◆ Why a shark is so thick skinned
- ◆ How sharks camouflage themselves

The shark has remained roughly the same for about 75 million years. That suggests evolution has done a rather remarkable job in making the shark one of the most adaptable and fascinating creatures on the planet. This chapter details the adaptations different kinds of sharks have made in size, shape, teeth, skin, and coloring in order to be successful in the underwater world. However, because there are so many different species of sharks, with different diets, habitats and reproductive methods, these adaptations take a variety of forms. In Chapter 2, I examined the traits that distinguished sharks from bony fish. In this chapter, I will be looking at some of the differences among shark species. There are some species, for instance, that prefer to dwell in shallow waters close to shore while others are found mostly in the deep.

From Whales to Pygmies: The Size and Shape of Sharks

With so many species of sharks (almost 400), you would expect them to come in a number of shapes and sizes. Many species measure less than 3 feet in length, but some of the high-speed, ocean-going sharks can reach 20 feet or more. Whale sharks are the largest species of shark; in fact they are the largest fish in the ocean. In 1925, a whale shark was caught in the Andaman Sea in the Gulf of Thailand that was estimated to be 60 feet in length, although the largest officially measured whale shark (caught off Bombay, India, in 1983) was just a little over 40 feet. Whale sharks can weigh as much as 20,000 pounds.

Basking sharks are the second largest species at 33 feet. Interestingly, both whale and basking sharks are harmless, gentle giants who feed on plankton. No one can say that about great white sharks, though. These fierce ocean predators (which served as models for the shark in *Jaws*) can grow up to 23 feet and weigh more than 7,000 pounds. At the other end of the scale is the spined pygmy shark, who lives in extremely deep water and feeds at midwater depths, who grows to the size of a medium cucumber, about 7 or 8 inches long. Most sharks are in the middle of these extremes. Approximately 50 percent of shark species are less than a meter (or about 40 inches) long.

The shape of a shark's body depends on the kind of life he leads. Predators such as great whites and hammerheads have bodies shaped like torpedoes with powerful tails that are custom-tailored by evolution to hurtle them through water after prey. Bottom-feeding sharks such as sand sharks have flexible, tapered bodies that are well suited to hiding among rocks and coral. Most sharks have two fins on their backs and a smaller fin on the undersides of their bodies. Chapter 5 provides a closer look at different kinds of fins and tails and explains how they help sharks move through the sea.

The Odds and Ends of Shark Heads

Sharks' heads come in a variety of shapes; they can be wide and flat or bulbous and long. Hammerheads, not surprisingly, derive their names from the odd shape of their heads, which do, in fact, have flattened heads that resemble the head of a hammer. The eyes and nostrils are at the tips of the head and can be up to 23 inches apart, which gives them a panoramic view of their environment—the better to spot prey. There are several different kinds of hammerheads. The scalloped hammerhead, for instance, (also known as kidney-headed shark) has a head that is flattened, scalloped, and wide. This kind of head is called a *cephalofoil*, and it makes the shark more hydrodynamic. These heads are also filled with a variety of sensory organs called electroreceptors, which, as the name suggests, can pick up electric impulses from potential prey.

The hydrodynamic shape of the head tends to direct the shark upward when the tail is flexed and probably helps maintain the upward thrust when the shark is swimming slowly to keep it from sinking.

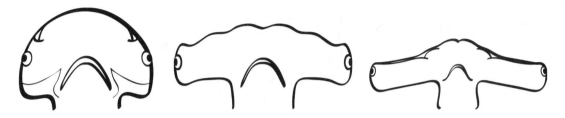

Sharks' heads come in all sorts of shapes, as shown in these three examples.

No matter what their shape, all shark heads are chock full of sensory organs—some specialized for detecting scents, others for detecting electrical impulses given off by prey. Although the shape of shark heads differs from species to species all shark heads have these traits in common:

- **Snout and mouth.** Most sharks have relatively blunt snouts with the exception of saw sharks, who have greatly elongated and toothy snouts. In most sharks the mouth is located on the underside of the snout, but in angel sharks, whale sharks, and a few other species, the mouth is found at the tip of the snout.

- **Tongue.** A shark's tongue, like the shark itself, is made out of cartilage. (Keep in mind, though, that cartilage isn't the only component of sharks; they are made up of other types of tissues as well.) It's found on the floor of the mouth in both sharks and other fishes and is relatively inflexible. Technically, a shark or fish tongue is called a *basihyal*. From what scientists can tell, the basihyal serves no function in most sharks, except for a species known as cookie-cutter sharks. These sharks use the basihyal to rip chunks of flesh out of their prey. These sharks actually suck the "cookie" out with the large flattened basihyal.

- **Nostrils.** Yes, sharks do have noses, but no, they do not use them to breathe— only to smell. Unlike human noses, shark noses are not connected to their mouths. The nostrils, which come in pairs, are found on the underside of their snouts. As water continually flows through the nostrils, it brings with it information in the form of smells that tip the shark off as to

What Does It Mean?

Barbels are whiskerlike projections, similar to those of a catfish, that are found in some species of sharks, such as the nurse shark. Barbels are located near the nostrils and mouth and act as tasters and smellers.

where he is likely to find his next meal. Some species also have whiskerlike feelers protruding close to the nostrils and mouth called *barbels*, which can enhance the shark's sense of taste and smell.

All the Better to Bite You with, My Dear

Evolution gave sharks one real weapon: their mouths. A shark mouth is a remarkable piece of engineering that basically relies on two components: teeth and jaws.

Types of Teeth

Shark teeth are not very different from those of predators that stalk their prey on land. Most sharks are *carnivores*—in other words, they eat the flesh of other creatures. Therefore, the teeth of many shark species have sharp points that are well suited for cutting meat. Some sharks have two different kinds of teeth—one kind for grasping prey and another kind for grinding it up. Some bottom feeders have teeth suited for grinding because they feed on shellfish. Many bottom feeders consume plankton as well, but they absorb it all at once. There's no need to take the time to chew the stuff.

What Does It Mean?

Carnivores are animals that mainly feed on the flesh of other animals. Mammals are carnivores and so are several species of sharks.

Shark teeth can be divided into two main categories: long and thin teeth or wide and serrated. Sharks such as the goblin shark and the sand tiger shark use their long, thin teeth to catch small fish. A single bite with teeth like these is usually sufficient to kill the prey. Then, without further ado, the shark swallows the fish whole.

But what about larger sharks who feed on proportionately bigger prey? As you might expect, their teeth are formed differently. Their wide, serrated teeth are built to cut like a hunting knife, slicing through flesh and bone with ease. Sharks such as the great white use their teeth to tear into their prey, ripping off large chunks of flesh with each bite (a gruesome spectacle, to be sure).

A third group of sharks use a combination of the two types of teeth by piercing a fish and holding it in place with their long, pointed teeth while chopping the fish into easily digestible pieces with their serrated teeth. There are all sorts of variations on a theme: dogfish sharks have strong, flat teeth for crushing crabs; sand tiger sharks have long, hooked teeth for snaring fish; and tiger sharks have serrated teeth to eviscerate larger prey.

Shark Facts and Stats

The great white shark has the largest teeth of all sharks.

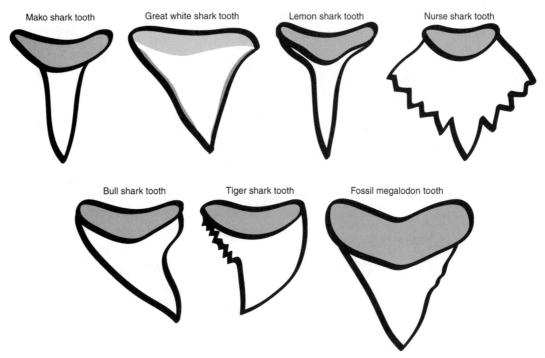

Mako shark tooth   Great white shark tooth   Lemon shark tooth   Nurse shark tooth

Bull shark tooth   Tiger shark tooth   Fossil megalodon tooth

Shark teeth come in a variety of forms; some are designed for grasping prey, others for slicing, but sharks do not use their teeth for chewing.

Teeth to Last a Lifetime

Shark teeth have the same basic consistency as our teeth: an outer layer of enamel, dentine, and a central pulp cavity. But similarities between our teeth and shark teeth pretty much end there. For example, we humans are born without teeth. But sharks already have fully developed teeth when they are born because even pups are left to their own devices after birth. We have two sets of teeth, and after childhood we've gotten all the teeth that we're going to get. Sharks continue to replace teeth as long as they live, and some sharks can live up to 40 years and there's evidence they can live far longer, possibly to 70 years. That's a lot of teeth.

Another difference is that we only have one row of teeth. Sharks, on the other hand, can have as few as 3 and as many as 15 rows of teeth. Whale sharks can have up to 3,000 teeth in 310 rows. These teeth are easily misplaced because they usually end up embedded in the body of the shark's prey. But not to worry—when a front tooth is lost, a back one replaces it the next day. These new teeth form in the gums and roll forward as needed in a process somewhat like a conveyer belt of teeth. Every 10 to 14 days, all of a shark's teeth are completely replaced.

The placement of the teeth in a shark's mouth is quite a bit different from how teeth sit in our mouths. Our teeth are planted in our gums. In sharks, developing teeth lie flat just above the gums and then move into the jaw as needed.

Shark Lore

In 25 years, a gray shark can produce up to 20,000 teeth! That accounts for why shark teeth are the world's most commonly collected animal artifact.

Shark Facts and Stats

Whale sharks have mouths that are four feet, six inches wide.

Say aaah! The shark's jaw is only loosely connected to its skull.

Infamous Jaws

No part of the shark's body is more famous (or more feared) than the characteristic hingelike jaws, which are only loosely attached to the skull. The great white shark, for example, has a bite that can exert 3.75 tons per cubic centimeter. Some sharks, such as great whites, can open their jaws so wide that they can eat prey that is bigger than their mouths. They can do this by pushing their top jaws forward while the lower jaw swings down. When the shark closes his mouth, the teeth of the lower jaw pierce the prey and clamp it in place while the teeth of the upper jaw begin to slice away.

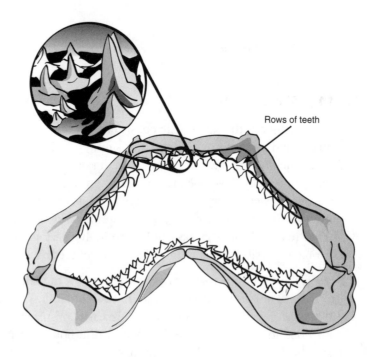

Rows of teeth

A Tenacious Grip: Two True Stories

What is it like to be bitten by a shark? In April 1998, in Florida, a 16-year-old boy found out the answer to that question when a nurse shark bit him. Nurse sharks are usually harmless; they frequently live in caves in warm, shallow waters and can grow up to 15 feet. They have broad heads and stout bodies and move sluggishly, spending most of their time on the seabed feeding on shellfish. Injuries are most likely to occur when curious divers move into their crowded space or touch them, and that's exactly what happened in this incident.

The boy had provoked the attack by grabbing the shark's tail, which was a pretty stupid thing to do. To defend itself, the shark latched onto the boy's chest with its teeth. In spite of the boy's desperate efforts, the shark refused to relinquish its grip. Finally, the shark had to be detached surgically. The boy lived. The shark did not.

In another case from several years ago, a pearl diver named Iona Asai was attacked while swimming in the Great Barrier Reef off Australia in about 30 feet of water. The diver turned to see a huge tiger shark heading straight for him. Asai had no time to take evasive action. A few moments later, the shark was gripping Asai's head in his fearsome jaws. Asai was able to escape by squeezing the shark's eyes until the shark surrendered its grip and swam away. Asai needed nearly 200 stitches to suture his wounds; he was lucky to survive. Three weeks after his operation, he returned to the hospital with an abscess. When surgeons opened the wound, they found a tiger shark tooth embedded in Asai's skull.

Denticles: The Shark's Armor

During the long evolution of sharks, they have developed a skin composed of tiny, hard, toothlike structures known as the dermal denticles or placoid scales. Not only are these structures formed like curved, grooved teeth, they also are made out of the exact same material as teeth. (Shark's teeth are modified placoid scales.)

If you moved your hand from a shark's tail to his head, his skin would feel much like sandpaper. However, if you moved your hand the other way (from head to tail), the denticles would feel relatively smooth because all of the spines of the denticles point backward (toward the tail). Sharkskin is also very thick. The skin of whale sharks, the largest of the species, can be up to four inches thick.

This rough, thick body armor offers sharks some significant advantages. For one, it helps the shark swim more quickly because the water channels through the grooves formed by the denticles' streamlined shape reduce drag by minimizing friction. For another, the shark's skin is so rough that prey can be injured simply by coming in contact with it.

The shark's placoid scales or denticles form a protective "armor."

From Top to Bottom: Two-Toned Creatures

As I mentioned in Chapter 2, sharks' coloration is designed for camouflage. Sharks usually come in two tones: darker on top and lighter on bottom. More specifically, most sharks have dark gray bodies and white undersides. This two-toned phenomenon is known as *countershading*. (By the way, countershading isn't limited to sharks; other animals also have adopted this strategy of protection and deception.) The darker color on top (the dorsal side) provides camouflage against potential predators because it blends in well with the darker waters. Seen from below, the lighter toned belly of the shark (the ventral side) can be obscured by the waters above when they are brightened by the sun. Of course, this color scheme not only affords shark protection against predators but also allows them to sneak up on their prey.

In addition to the typical shark countershading, whale sharks have a mixture of pale polka-dot-like spots and lines on their backs that contribute to their camouflage. To some observers, the pattern resembles a school of fish; others think that it resembles reflections of sunlight on a shallow reef.

Some species of sharks have developed even more elaborate color schemes. Bottom-feeding sharks such as the angel shark are camouflaged so that they blend in with the sand, rocks, and mud on the ocean bottom where they live and feed. For the same reason, wobbegongs, another type of bottom feeder, are covered with splotches, spots, and lines. Wobbegongs are masters of disguise: in addition to their spotted or striped skins, they also sport tassels or frills on their heads that could easily be mistaken for seaweed by some unsuspecting prey.

In some cases, a shark's coloration can vary, possibly because of a change in weather or water conditions. Some changes in color can occur when the shark is removed from the water. For example, the dusky black of the basking shark can turn to brown or blue along the back, becoming lighter on the sides and on the belly. The lower part of the snout, which was dull reddish to begin with, can turn dull white. In general, though, the palette of shark colors is fairly drab, ranging from blacks and grays to browns and reddish browns.

The Least You Need to Know

◆ Sharks come in all sorts of sizes, ranging from over 40 feet to a few inches; nearly half the species measure only about a yard in length.

◆ A shark has only one major weapon: his mouth.

◆ Sharks have a skin made up of a thick matrix of sharp protective scales known as denticles.

◆ Sharks are colored for camouflage. Many sharks are countershaded, which conceals them from predators and prey from below and above.

Chapter 4

Exploring Sharks from the Inside

In This Chapter

- What makes sharks cold-blooded
- What goes on in a shark's brain
- How sharks see, hear, and smell
- How sharks' extra senses lead them to prey

Now that you have an idea what the outer shark looks like, it's time to examine a shark internally. This chapter describes the shark's regulatory system: how a shark breathes, sees, hears, and smells (as you might suspect, a shark's olfactory sense is extraordinary). You'll also find out if it's possible to answer the question: Just how smart (or dumb) are sharks?

Cold- and Warm-Blooded Sharks

Most sharks are cold-blooded or technically heterotherms or *poikilotherms*. Cold-blooded sharks do not generate heat by digesting food like warm-blooded mammals do, but instead have variable temperatures. The body temperature of most sharks matches the temperature of the surrounding water. If the temperature of the water changes, the shark's body temperature changes as well. (Reptiles, who are cold-blooded, modify their body temperature according to the environment. For instance, lizards bask in the morning sun to warm themselves.) By contrast, warm-blooded (*homeotherms*) animals generate heat internally and maintain a relatively constant body temperature that is higher than the average temperature of the environment.

Important exceptions to the cold-blooded rule are several *pelagic* predators such as the mako, the blue, and the great white sharks, all of whom are partially warm-blooded.

What Does It Mean?

Pelagic refers to creatures that wander far out into the oceans. This group of animals includes mako sharks, great white sharks, and blue sharks, as well as whales, tuna, and dolphins.

At least eight known species of sharks are able to raise their body temperature above the water temperature by as much as 18 degrees Fahrenheit when they require energy for short bursts of energy while hunting. When sharks swim at rapid speeds, their muscles generate heat, which is then transferred between adjacent arteries and veins to the muscles. As their body temperatures climb, they gain more energy, which in turn enables them to accelerate even further.

The Thinking Shark

Sharks and rays have very large and complex brains. Surprising as it may seem, the ratio of the sharks' brains to body mass is higher than most other fish and is comparable to many other vertebrates, including some mammals. But like every other shark characteristic, brain size and complexity depend on the type of shark species. Large, highly active sharks such as great whites and scalloped hammerheads have proportionately bigger and more complex brains than bottom feeders, whom shark writers commonly describe as "sluggish."

Scientists have learned which parts of the shark brain are in charge of body and head movements, which parts process and coordinate sensory input, and which are responsible for hearing, vision, and smell. Through the study of shark brains, scientists have discovered just how crucial smell is to the sharks' survival. Nearly a third of the shark's brain is devoted to smell. After all, the sharks' heightened olfactory sense is crucial to guiding them to their prey, as are other senses such as electroreceptors.

Yet much about the shark brain remains a mystery. Studies have given scientists some idea about which parts of the shark brain regulate behavior, and sharks can be trained, showing intelligence that is put to use in experiments in smell, electric field reception and related studies in the lab. Researchers demonstrated as early as 1975 that lemon sharks learn faster and retain a conditioned response longer than a cat or rabbit. (When an animal is trained to associate the ringing of a bell with food, the bell ringing will evoke the same response even in the absence of food: This is an example of a conditioned response.) All the same, they probably will never learn how to perform tricks (or would not want to even if they could) as dolphins or sea lions do to the delight of aquarium audiences. But no one is certain what kind of intelligence sharks have—whether it is on the level of an elephant's, say, or a dog's, or is far more primitive.

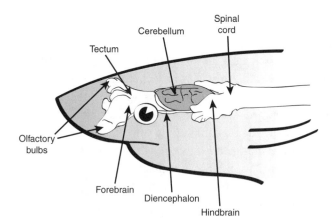

Researchers can identify the parts of the shark brain but they can't say how intelligent they are.

Gills: Getting Oxygen into the Bloodstream

In Chapter 2, I noted that although sharks have noses, they don't use them to breathe. Instead they use gills to breathe by extracting dissolved oxygen from water. Gills are paired respiratory organs found in many forms of marine life. They usually grow out of the body wall and are filled with blood vessels. Although gill structures vary, all gills are usually immersed in water; dissolved oxygen flows into the gills from the outside, and carbon dioxide is expelled in the other direction.

What Does It Mean?

Spiracles are a special type of gill slit found in some species of shark, located just behind the ears, used to filter oxygen from water while they eat. Typically, sharks have five to seven gill slits. Because most (but not all) sharks lack muscles to pump water through the gills, these species need to keep in motion for respiration—a process known as ram ventilation.

In sharks, oxygenated water first enters the mouth, then courses through the gill opening, and then passes over tiny *gill filaments* before being pushed out again through gill slits located behind the head. In bony fish, these slits are covered; in most sharks the slits are easily seen. Sharks have five to seven gill slits on each side of their head. Bony fish, by contrast, have only one gill on each side.

Some sharks have small openings called *spiracles* located behind their eyes, at the top of the head. These openings are like immature gill slits. The most active, fast-swimming sharks either have one or two very small spiracles or none at all, which suggests that they serve little practical function in those sharks.

Pulling Water Through the System

Gills are crucial in getting oxygen into the shark's bloodstream (and thence to all the tissues and organs). However, because sharks lack muscles to draw water across the gills, they need to find a way to move water through their respiratory system. The solution? They swim. The forward swimming motion of the shark keeps the water flowing across the gills, ensuring a constant supply of oxygen. This process of swimming to breathe is known as *ram ventilation*. Sharks that expend a particularly high level of energy rely on ram ventilation almost exclusively, which means that they must constantly be in motion if they want to keep breathing.

However, some species of sharks are capable of pumping water through their gills by opening and closing their mouths. The muscles they use to perform this task are collectively called a *gill pump*. The process is similar to the way in which our lungs work. Most of the bottom dwellers have gill pumps.

Absorbing the Oxygen

Once the water is gone, what happens to the oxygen? That's where the gill filaments come in. These filaments are covered with microscopic blood vessels called capillaries. Because these capillaries contain less oxygen than the surrounding water, an imbalance results. To restore the balance (a process known as *osmosis*) and make the oxygen level equal inside and outside the shark, the oxygen enters the shark's bloodstream, which disperses the gas throughout the body.

Keeping the Beat: Heart and Circulation

Humans have four-chambered hearts. Shark hearts are simpler; they have just two chambers: an atrium (also called the *auricle*) and a *ventricle*. Relatively small compared to the rest of a shark's body, the heart looks like an S-shaped tube and is located in the shark's chest close to the head.

The heart pumps the blood through the respiratory or branchial arteries to blood vessels in the gills in order to pick up oxygen that has been collected from the water passing through the gills. The oxygenated blood then is circulated through the bloodstream.

In order for this system to work, the heart needs to get the blood to the blood vessels in the gills in the first place. The problem is that the shark's small, two-chambered heart isn't strong enough to do this by itself. Because the heart creates such low blood pressure, many sharks need to keep swimming in order to produce the muscle contractions necessary to maintain blood circulation. Basically, sharks need to swim to maintain blood circulation just as they need to swim to keep the oxygenated water flowing across the gills in order to get the oxygen into the blood. Either way, the shark can't stop. In effect, motion and life are one and the same for sharks.

How the Shark Senses the World

Sharks have exquisitely honed senses (some unique to them alone) that give them an edge in the intensely competitive underwater world in which they live. Of all these senses, the sense of smell is the strongest. The shark's ability to detect nearly indiscernible scents over considerable distances is one of the main reasons sharks are such successful predators. But sharks also have extra senses that enable them to pick up electrical impulses, which not only helps them find prey but may also help them navigate across thousands of miles of ocean.

Swimming Noses

Sharks were once known as "swimming noses" when it was believed that their sense of smell compensated for their poor vision. This misconception arose when scientists plugged the nostrils of a shark and found that he had difficulty finding his prey. The scientists reasoned that sharks' keen sense of smell must be crucial and without it they were severely handicapped. Well, they were right, but they were also wrong! All of the shark's senses are highly refined, but they work together; as soon as you eliminate one sense, the other senses suffer as well, throwing the shark's navigational system completely out of whack. As it turns out, sharks have a fairly good sense of vision and hearing although smell is certainly paramount.

As I mentioned in Chapter 2, sharks can detect even faint scents of blood or body fluids from a considerable distance. Some experts estimate that sharks can pick up animal odors up to nearly 2.5 miles. To put it in another perspective, a great white shark would be able to detect a single drop of blood in an Olympic-size pool.

The smells are carried on ocean currents, which form an odor corridor. As the shark moves, water flows through the paired forward-facing nostrils on the underside of his snout, entering the nasal passage and then moving past folds of skin covered with sensory cells. (The nostrils are dedicated exclusively to smell, not breathing.) A special olfactory groove, which is a slit in the shark's mouth, allows the shark to follow the path of the telltale odor through the currents.

Shark Facts and Stats
Although sharks have a very keen sense of smell they are not the olfactory champions that catfish, eels, and salmon appear to be. These creatures are all capable of locating their home stream after a year or more at sea by smell alone.

A shark's sense of smell is even more remarkable in that it can detect the direction from which a particular odor is originating. You can tell where sounds are coming from because of the placement of your ears on either side of your head. In much the same way, a shark uses its paired nostrils to register the direction of a scent. An odor coming from the left of a shark reaches his left nostril an instant before it gets to the right one. That gives the shark the clue he needs to head in the right direction (or the left direction, as the case may be).

Hearing Down in the Depths

Sharks also have an acute sense of hearing, especially for low-frequency vibrations beyond the range of human capacity. These low-pitched sounds are often the distress sounds of wounded prey. Experts differ on just how far sharks can register sounds, and the range probably depends on the species. Some sharks may be able to hear relatively quiet sounds as far away as 1,000 yards (about the size of a football field); others may be able to hear louder sounds from a couple miles away.

Sharks have a hole on the top of each side of their head called *endolymphatic pores.* These pores are the only external sign that the shark has ears at all. These pores contain ducts that lead to a series of semicircular canals, which give the shark its auditory capacity. Many tiny openings or pores around the shark's head also allow him to sense animals moving in the sea.

Seeing in the Dark

Although shark vision is much better than scientists originally believed, it varies in acuity, depending on the needs of the shark. Some sharks have a good ability to see in dim light; in many ways, their visual capacity is similar to that of a cat's. For bottom feeders such as sand sharks and wobbegongs, vision is less important in hunting prey, and so their eyesight is commensurately weaker.

Similarly, shark eyes vary in shape, size, and position among different species. Sharks that live deeper in the oceans, for instance, usually have larger eyes than those living nearer the surface, and their eyes tend to be emerald green in color, an adaptation that allows them to discern luminescence of other deep-water creatures that might make good prey. By the same token, sharks used to shallower waters tend to have smaller eyes because they have the benefit of the sun to aid their vision.

The Anatomy of Shark Eyes

In many ways, shark eyes aren't so much different from our own. They have a large, spherical lens, a cornea, a retina (containing both rods and cones), an iris, and a pupil. What distinguishes shark eyes and accounts for sharks' night vision is a mirrorlike layer in the back of the eye called the *tapetum lucidum*. This layer serves as a kind of light amplification device by doubling the intensity of incoming light. Moreover, sharks can control the amount of light reaching their eyes by dilating or contracting them, which is an ability that no other fish has. Although sharks see in color, light intensity is more important. We know this because the shark's retina has a greater proportion of rods (light intensity sensors) than it does cones (color sensors), making sharks sensitive even to small gradations in light.

In addition, most sharks have a fairly wide field of view owing to the fact that their eyes are positioned on each side of the head. Scientists describe this positioning as having lateral eyes. Hammerheads are the most extreme example: Not only are their eyes spaced wide apart—up to 23 inches in some cases—but they actually protrude out from the head.

Some sharks, the great white in particular, have a special kind of eyelid, known as a *nictitating membrane*, that protects the eye from being injured by thrashing prey while the shark is feeding. A moveable inner eyelid, this membrane is found in many animals including amphibians, birds, and mammals. This third eyelid serves to protect the eye against injury. In the rabbit, for instance, the membrane helps keep the eye moist. In the American dipper, an aquatic songbird, the membrane shields the bird's eyes from water spray of rapids and waterfalls.

The shark's eye is designed so that it can amplify dim light at lower depths. Note the nictitating membrane or third eyelid.

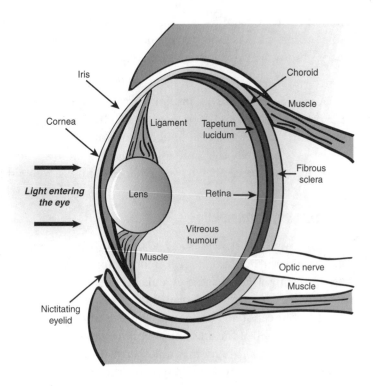

The Bonus Package: Extra Shark Senses

Some species of sharks are capable of migrating hundreds of miles across the oceans. How do they know where they're going? How do they know when they get there? Scientists have concluded that at least some, if not all, of these sharks are able to navigate using their own internal compasses. Which is to say that sharks are sensitive to Earth's magnetic field. And that's not all. Sharks can also detect electrical fields.

An Electrical Experiment

To determine whether sharks could detect electricity, scientists conducted an experiment in which they trained a group of sharks and rays (remember that rays are members of the same branch of fish that sharks belong to) to eat in an area directly over a pair of electrodes buried in the sand bottom. The sharks couldn't see the electrodes and weren't aware they were there—at least at first. Whenever the sharks were fed fish the current was turned on a tiny amount, just four tenths of a microvolt.

Then the scientists tricked the sharks and rays: they turned on the current but withheld the food. Without being anthropomorphic, let's just say that the sharks and rays were extremely unhappy about this turn of events. They quickly swarmed about the buried electrodes, uncovered them, and snapped at them as if they were going to make them answer for this outrage. The scientists had succeeded in demonstrating that the sharks were in fact capable of sensing even minute charges of electricity and could trace the current to its source.

The Ampullae of Lorenzini

Every creature on the planet emits electricity in small amounts. This electricity is produced by regular muscle contractions. Evidence suggests, however, that sharks are better equipped to register these electric fields than any other animal. The explanation is found in a special cluster of electrically sensitive receptor cells in the shark's head called the *ampullae* of Lorenzini.

Sharks and rays were among the first animals to be identified as having electroreceptor organs. As one expert on sharks once put it, a "shark is like the Starship Enterprise, bristling with sensors." The ampullae are distributed around the shark's head and are large enough to be seen with the naked eye, but their function was not discovered until fairly recently. They are connected to pores on the skin's surface through a network of small jelly-filled tubes. Scientists are still uncertain exactly how the ampullae work and there is some dispute about how far this electrical detection system extends. Some scientists believe that a shark can register an electric field produced by a 12-volt car battery in the middle of the Atlantic Ocean. The current flowing across the ocean—1/1,000,000,000 volt per square centimeter—would still be detectable by sharks. That means that a shark could find even a well-camouflaged or hidden prey simply by picking up the electrical field the prey emitted.

Sharks also use their electroreceptors to orient themselves. Any object—solid, gas, or liquid—through which electricity can flow is known as a conductor. But every conductor resists an electric current to one degree or another. Sharks can detect the differences in resistance of objects that happen to enter their electric fields, providing them with a kind of electric roadmap or compass underwater. The ampullae of Lorenzini act as an insulated core

What Does It Mean?

Ampullae were clay jars used by the ancient Romans to store grain, oil, and wine. Scientists named the shark's electrical sense organs after them because the organs' shape resembled the shape of the jars.

conductor. Once an electrical field is created by an organism or by the environment it emits a signal which reaches the sensitive receptor cells; this signal is converted to a chemical message which is then conveyed by nerves to the central nervous system. There the brain analyzes the signal and responds accordingly. Is there prey in the vicinity? A larger object that might necessitate a change in direction? The shark's response itself will either change the electric field or else create a new one altogether.

The ampullae of Lorenzini are specialized jelly-filled organs that allow the shark to detect electric impulses given off by the muscle contractions of prey.

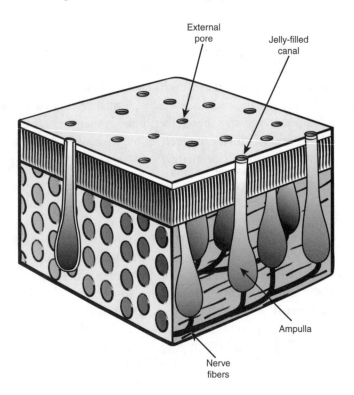

External pore

Jelly-filled canal

Ampulla

Nerve fibers

The Lateral Line

As if sensitivity to electric fields were not enough of an added bonus to the usual repertoire of senses, sharks have another unique sense organ known as the *lateral line*. Essentially, this "line" consists of fine, fluidlike tubes that contain nerves positioned beneath the shark's skin and running along both sides of the body from head to tail. These tubes are lined with hairlike protrusions that connect to sensory cells. Water gets into these main tubes through pores on the skin's surface. The water also brings important information. When any creature (or object such as a boat) approaches the shark, it sets off a vibration, which causes the water coursing through the lateral line to move back and forth, an action that stimulates the sensory cells. This stimulation alerts the shark to the presence of potential predators or prey. The reception of the vibrations in the water is basically an additional low frequency hearing system.

The lateral line, running down the side of the shark, is full of nerves that alert the shark to vibrations of moving objects in the environment.

If you want to get a better sense of how the lateral line operates, try this experiment. Blow steadily on the palm of your hand and note the feeling of the air moving across it. Now hold one of your fingers between your mouth and your hand and move it back and forth so you interrupt the flow of the air. Notice the change in the feel of the air on your hand. This feeling gives you some sense of how a shark detects changes in water pressure. This sense of "distant touch" gives the shark the ability to register the direction and intensity of vibrations from a suspicious presence in his area and enables him to determine its speed, size, and form. A thrashing prey, for instance, would announce itself with a distinctive pattern of vibrations, ensuring a quick end to his agony.

By themselves, no one of a shark's sense organs would be adequate for effective hunting. The combination of all these senses is what makes the shark a deadly predator. The electroreceptive organs like and the ampullae, however, give sharks the ability to detect other living creatures even if their other senses didn't work.

The Least You Need to Know

♦ Sharks breathe through gills that filter out the dissolved oxygen in water and distribute it to the bloodstream.

♦ The most important sense a shark possesses is that of smell.

♦ Sharks have special senses that enable them to detect electric and register the vibrations in their immediate environment made by other creatures or objects.

5

Hunting and Feeding

In This Chapter

- ◆ How sharks swim
- ◆ What types of fins sharks have and what they do
- ◆ How and what sharks eat
- ◆ How the shark's digestive system works

Chapters 3 and 4 described the shark inside and out. You learned how sharks obtain information from the outside world by using their specialized senses. Now it's time to consider the shark in motion. As you learned in Chapter 4, sharks have to stay in motion in order to keep oxygen coming in and ensure that oxygenated blood reaches every part of their bodies. This chapter examines the mechanics of the shark's movement by analyzing how the shark's fins and tail function, and how a shark swims (or if you prefer, flies) through the water. When a shark moves, of course, he is usually in search of food. So this chapter also looks at what sharks eat and what kind of diets various species maintain.

Bodies in Motion

Sharks are masters of motion, as well they should be. If they didn't move continuously they would sink like a stone to the ocean bottom. Some species can achieve extraordinary bursts of speed—up to 40 miles an hour or more for some pelagic sharks—while others coast at barely perceptible speeds along the ocean floor. The faster sharks stand out from the other fish in the sea because they don't appear to swim through the water as much as they seem to fly. But whatever their speed, they all rely on their fins to move and navigate through the water.

Fins with Functionality

Sharks may have up to five different types of fins:

- **Paired pectoral fins.** These fins, located behind the head, give sharks lift as they swim.

- **Paired pelvic fins.** These fins, located near the tail, provide sharks with stability as they swim.

- **Paired dorsal (back) fins.** Most sharks have dorsal fins, but two exceptions exist: frilled sharks and cow sharks (technically known as *Hexanchiformes*) have only one dorsal fin. In some species, the dorsal fins have spines. They also provide lateral stability to prevent rolling.

- **Anal fins.** Anal fins offer additional stability. With the exception of angel sharks (*Squatiniformes*), saw sharks (*Pristiophoriformes*), and dogfish sharks (*Squaliformes*), all sharks have an anal fin. These sharks are modified for reproduction.

- **Caudal or tail fin.** This fin is found at the rear of the shark. This fin is responsible for forward propulsion.

Sharks can have up to five different types of fins—two pectoral, two dorsal, two anal and one caudal or tail fin.

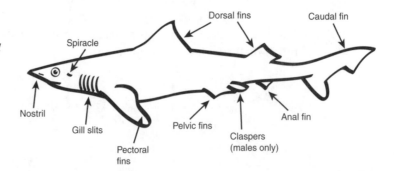

Fins perform a number of functions; for example, they can steer and brake and help the shark maintain balance. The pectoral fins alone, for instance, serve no less than three functions:

- They provide lift as sharks move up and down in the water.

- They provide stability when sharks are swimming at a constant depth.

- They aid in steering and turning.

When I said that some sharks appear to fly through the water, I wasn't just speaking metaphorically. The pectoral fins near the head resemble the wings of an airplane, and like the wings of a plane, these fins serve a balancing function. As a plane flies forward, air flows over and under the wings. Similarly, the forward movement of a shark pushes water around the fins, creating lift.

The pectoral and pelvic fins on the sides of the shark's body occupy approximately the same position as the main wings and horizontal tail wings of a plane. The shark can move these fins to different angles, which changes the flow of water moving around them. By raising a fin sharks can create greater water pressure below the fin than above it. This action produces upward lift. By tilting the fin down, sharks do the reverse, applying greater pressure above the fin than below it and thereby pushing themselves down. Sharks use their pelvic fins to swim in a level position. (In male sharks the inner edge of each pelvic fin has special sexual organs called *claspers*. Chapter 12 discusses the reproductive behavior of sharks.)

The vertical dorsal fins found on the shark's back (often together with the vertical anal fin) function much the same as the vertical stabilizer wing on a plane. These fins help maintain the shark's balance, and when they are moved from one side to another, they can also turn the shark to the left or right.

The Tail Fin

Some sharks, notably the great white shark, rely exclusively on their tails (or caudal fins) to propel themselves through the water, typically in a side-to-side motion like the movement of a snake crawling in the grass. They use their other fins only for balance. The tail works in tandem with the muscles of the body and the flexible cartilage skeleton to give the shark a powerful and smooth swimming motion. The tail acts as the shark's propeller; the shark swings it back and forth to move forward.

Fast-swimming predators, such as the great white and mako sharks, have tails with lobes that are similar in size. In other words, their tails are symmetrical. The slower swimmers, by contrast, have tails that are more asymmetrical. The colorfully named bugeye thresher shark, for instance, has such a tail; the top lobe is far larger than the bottom lobe, and the top lobe is so long that it is half the length of the rest of the shark's body.

The thresher shark has a tail or caudal fin that is practically as long as the rest of his body.

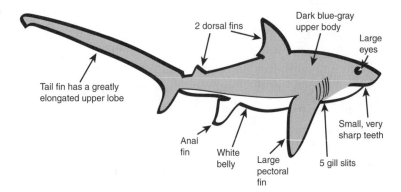

2 dorsal fins

Dark blue-gray upper body

Large eyes

Tail fin has a greatly elongated upper lobe

Anal fin

White belly

Large pectoral fin

Small, very sharp teeth

5 gill slits

Tails (caudal fins) are differently shaped, depending on the lifestyle of the particular species. Mako sharks, for instance, have crescent-shaped tails to help them reach great speeds. Threshers have tails shaped like huge scythes, which they use to corral and stun their prey.

How Fins Limit the Shark's Movement

For all their usefulness, fins also limit the movement of the shark. That's because they are so rigid and lack flexibility. This rigidity, created by rods made of cartilage inside the fins, gives shark fins structural support. However, it also means that sharks can't stop suddenly or swim backward because the shark's pectoral fins cannot bend upward to stop or reverse course. If some object gets in a shark's way, he has to swerve to one side or another in order to avoid it because he can't stop. If a shark needs to move backward, he has to rely on gravity by falling and then resurfacing in the desired location or turn around in circles. Although the lack of movable parts might make sharks a bit less agile, this same deficit also means that they don't need a lot of space to perform certain maneuvers such as turning around.

How Sharks Feed and Digest

If sharks have one overriding obsession it's food. (Some humans share this obsession.) Sharks occupy the top rung of the food chain in the sea; they are the apex predators. Larger fish may eat smaller fish, and smaller fish may eat shellfish and crabs and plankton, but the shark eats them all. In this section you'll find out how sharks eat, digest, and excrete their food.

Feeding Habits

The majority of sharks feed on live fish, but many species of sharks eat anything that strikes their fancy, including other sharks (so long as they're smaller). Many sharks can consume seals, stingrays, turtles, and seagulls with equal abandon. Some sharks, such as makos, have an even more lavish diet at their disposal because they can live in warm seas where far more animal and marine life is available to please their palate. Bottom and filter feeders have different strategies altogether because their diets are based on small maritime life and shellfish.

Sharks don't chew; they just swallow their food whole. But many of them first pierce, rip, and tear their food, especially when the prey is big and meaty. Sharks have astonishing teeth and often several rows of them, which are lost and replaced throughout their lives. The type of teeth they have influences their diets. Smooth dogfish sharks, for example, have strong, flat teeth for crushing crabs while sand tigers have long, hooked teeth for snaring fish. Tiger sharks use huge serrated teeth to tear off meat from larger prey. Goblin sharks have blunt back teeth that are eminently suited for crushing oysters.

> **Shark Facts and Stats**
>
> Sharks eat about 2 percent of their body weight each day—a bit less than humans eat. Because most sharks are cold-blooded, they don't need as much whereas humans need some food to keep their bodies warm.

Paradoxically, the biggest sharks shun larger prey. They are filter feeders who sieve tons of water through their mouths and gills for food, and their diet consists mainly of plankton. The so-called gentle giants, whale sharks and basking sharks, are filter feeders that take in huge quantities of water through their gaping mouths. As the water passes through their gills, they strain the plankton and other nutrients out using special organs for filtration. But these filter feeders differ from one another in significant respects, too. Whale sharks, for instance, use their numerous minute teeth to trap food, but basking sharks are content to cruise along the surface of the water with their mouths wide open, ready to consume whatever comes their way. Basking sharks, which favor temperate coastal waters, forage mainly for zooplankton.

Although filter feeders may give the impression that they're eating their dinner without having to do anything to earn it aside from opening their mouths, don't be fooled. Keeping their mouths open requires a great expenditure of energy because it increases drag, thereby making swimming more difficult. Researchers have found that plankton eaters need to forage in waters with relatively large concentrations of zooplankton just to meet the energy costs of feeding.

Like corporate executives, these sharks should perform a kind of cost-benefit analysis. Is it worth making the effort if the task consumes more energy than the amount that gets replenished through filtering? Basking sharks, some scientists theorized, live on an "energetic knife-edge." The annual disappearances of these sharks from coastal waters may be due to just this phenomenon. When cold weather causes a depletion of plankton, some scientists believe, basking sharks migrate to deeper waters where they pass the winters in a state of suspended animation where they sustain themselves at the lowest possible metabolic rate.

> **Shark Lore**
>
> Most sharks swim and feed alone. Some of the major exceptions are scalloped hammerhead sharks and blue sharks, who often swim in schools.

> **Shark Facts and Stats**
>
> The biggest meat-eating shark is the great white, which grows to 21 feet long, though some great whites have reportedly been measured at close to 40 feet.

Going After Plankton

What is plankton exactly? Generally speaking, plankton includes any number of marine and freshwater organisms that are found near the surface of the water and are carried by winds, tides, and currents. Plankton comes in two basic varieties: *phytoplankton* and *zooplankton*. The former consists of photosynthetic organisms, including several different types of algae. The latter variety is made up of *protozoa* and small crustaceans, jellyfish, worms, and mollusks. In addition, zooplankton also includes the eggs and larvae of many animals that inhabit the sea and fresh water. The amount of plankton in a particular area varies depending on the density and stability of the water. A liter of lake water, for example, can contain more than 500 million planktonic organisms. Plankton forms the major component of the diet of the filter feeders, which include whale sharks, basking sharks, and megamouth, a shark that more than lives up to its billing.

> **What Does It Mean?**
>
> **Protozoa** are single-celled organisms that are propelled by minute, hairlike projections called cilia.

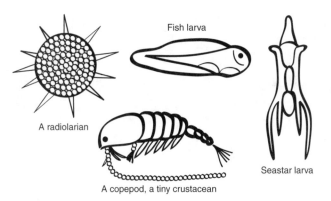

Fish larva

A radiolarian

A copepod, a tiny crustacean

Seastar larva

Plankton is composed of a variety of microscopic marine life; in addition to zooplankton there is another kind of plankton—phytoplankton—made up of algae and other microscopic plants.

Digesting Food

The shark's digestive system is usually an efficient machine that can digest fishes whole and even some mammals, as well as hard-shelled mollusks and crustaceans. Sharks' U-shaped stomachs contain strong acids and enzymes that dissolve most of what they eat. The combination of these acids and enzymes produces a soupy mush that is easily absorbed by the body. Only this liquid mush enters the intestines. Anything that can't be digested (large bones, say) is filtered out by a pyloric valve, a kind of screening device located between the stomach and the intestines. Large indigestible material, however, remains in front of the pyloric valve and is ultimately vomited to the outside. The intestines are where the food (in the form of liquid mush) is absorbed into the shark's body. Another important valve called the spiral valve serves to slow digestion and increase food absorption.

A shark's intestine is short and straight in contrast to those of most animals (including humans) who have long, coiled intestines. Although sharks have shorter intestines than other animals, shark intestines are arranged in such a way that the surface area is expanded. The arrangement differs from species to species. For example, some shark intestines are arranged in folds, some are in a spiral pattern that resembles a spiral staircase, and others are enclosed within a cylinder. Nevertheless, all of the different intestine arrangements have the effect of making more space available for food absorption.

The next stop in the digestive process is the *cloaca*. The cloaca is a rear chamber into which the digestive tract empties. The cloaca also receives wastes from the urinary tract and eggs or sperm from the reproductive system. All these wastes are eliminated from the body through the anus. A special salt-secreting gland, the rectal gland, helps eliminate excess salts absorbed from food and surrounding seawater.

The shark's stomach contains acids and enzymes that help digestion, turning food into mush that is then passed into the intestines and eliminated through the anus.

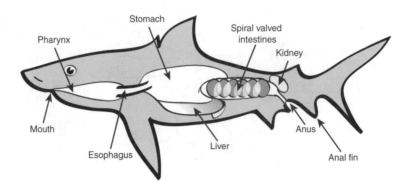

Absorbing Water

Unlike bony fish, sharks don't drink water. Instead of drinking it, sharks absorb water from the surrounding waters by osmosis. In this process, water flows through a semi-permeable membrane (in this case, the gills) from an area of higher concentration of saltwater to an area of lower concentration of saltwater, which has the effect of equalizing the concentrations within and without the shark. Any excess salt is secreted through the rectal gland.

What Does It Mean?

Urea is a colorless, crystalline waste product of protein metabolism that is often found in the urine of many species, including humans. In sharks, urea passes through the blood and collects in the gills where it is then excreted.

The blood and tissues of sharks (and other cartilaginous fish such as rays and chimaeras) are extremely salty. This means that they have high concentrations of *urea* and salts in their body. In fact, sharks and their relatives are slightly saltier than the sea—a phenomenon known as *hyperosmotic*.

Because most sharks require so much salt, they are unable to live in fresh water. However, some sharks, such as bull sharks, can lower their salt concentrations sufficiently to survive in fresh water.

Peeking into the Garbage Can of the Sea

No account of shark diets and digestion would be complete without a brief catalogue of the improbable and bizarre objects that have been found in sharks' stomachs. Sharks have an efficient digestive system, but their bowels are underdeveloped. That's why so much junk ends up undigested and unexcreted in the shark's stomach. Sharks often rid themselves of nonnutritious and nondigestable items by vomiting, but not always. Some things are simply too large to be regurgitated. Tin cans, car tires, shoes, dogs, and even a chicken coop with feathers and bones have all been found inside sharks. Here are some of the other objects and creatures that have been recovered, in whole or in part, undigested (and often indigestible) from shark stomachs:

- Twenty five quart bottles of Vichy water bound together with a wire hoop
- Three bottles of beer
- A nearly whole reindeer
- Six horseshoe crabs
- A blue penguin
- Porpoise parts
- A 100-pound loggerhead turtle
- A handbag with three shillings inside
- A full-grown spaniel
- A Galapagos seal pup
- A 25-pound lump of whale blubber and seven strands of whalebone

And I shouldn't forget to mention the tiger shark in the Australian aquarium that threw up a hand that turned out to be the solution to a murder (more about that in a later chapter), and another which vomited up the head of a person in Hawaii.

Finally I quote a stomach-turning excerpt from the "Natural History of the Fishes of Massachusetts" by Jerome Smith, which was published in 1833. "In the records of Aix, a seaport in France, in the Mediterranean Sea," Smith begins, "is the account of a shark, taken by the fishermen, 22 feet long, in whose stomach, among other undigested remains, was the headless body of a man, encased in complete armor."

The Least You Need to Know

- A shark's fins provide balance and allow sharks to turn, push downward, or create lift.
- Though the diet of most sharks consists of fish, feeding habits differ depending on the species, ranging from plankton, mollusks, and small fish to sea lions and elephant seals. Filter feeders consume mainly plankton, and bottom feed.
- The shark's digestive system turns the food into a kind of mush that is filtered and passed into the intestines where it is absorbed.
- Sharks' reputations for being omnivorous is a result of so many bizarre and often very large objects and creatures being found in their stomachs.

Part 2

Categorizing Sharks

Sharks come in all shapes, sizes, and configurations; there are nearly 400 species, and it's likely we haven't found them all. The very variety of sharks and the startling difference among sharks in behavior, habitats, diets, and reproductive methods have proven a boon and a headache to researchers. The next four chapters introduce you to several species including such celebrities as the great white and the largest shark of all—the whale shark.

Chapter 6

The Gentle Giants: Megamouth and Whale Sharks

In This Chapter

- The science of shark names
- The megamouth shark
- The whale shark
- A personal encounter with a whale shark

In this chapter, I'm going to introduce you to some of my favorite sharks—the biggest sharks (and biggest fish) in the sea. I call them gentle giants because these two species—megamouth and whale sharks—are actually very docile, posing no harm to humans or any other mammals. They thrive on diets of plankton (tiny marine life) and small fish, not quite the image most people have of sharks as menacing predators. In spite of its huge bulk, megamouth managed to remain hidden from the world until only a few decades ago. And while the whale shark has been known for many years we still have a great deal to learn about it. Researchers are still trying to determine its migratory patterns. Before I discuss these two species it might be helpful to consider how shark species get their names. Whale sharks resemble actual whales, but as you'll see, the nomenclature isn't always so obvious.

Naming Sharks

Names like the wobbegong, the bugeye thresher, the goblin, the dogfish, the tiger, and the zebra shark are not easy to forget. A number of different systems have been used to name sharks, and not all of them are exactly scientific. The scientific names, on the other hand, are pretty well regulated by rules, but the common names are up for grabs.

Some sharks, for instance, have been named after other creatures. In addition to dogfish, tiger, and zebra sharks, there are also crocodile sharks, bull sharks, catfish sharks, and even cow sharks. Colors, too, have provided a fertile source of nomenclature. Thus, you find the great white, the blue, the blacktip, the whitetip, the silvertip, the gray reef, and the lemon shark.

Sometimes sharks are named because they have features that bring to mind other associations. These sharks include angel sharks, silky sharks, bramble sharks, spinner sharks, hammerhead sharks, basking sharks, and nurse sharks.

You don't have to inquire very deeply to figure out the origin of the name megamouth, which I talk about in this chapter. Cookie-cutter sharks also derive their name from their mouths, which are typically round with wedge-shaped teeth on the lower jaw that the sharks use to carve out cookie-shaped pieces of flesh from their prey. On the other hand, the origin of the name nurse shark is more of a puzzle. One possibility is that someone observed sharks giving birth to live young and mistakenly believed that the mother was "nursing" her newborn pups—a terrible misconception given the fact that nurses, like other sharks, tend to consume their young if they don't swim away with dispatch. Etymologists (those who study the origin of words) have another opinion. In the *Oxford English Dictionary* you learn that the use of the letter "n" if used before a word beginning with "h" was often transferred to the adjoining word. Such words as huss and hurse, for instance—names for dogfish and other sharks—that were ordinarily preceded by a "n" gradually evolved into nurse. Evidence extending back to the sixteenth and seventeenth centuries suggests that the words "nurse" and "nurse-fish" were used to designate dogfish, a name commonly applied to a number of small sharks. Later the term "nurse" was applied to any large fish, not only sharks. It was only beginning in 1768, with the first voyage of Captain Cook, that the term was applied exclusively to sharks.

Sharks That Aren't Sharks

Some types of fish, which bear some resemblance to a shark, have been mistakenly called sharks—and the name has stuck.

- The iridescent shark (*Pangasius sutchi*) is actually a type of catfish that superficially resembles a shark. It is an aggressive fresh-water fish that preys upon smaller fish. The iridescent shark is a popular home aquarium fish.

- The bala shark (also called the silver shark or tricolor shark) is no shark at all but rather a type of minnow and a bony fish. They are much more closely related to goldfish than to sharks and are popular in home aquariums. Growing to about eight inches, they originally came from Southeast Asia and may be an endangered species in the wild.

- The rainbow shark is another misnamed shark; it is a type of algae-eating minnow (a cyprinid) that bears a superficial resemblance to a shark (and is often confused with the red-finned shark—another nonshark). Although its principal diet is algae, it can be an aggressive fish and will eat smaller or weaker fish. Like other nonshark "sharks," the rainbow shark is a popular home aquarium fish. It grows up to six inches and is native to Thailand and Indochina.

- The guitar shark (also known as sharkfin, guitarfish, and shovel-nosed shark) is a closely related part of the ray family. While not a shark, it tends to move like a shark in the water with the typical swaying movement but once it gets to the bottom it acts like a ray. Guitar sharks aren't dangerous but they can grow big and often swim up close to divers.

- Banjo sharks are members of the ray family and are not sharks. They inhabit the coast of Australia and are characterized by a striking pattern and are quite docile.

These suggestive names underscore the great diversity to be found among the hundreds of species of sharks. Chapter 2 described the great variety of shark sizes, but a similar variety can be found in color, shape, behavior, and abilities. Sharks even have personalities that differ not only between species but also vary individually within a species. And a great deal remains to be discovered about sharks. The great depths of the sea undoubtedly hold many surprises about these creatures that you can scarcely imagine.

Sharks that have escaped detection for centuries are finally being discovered; the most recent example of this phenomenon is the megamouth. Scientists still disagree over how many sharks have been found to date, and there is little consensus over how species of sharks should be catalogued. Different sharks, for instance, go by the same name in different countries. Nurse sharks of Australia, for instance, are different species from nurse sharks in the Caribbean and the Atlantic. And although most scientists are in accord that the Lake Nicaragua and Zambezi shark are both bull sharks, some researchers still beg to differ.

Cookie-cutter sharks derive their name from the cook-ielike shape of flesh that they tear out of their prey.

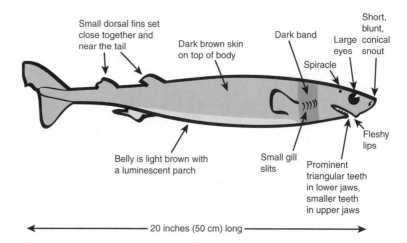

Small dorsal fins set close together and near the tail

Dark brown skin on top of body

Dark band

Large eyes

Short, blunt, conical snout

Spiracle

Belly is light brown with a luminescent parch

Small gill slits

Prominent triangular teeth in lower jaws, smaller teeth in upper jaws

Fleshy lips

20 inches (50 cm) long

Open Wide: The Megamouth

Scientists consider the megamouth to be one of the most unusual sharks. What makes the megamouth story so fascinating is the fact that the species wasn't discovered until 1976. Its elusiveness is accountable to the fact that it dwells at great depths and seldom gets anywhere close to the surface during the daytime. As of April 2002, only 12 of these enigmatic creatures have ever been found.

One of the reasons megamouth sharks are such strange creatures is that, although they belong to a taxonomic order famously renowned for its teeth, they have very small teeth that are used to filter food. Their mouths appear to be set into perpetual grins stretching three feet wide. These grins are filled with organs that some experts believe may attract prey to their doom.

Megamouth has a cylindrical (but soft and flabby) body that tapers towards the tail with small gill openings and measures about 14 to 16 feet long. Megamouth's body also lacks any particular pattern. The head is bulbous, wide, and long, and the eyes—in marked contrast to the expansive mouth—are very small.

Where Megamouths Live

Megamouths seem to be well traveled. One shark was found in Australian waters, stranded on a beach. Five others have been sighted in Japan, two in California, one in Brazil, one in the country of Senegal in West Africa, and another in the Philippines. The first of the species to be discovered was caught in scientific nets of a U.S. Naval research vessel working at a depth of about 470 feet in Hawaii.

Evidence suggests that these sharks inhabit depths from 450 to 4,000 feet and feed near the surface at night. That means that recreational scuba divers, who rarely dive below 130 feet, would be unlikely to ever encounter a megamouth (surely it would be a memorable experience if they did). The megamouths' deep-dwelling habits are no doubt the reason they kept their identity hidden for so long.

The megamouth, which can grow up to 14 feet in length, wasn't discovered until 1976.

How Megamouths Feed

Although the megamouth may look intimidating, given its bulk and its preposterously large mouth, the truth is that these sharks are quite timid. These tropical, deep-sea feeders swim in stiff, slow movements and sustain themselves on plankton and jellyfish.

To learn more about the habits and migrations of megamouth sharks, scientists undertook a *tracking study* of the sixth megamouth ever sighted, which was captured and tracked in Dana Point, California, in October 1990. The study resulted from a question raised by well-known shark researcher Dr. Eugenie Clark only a few years after the megamouth was first discovered. Here, she said, is "an entirely new species that has yet to be named scientifically."

What Does It Mean?

A **tracking study** refers to a research program in which an animal is caught, tagged (often with a tiny radio transmitter), and then released. This procedure allows scientists to monitor an animal's movements and behavior.

It feeds on plankton, yet it is known to be a deepwater fish. That presented a paradox. Plankton is generally found near the surface of the sea. So how, Clark asked, "does megamouth find sufficient food to survive at great depths?"

The study seemed to suggest an answer, revealing that the shark descends to about 400 feet during the day and then at night rises to about 60 feet below the surface where a plentiful supply of plankton is more likely to be found.

Megamouths are rarely found because they live at such great depths; most specimens have been found off Japan or California.

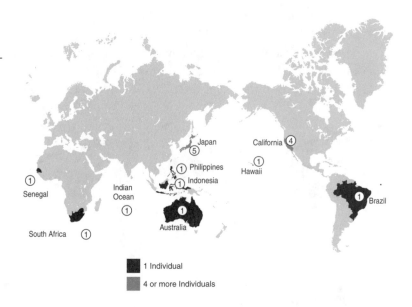

The Whale Shark: The Largest Shark of All

Taxonomically speaking, the whale shark is called *Rhincodon typus*. Whale sharks are the largest sharks, about the size of a bus. Their maximum length is about 45 to 50 feet, and they can weigh twice as much as an elephant, or about 27,000 pounds. They get their name from a superficial resemblance to whales with which they are sometimes confused. The largest fish on the earth today, it boasts of a mouth that's nearly as great as the breadth of head, up to five feet wide. It is dark gray to a reddish or greenish brown on its back and sides. It has white or yellowish spots and a number of narrow white or yellowish transverse stripes. Its belly and lower parts are white or white yellow. Whale sharks have five gill slits, an anal fin, and two dorsal fins.

The whale shark is distinguished from other sharks by its very broad head and wide mouth located at the front of the head, rather than underneath the head as in other species. Its olfactory opening is just above the upper lip, hidden in a nasal groove. Its eyes are small and when the whale shark closes an eye it has to rotate it and suck it back into its head.

Whale sharks give birth to live young. One female, caught off Taiwan, contained 300 embryos in her uteruses. (Sharks have two uteruses; in humans the uterus is the womb.) Whale sharks don't reach maturity—sexually capable of reproducing—until later in life, between 25 and 30 years of age. This finding has led some marine biologists to estimate that Whale sharks may live well over one hundred years.

> ### Shark Facts and Stats
>
> The whale shark has the biggest mouth of all sharks.

A great deal about this enormous shark remains mysterious. Only rarely have marine biologists had the opportunity to examine its internal organs. Most specimens have quickly putrefied after being caught. Biologists believe that the shark has a small gullet, meaning that while it might be able to take large objects into its mouth it would be unable to swallow them.

> ### Shark Facts and Stats
>
> The whale shark's liver is massive; in a 36-foot whale shark the liver weighs 1 ton, about 9 percent of the total weight of the shark.

The Eating Habits of Whale Sharks

In spite of their size and massive proportions, whale sharks have a decidedly benign temperament, displaying none of the aggressiveness of other ocean-going predators. Their teeth aren't very sharp, and for good reason: The whale shark is a filter feeder.

Whale sharks usually feed on or just below the surface. It prefers a diet of plankton, fish larvae, krill, squid, and sardines. It absorbs these tiny organisms, some only one millimeter in diameter, out of the water through its five relatively large gill slits. They have a fine mesh of rakers attached to these gills to help them strain food. (Only the basking shark, another large species, has bigger gills.) When the shark is feeding its gills flare out as the shark pumps large volumes of water through the gills. Opening its mouth, it draws in a large amount of water, which it then expels through the gill slits. Whale sharks can feed actively: When the sharks spot schools of fish or blooms of plankton, they rise up vertically through the schools, catching their dinner as they climb. If the concentrations of food are heavy enough, it will remain in the vertical position and feed for long periods of time. Sometimes, though, this shark will feed passively, cruising beneath the surface with its mouth agape.

Where Whale Sharks Live

Whale sharks prefer temperate waters along the equator where there are pockets of nutrient-rich colder water. These conditions are favorable for blooms of plankton on which the sharks feed. They are often seen with schools of pelagic fish, especially trevally (jacks). Whale sharks are usually seen in small schools or alone during certain seasons. They frequent the waters of western Australia in March and April, for instance, during the coral spawn. They have also been frequently sighted in November and early December off Australia's southern Queensland coast. Whale sharks also gather in the Seychelles in the Indian Ocean in August and November. Whale sharks have been sighted off Mozambique and South Africa between October and March, which is summertime in southern Africa. Whale sharks have been observed in the Sea of Cortez near Cabo San Lucas and along the Mexican coast to Acapulco between March and August, and in Bahia de los Angeles, Baja California, Mexico, they are most common from August to October. Although it is known that whale sharks travel for great distances—one was tracked for 14,000 miles over 40 months—their migratory patterns are unknown.

> **Shark Facts and Stats**
>
> The skin on the back of the whale shark is the thickest and toughest of any species in the world.

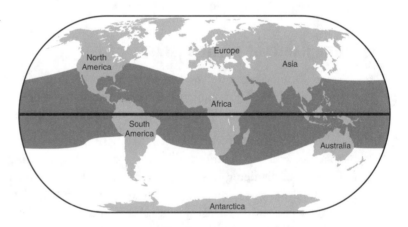

Whale sharks prefer temperate waters near the equator where they can find ample food sources.

Why Are Filter-Feeders So Big?

Why are plankton feeders—megamouth, for instance, or whale sharks—so large? One possibility: food storage. Zooplankton is scattered and forms in patches—and it's seasonal, meaning that this source of food may not always be available. So the animal needs to get as much as he can in a single helping to make it through the barren periods when the plankton is sparse or nonexistent. Even during the summer, for instance, when plankton levels are at their peak, basking sharks—another large filter-feeder—can barely get enough food to sustain themselves. When winter comes, and plankton levels drop off, basking sharks will actually molt (the only shark known to do so), shedding their gill rakers, specialized organs that sieve water and then apparently goes into a form of hibernation; it sinks to the bottom and remains there until spring when it regrows the gill rakers.

Having a large size may also give these sharks a greater foraging range, their ability to swim over long distances facilitating their ability to find new sources of zooplankton. Whale sharks appear to migrate over vast distances in the eastern Indian Ocean in search of new plankton blooms. (There is some evidence that they are able to find these blooms from great distances because they smell a particular chemical compound given off by the zooplankton.) Similarly, a larger mouth is associated with increased water processing—a principal function of filter feeding is to sieve water for food. Basking sharks, for example, can filter more than 1,650 tons of water for plankton an hour. In addition, a large body confers protection against potential predators even if these sharks are not particularly aggressive.

Close Encounters of the Shark Kind

I have been lucky enough to be able to see a whale shark in person while scuba diving near the northernmost Galapagos Islands of Darwin and Wolf, about 600 miles west of Ecuador in the Pacific Ocean. Surrounded by vertical cliffs that make landings inaccessible, these islands are visited almost exclusively by divers.

Darwin's Arch is a celebrated shark diving location in the Galapagos, the archipelago off the coast of Ecuador made famous by Darwin in his theory of evolution.

Dive operator Marc Bernardi has found that because most sharks swim into the current, dropping into the water upcurrent from a pinnacle where you are most likely to spot a shark gives the diver a better opportunity to see the shark from the front. As he says, "They swim like dinosaurs, gliding majestically, but if you try to swim after them, it's so long, Jack."

> ### Shark Facts and Stats
>
> Divers usually leave their tank and gear behind when a whale shark has been sighted, partly because they don't have the time to put the equipment on, but more importantly, to avoid frightening the shark with air bubbles from the regulator.

Along with the other 14 people in my group, I dived to a depth of 60 feet, where we clung to the barnacle-covered rocks of the seamount, trying to avoid being swept away by the strong current. As a shadow darkened the ocean above us, our attention was diverted to an unparalleled underwater parade: Bottlenosed dolphins were escorting a 40-foot-long, wide-mouth whale shark. Its giant body was gliding gently just below the surface.

As I watched, the shark's wide-open mouth scooped krill from the plankton-rich waters. Dozens of remoras clung to the shark's huge tail fin, as they busily cleaned microorganisms from the animal's huge polka-dotted hide. Below the dolphins' entourage, schools of hundreds of scalloped hammerheads swam in jigsaw patterns, their necks scarred by bites incurred during mating rituals. On any other dive, swimming with hammerheads just an arm's length away would have been a thrill. But not this time. The whale shark overshadowed them so much that I was as nonchalant about the hammerheads' presence as if I'd found myself among guppies in an aquarium.

> ### Shark Facts and Stats
>
> Remoras have a symbiotic relationship with whale sharks and other large fish. They attach themselves for a free ride while cleaning parasites from the shark. They even have been known to attach themselves to a diver's tank, a sight good for a laugh. They are found in tropical and temperate waters throughout the world. Remoras range in size from 7 to 35 inches and are generally brown or gray in color.

For the next five minutes, our group watched in awed silence. This thrilling underwater experience was over much too quickly. As the shark glided out of sight, I wanted to swim after it. I didn't want to see it disappear in the density of the plankton. Fortunately, my group ran into the whale shark again the following morning accompanied by schools of scalloped hammerheads, which were enveloped in turn by schools of small, reddish Creole fish.

On the same trip, Galapagos naturalist Ruli Menoscal and I had a rather harrowing encounter with another type of shark that, unlike the whale shark, is not so congenial toward human intruders. As Ruli and I ascended from one dive, a Galapagos shark began to follow us. Ruli signaled me to keep a close eye on this one. The 8-foot shark began circling us in a tight ring maybe 10 feet away.

Back to back, we turned in circles, following the pattern charted by the shark. As we made our ascent from 60 to 50 then to 30 feet, the shark rose with us. The shark's eyeballs seemed to close in on us. I was scared, particularly because I made for a bigger and therefore juicier target than Ruli. Curious sharks had followed me on dives in the past. On those occasions I had ascended as quickly to the dive boat as prudence would allow. This was different. Here there was nowhere to go. When we surfaced, we would be at the mercy of the current until we could be spotted and retrieved by our dinghy. We were easy pickings.

Shark Lore

The chances of diving with hammerheads are good throughout the Galapagos. Chances of sighting schools of these sharks on the long boat trip to Darwin or Wolf islands are almost 100 percent.

At 15 feet we needed to stabilize our ascent for a three-minute safety stop in order to get rid of nitrogen from our bodies. This is a common practice divers follow to prevent the bends. But we also knew that we would have to confront this huge Galapagos shark. Still, we had no choice. Fortunately, when we paused, the shark was content to make one final circle before heading off into the blue. Phew!

Other divers in our group also reported being followed up to the surface by Galapagos sharks. We all agreed that this was a more frightening experience than being surrounded by a thousand hammerheads and one magnificent whale shark at a depth of 60 feet. Bernardi feels that Galapagos sharks don't establish "prey-predator" boundaries like other sharks, which makes them curious. In his 13 years of leading trips to the Galapagos Islands, he has had lots of divers surrounded on the surface by Galapagos sharks without any incidents other than frightened divers.

For me, finding the whale shark was the realization of a lifetime goal. Yet my experience in the Galapagos only whetted my appetite. Yes, I can say that I have "been there and done that," but that hardly conveys the sense of exhilaration and excitement I felt once I caught a glimpse of such a fabulous creature. I can only imagine that encountering a megamouth ascending from the deep would be an equally great thrill.

The Least You Need to Know

- ◆ Species of sharks derive their names in a variety of ways: from their resemblance to other animals, for example, or from their color.

- ◆ Megamouth, a filter feeder who lives at great depths, was first discovered in 1976; only 12 megamouths have ever been found.

- ◆ Whale sharks, another filter feeder species, are the largest species of shark and the largest fish in the sea, measuring up to 45 feet and weighing twice as much as an elephant.

- ◆ Marine biologists still have a great deal to learn about the whale shark, including its migratory patterns.

Chapter 7

Sharks with Bad Reputations

In This Chapter

- Meet the great whites
- The true-life story that inspired *Jaws*
- Why bull sharks are so dangerous
- The trouble with tiger sharks
- The lethal role of oceanic white tips in disasters at sea

The previous chapter examined two of the "gentle giants," the megamouth and the whale shark, who are humongous filter feeders who subsist on diets consisting largely of plankton, small crabs, and small fish. As their sobriquet suggests, these sharks are harmless to humans. This chapter takes a look at some predatory sharks who pose a potential threat to humans (and many other species) and as a result have garnered the most attention.

These sharks have attained the status of celebrities, in large part because of Steven Spielberg's movie *Jaws*, the first real Hollywood summer blockbuster, which was based on the best-selling novel of the same name by Peter Benchley. But as Benchley points out in his latest book (a nonfiction look at sharks), the danger that sharks present to humans is vastly overblown. Of the 375 to 400 species of sharks, only 11 have ever been known to attack humans, and only 3 of those are man-eaters. Sharks can be dangerous to be sure (and Chapter 18 talks about sensible precautions to take to avoid running into unpleasant encounters with them), but the vast majority of sharks prefer to mind their own business and have no interest in making their meals out of us.

The Great Whites

The great white is the undisputed star of the sharks, the best-known and one of the most feared (although that reputation is not always so deserved). When you say the word "shark," the image of the great white is the first thing that leaps into people's minds. Among Australians the great white is known as the white pointer. Tabloid writers, with an eye to selling papers, have called this shark the white death, while divers who have seen the shark close up call him Whitey. For scientists, the great white is *Carcharodon carcharias*.

Whatever name these sharks go by, they are the largest and strongest predatory fish in the sea and average 18 feet in length, though they can grow to about 25 feet. (One great white reputedly measured 30 feet, but this measurement has never been verified.) They can weigh more than 4,000 pounds, and some have been caught that weighed more than 7,000! The tops of their bodies can be brown or charcoal gray, even occasionally blue or indigo. Their bellies, however, are always white.

Stouter than most sharks, great whites are distinguished by their large, jet-black eyes and crescent-shaped tail fins. They have large, serrated teeth that are the largest teeth of all sharks, and they can eat just about any animal, including *pinnipeds*. Yet most evidence suggests that great whites don't fancy humans. Great whites may be the only sharks with the rather unsettling habit of poking their heads above water to scout out where their next meal might be found. They are also one of the few sharks that are warm blooded (their body temperatures are higher than the surrounding water), so they can draw on extra reserves of energy when speed is of the essence.

What Does It Mean?

Pinnipedia is a taxonomic classification of sea mammals that includes seals and sea lions.

To navigate and find prey, great whites have a particularly refined detection system that is superior for seeking out other creatures as well as other sharks. The ampullae of Lorenzini, those jelly-filled tubes discussed in Chapter 4, allow them to pick up electrical charges as small as .005 microvolts, which can signal a heartbeat or gill action of prey hiding only a few feet away.

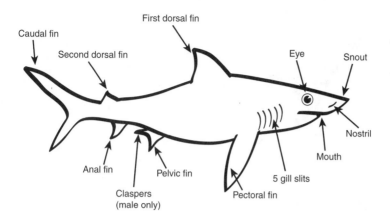

Great whites can grow to 25 feet in length or longer and can weigh up to 7,000 pounds.

The Great White Life Cycle

Great whites are exceptionally long-lived. Some researchers estimate that these sharks can live to 100 years old. But their longevity comes at a cost; they do not develop until late in life, reaching maturity at 10 years old or later.

In contrast to other sharks who lay eggs, the great white gives birth to live young. Great whites also have very few pups at a time. Once born, the shark is on his own. Newborns are believed to be around 4 feet long, and they grow about 10 inches a year.

What the Great Whites Eat

Great whites begin life by feeding on fish, rays, and smaller sharks. As great whites mature, their palates begin to show a preference for marine mammals and whatever they can scavenge from large animal carcasses. They begin preying on small harbor seals, but as the sharks get larger, they ambitiously begin to prey on meatier sea lions, elephant seals, and even small whales. Great whites prefer to attack from below, taking their victims by surprise as they inflict a large, potentially fatal bite. The prey often die from the massive trauma or blood loss, but not always. The sea is full of marine animals with scars from bites that missed their mark. Great whites are also scavengers, favoring the carcasses of whale sharks and the fat-rich blubber layer of dead whales.

Shark Lore

The great white shark has 3,000 teeth in total.

Great whites typically bite into their prey only once— and that's usually enough— and then wait for their prey to bleed to death.

Where the Great Whites Swim

The great white is found in both temperate and colder seas along shorelines or islands. The majority of large great whites have been found in south Australia. In the United States they have most frequently been sighted off Massachusetts, New York, and California. Sharks also hunt along the coast of Oregon and have occasionally been sighted as far north as the Gulf of Alaska.

During the fall, many great whites migrate to southern California where females give live birth to their offspring. This area is rich with the sharks' favorite food sources: the northern elephant seal, the California sea lion, the Steller sea lion, and the harbor seal.

Great White Attacks

Although bull, mako, and tiger sharks have attacked humans, the great white shark probably has the worst reputation for attacks. To some degree this rap is undeserved. All evidence indicates that great whites don't like the taste of human flesh and that if they take a bite out of a swimmer, surfer, or diver, it's because they've mistaken it for a pinniped or some other sea creature (though that's hardly much of a consolation for the victim). Especially in murky water these sharks can be confused as to the nature of the prey.

Scientists term the great white's feeding behavior as "bite, spit, and wait," which is kind of similar to the process of wine tasting. Great whites have a remarkable ability to determine the potential caloric value of what they've just bitten. One taste answers the question: Is this creature worth the energy to keep eating or not? Even if the shark is satisfied that the creature will make a tasty meal, he doesn't necessarily resume his attack. If the initial bite has done its job, the shark can sit and wait for the creature to bleed to death and then resume eating it.

Most researchers believe that great whites dislike the taste of humans and know after the first bite that they have made the wrong choice. There are exceptions, though. In 1909, in an incident that still leaves shark experts baffled, a 15-foot great white caught off Sicily contained the bodies of two adults and a child. Yet most reports of human attacks by great whites provide corroboration for the experts' theory: about 70 percent of great white shark victims survive simply because they have escaped with only one misplaced bite. But only one shark bite can sometimes prove to be one shark bite too many.

Nonetheless, the media has grossly inflated the danger that the great white poses to humans. Every year the great white is responsible for two to three nonfatal attacks on divers and swimmers. California takes first place in the greatest number of great white attacks with almost 70 attacks to date; South Africa is second, and Australia is third. Surfers, swimmers, and divers in the United States have little to fear, however, because only about 100 great whites live in American coastal waters. There are so few that the great white was placed on the protected species list for the state of California in 1992. That means the shark is legally protected from unlawful killing.

Diving with Great Whites

The September 1997 issue of *Sharks and Divers* ran an astonishing account by a diver named Jeremiah Sullivan who swam with a great white off the southern Australia coast. (He provided some photos as corroboration, one of which showed him holding the tail of a 16-foot great white and using it to tow himself around as if the shark were a lovable, if oversized, pet.) The diver reported:

> I was so close to him I could stroke his torso as he swam by—he seemed quite unconcerned. On his next pass I tested him further by hooking my right hand around the upper lobe of his tail. When his momentum jerked me into his slipstream, he didn't so much as flinch. ... The only acknowledgment of my presence was a slight but very deliberate glance over his right side as he towed me out to sea. ... I turned towards the big boy ... everything was quiet ... he cruised up, looked at me sideways, and appeared to say, "Oh, Jeremiah, it's you!"

Taste of the Bizarre _____

Great whites don't have many predators, but they reportedly have been attacked by orca (killer) whales. In one case, the whale gave the kill to her calf without showing any interest in eating the shark herself.

The Story Behind *Jaws*

No account of the great white would be complete without talking about the book and movie named *Jaws* that brought the great white so much fame. Peter Benchley, the author of the novel, wrote that he was inspired by a *New York Daily News* story from 1964 about the capture of a 4,550-pound great white off Long Island. He carried around the yellowed clipping in his billfold and regularly showed it to any book editor he encountered. Finally, one editor bit and provided a contract and a desperately needed advance. Only hours before the book was to go to press (it was published in 1974), Benchley and his editor were still arguing over the title. They had more than 100 possibilities, none of which satisfied them. The title *Jaws* was a compromise; they settled on it because it had the advantage of being short. No one involved with the book, including the author himself, had any idea just what an inspired title it would turn out to be.

Some reports suggest that Benchley, an experienced diver himself, also drew on a series of shark attacks near Mattawan, New Jersey, for his material. The first attack took place on July 1, 1916. The victim was a 25-year-old man who was swimming just a few yards from shore. Although he was pulled to shore by another swimmer, he died that night. The second fatal attack—this time on a hotel bellboy—occurred five days later. Although the first attack had barely attracted any notice, the second made the front page of *The New York Times*.

Local businesses, concerned that the summer tourists might stop coming, called for official action. The mayor of Spring Lake, the community closest to where the attacks had occurred, organized a boat patrol. Men stood on the boat's deck with rifles at the ready as they dragged the water for the offending shark. But the shark did not oblige them by appearing.

Shark experts of the day seemed curiously sanguine, voicing their belief that sharks were very unlikely to ever attack a swimmer and expressing doubts that a shark's jaws were powerful enough to bite through a human leg bone. The experts were wrong.

On July 12, a retired seaman sighted the shark in the Mattawan creek, which was 11 miles inland. He phoned the chief of police to say that he'd just seen a large black shadow moving along the creek. Many people thought he was crazy. How could a shark get into a creek, after all? Unaware of the threat, a 12-year-old boy dove into the creek, only to have a great chunk of his hip and leg devoured by the predator. He didn't survive the night. Even as the local authorities were considering the idea of dynamiting the creek, the shark attacked a fourth victim, a 14-year-old boy who was not fatally hurt. The shark attacks had by now attracted national attention. The cabinet met in Washington to consider a response to the spate of attacks. President

Wilson gave orders to the coast guard to use every means to eliminate the shark from U.S. coastal waters. In spite of the presidential directive, the shark was never caught.

Shark experts believe that the marauding shark was unlikely to be a great white because great whites do not inhabit fresh water. Rather, experts believe that the killer was a bull shark, who can flourish in salt water and survive in fresh water.

The film version of *Jaws*, directed by Steven Spielberg, was an enormous success, driving up paperback sales of the novel to nine million copies. Because sharks, unlike dolphins or whales, aren't in the habit of cooperating with humans, even when it means a star turn before the cameras, Hollywood technicians invented "Bruce," a 25-foot mechanical shark. Although Bruce was longer than most great whites, the result was credible enough to scare the living daylights out of countless moviegoers. For those who depended on the scuba diving industry for their living, the movie was an unmitigated disaster because it made so many people afraid to venture into the water.

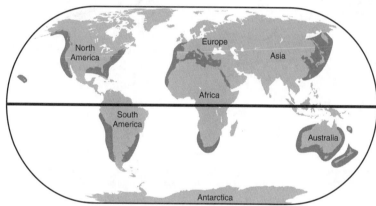

The great whites are found in temperate waters all over the world but they are concentrated in certain regions; the population of these sharks is unknown.

Great white sharks inhabit temperate
coastlines world-wide

Bull Sharks

Bull sharks are great wanderers and remarkably adaptive animals. They are equally at home in salt water, fresh water, and brackish water. They have a well-deserved reputation as aggressive, fearless, and territorial creatures. They go by an astonishing number of names, too. Bull sharks are known as cub sharks, Ganges sharks (in India), river sharks, Nicaragua sharks (in Central America), Zambezi sharks (in Africa), shovelnose sharks, slipway gray sharks, square-nose sharks, Van Rooyen's sharks, and *Carcharhinus leucas* to taxonomists. In Australia alone the bull shark is known variously as the freshwater whaler, the Swan River whaler, and the river whaler. This proliferation of names causes confusion because people are under the impression that these names all represent different species of sharks.

Bull sharks are stout and heavy-bodied with a short nose and two dorsal fins, one much smaller than the other. They have broad, serrated, triangular upper teeth and, unsurprisingly, very powerful jaws. It is gray on the top half of its body and off-white on its belly. Some have pale stripes on the side of their bodies. Males are relatively diminutive compared to females, measuring only about 7 feet to the females who can grow to about 11 feet in length. They also weigh much less—approximately 200 pounds whereas females may weigh as much as 500.

Bull sharks are among the most adaptable species, capable of living in fresh water as well as salt water.

Shark Facts and Stats

Bull sharks prefer to breed in the brackish waters at the mouths of rivers, usually in the summer months. They give birth to live young after a year of gestation. Until they are born, the embryos are nourished inside the mother. (To find out more about the various ways in which sharks reproduce please turn to Chapter 12.) Pups are born in litters of up to 13 and measure about 28 inches. Bulls reach sexual maturity between the ages of 8 and 10.

What Bulls Eat

The bull shark is a large, fierce predator known for eating just about everything else. They also seem to find humans more savory than great white sharks do, to the detriment of the former. A typical bull shark diet consists of fish, young sandbar sharks, rays, turtles, echinoderms, birds, mollusks, and dolphins. Remains of humans and hippopotami have been found in bull sharks' stomachs. Bull sharks mainly hunt in murky water close to shore and prefer to do so alone.

According to divers, bull sharks stage their attacks by circling the intended victim. They circle wide at first, but they gradually narrow the radius, coming closer and closer to their prey.

> **Shark Facts and Stats**
>
> One of the bull shark's favorite treats is baby sandbar sharks.

Where Bulls Live

Bull sharks usually prefer water that is waist-deep to about 90 feet below the surface, although they have been found at much greater depths. They are one of the few shark species to thrive in fresh water as well as saltwater. Most bull sharks do not migrate, though many bull sharks in South America are known to migrate thousands of miles from the Amazon River to the Atlantic Ocean. The tendency for bull sharks to swim up and down the Amazon, making journeys of up to 3,000 miles is hardly an aberration. They have also been spotted in the Mississippi and Congo rivers, and inland lakes such as Lake Nicaragua. Water with a high salt content doesn't deter them, either. A bull shark's favorite haunts, though, seem to be shallow rivers and inlets. Bull sharks seldom venture far out to sea although from time to time they have been sighted in the middle of the ocean.

Researchers used to think that the bull sharks in Lake Nicaragua must be a separate species altogether. What other explanation could there be as there appeared to be no way for the sharks to move in or out of the lake? But the sharks proved to be more ingenious and dexterous than the researchers imagined. They discovered that bull sharks could jump along the rapids like spawning salmon and make their way to the lake and back to the ocean at will.

> **Shark Facts and Stats**
>
> Some shark researchers fear that the culling of shark populations along the East Coast of the United States might have inadvertently helped increase the population of bull sharks, which are far more aggressive than most species. The reasons are simple. Although many sharks offshore have been caught, bulls escape commercial fishing lines and nets because they tend to frequent shallow waters shunned by other shark species.

Bull Shark Attacks

Bull sharks are responsible for several fatal attacks on humans that were previously blamed on great whites and gray nurse sharks who are largely harmless to humans.

In 1975, a ferry sunk in the Ganges-Brahmaputa delta in India, and 190 crew members and passengers were thrown into the water. Before they could be rescued, bull sharks killed nearly 50 of them. In Africa, where the bull shark is known as the Zambezi shark, several swimmers in shallow waters have become victims of bull sharks. In a case reported in 1970, a fisherman was attacked while working in about 5 feet of water. The bull shark took his arm. As the fisherman struggled underwater, the shark came back for his head.

For some reason, bulls seldom seem to go after divers. With divers, the sharks might want to take a closer look; but once their curiosity is satisfied, they swim away.

Taste of the Bizarre

Bulls have been known to cruise the Ganges River in India where they've taken several lives over the years. They also feed on corpses that are set afloat on the river as part of Hindu funeral rituals.

Shark Lore

In Australia, bull sharks are responsible for a large number of attacks and deaths. Most of these attacks were previously blamed on great whites, gray nurses, or bronze whalers.

At certain times in the islands surrounding Papua New Guinea, bull shark attacks on humans have occurred as often as once a month. In March 1998, there were two shark attacks in the same weekend, both of which occurred 16 to 20 miles upstream on the northwest coast of Papua New Guinea. In one case, a bull struck a teenage girl who was washing clothes at river's edge in water only several feet deep. The shark grabbed her thigh, which severed her leg. She died of blood loss. The next day, a few miles away, a young man was swimming across a river when he was grabbed around the waist by a shark. He died of massive internal injuries and blood loss. The villagers used nets to try to catch the sharks. They succeeded in getting one, which was reported to have human remains in its gut. Whether one or two sharks were involved in the attacks was not known.

Bull sharks have found their prey closer to home, too. A shark suspected to be a bull shark attacked two men swimming in shallow water near a popular beach in Alabama in June 2000. The first attack occurred early in the morning when the shark struck a local school principal, taking his arm and then pursuing him as he ran to shore. A second swimmer, who did not realize what had happened, was subsequently bitten in the thigh area. The second victim hit the bull on the nose several times and then tried to make a run for it. He, too, was followed all the way to the shore. About a week later possibly the same shark attacked a 22-foot boat in nearby waters.

Tiger Sharks

Tiger sharks (*Galeocerdo cuvieri*) are considered the second most dangerous shark (as far as humans are concerned) after bull sharks, but they are not quite as nomadic. Their most distinguishing characteristic is the shape of the teeth—curved cusps with finely serrated edges. Their strong, serrated upper teeth are hooked or shaped like coxcombs, meaning that the point of the tooth is turned to the side. They have broad heads and large mouths.

Their coloration varies from light or bluish gray to black above to dirty yellow or white below. Juveniles, which measure up to about 71 inches, have mottled skin: their dorsal fins are covered with dark spots on a lighter background. But as the sharks mature, the spots blend together to form vertical bars or stripes, which gives them their distinctly tigerlike appearance. When they get older still, though, these stripes tend to fade except in flanks near the tail.

Adult tigers are among the largest sharks, reaching a length of 11 to 14 feet with some specimens exceeding 18 feet. They can weigh up to 2,000 pounds.

Tiger sharks are among the largest sharks, averaging between 11 and 14 feet in length and weighing up to 2,000 pounds.

What Tigers Eat

When tiger sharks feed, they really go to town. When they attack they are powerful—and fast. In Chapter 4, we mentioned all the strange objects that have been recovered from the stomachs of sharks, such as antlers, rubbish, license plates, the head of a crocodile, a chicken coop, and even a headless body in Medieval armor. All of these items were found in the bellies of tiger sharks. For the most part, however, the tiger shark feeds on such marine animals as turtles, clams, horseshoe crabs, many bony fishes, reptiles, moray eels, smaller sharks, and seagulls. Tigers have even been known to prey on gray nurses and even other tiger sharks. It is one of the few species of sharks that will scavenge dead animals.

How Tigers Live

Tiger sharks prefer temperate and tropical coastal waters and are prone to feed at lagoons and shallow waters at night, most commonly along the coasts of South Africa, the Philippines, Australia, the Indian and Pacific Oceans, and in the Caribbean waters. It adapts to a variety of different habitats including rivers and small lagoons. Although they prefer shallow water they have been sighted at depths of up to 450 feet.

> **Shark Facts and Stats**
>
> Although tiger sharks generally prefer to stay in one place, they have also been known to swim distances measuring several hundred miles.

Tigers give birth to live young in litters of 10 to 80 pups after a gestation period of nine months—the same as humans. Pups are slender and measure about 2.5 feet in length at birth. Like many other sharks, they develop slowly.

Tiger Shark Attacks

Tigers have been primarily responsible for attacking humans around the Hawaiian Islands in recent years. In one case, in 1999, a couple was attacked while kayaking off the island of Maui. They unfortunately tipped over, and as they floated, a tiger shark attacked the wife and severed her arm. As the husband struggled to stop her bleeding, the woman died. Forced with the decision to let her go in order to save himself, he eventually succeeded in making it to shore. Two other tiger shark attacks were recorded in 1999, but neither of them was fatal. On average, Hawaii experiences two tiger shark attacks every year.

Curiously, divers, unlike surfers or swimmers, don't seem to be nearly as imperiled by tigers (or bulls, as we mentioned earlier). In one incident, a diver making a decompression stop (to prevent getting the bends) was surprised by a tiger that approached him from behind. The diver accidentally turned around and bumped the shark. When he realized what he had done, he shot to the surface and climbed on the boat without getting bent. Nothing untoward happened to him. The shark clearly could have taken a chunk out of the diver if he so chose, but for whatever reason he decided to forego the opportunity.

> **Shark Lore**
>
> The largest tiger shark ever found measured 18 feet, but these sharks may grow even larger.

One of the strangest stories involving a tiger attack on a human occurred in 1944 when a fisherman near Florida caught a large tiger shark. When he opened up the shark, he found most of a man's torso from the ribs to the knees. But who the man was and how half of him came to end up in the belly of a tiger shark was never discovered.

The Oceanic White Tip

Oceanic white tips (not to be confused with the smaller white tip reef sharks, to which it is not closely related) are among the most aggressive of all sharks. The oceanic white tip (*Carcharinus longimanus*) is a large, thick-bodied, slow-moving shark with very large, paddle-shaped pectoral fins. It derives its name from the white tips on its pectoral and dorsal fins and tail. This color pattern may be absent on young sharks. On unborn sharks the color pattern is actually reversed and the shark has black tips to its fins. As adults, they usually grow to about 10 feet long. They have litters of up to 15 pups with the number of pups increasing with the size of the mother after a one-year gestation period.

Typically the oceanic white tip gives no sign of his intentions but rather will approach divers—usually it's just to have a look, but on occasion they can attack without warning. It is known to bite with no apparent reason and the fact that it is so unpredictable makes it dangerous. (Some shark researchers maintain that it is the most dangerous shark they have ever worked with.) These sharks have been implicated in many attacks on humans, especially victims of ship-wrecks or survivors of plane crashes at sea. One glance at its strong, wide triangular, serrated upper teeth will offer convincing evidence that it is capable of doing a lot of damage. It will eat just about everything.

> **Shark Facts and Stats**
>
> There are several contenders for most dangerous shark, but some experts give the honor to oceanic white tip sharks. According to the great explorer Jacques-Yves Cousteau, oceanic white tips are "the only species of shark that is never frightened by the approach of a diver, and they are the most dangerous of all sharks."

When Divers Invade Their Territory

The oceanic white tip lives far offshore in all tropical and subtropical waters in depths up to 500 feet, though they have been found in waters as shallow as 12 feet deep. These sharks are often attracted to waters where there are dead whales and are known to follow pods of pilot whales, dolphins, and schools of large fish such as tuna. There are unconfirmed reports of divers jumping in to dive with whales or dolphins, only to discover—to their great distress—that they were among oceanic white tips. Not all divers have come out the worse for their encounters with these sharks. Here is an excerpt of an account of one of these encounters, posted by a diver named Donald Paschal:

> We were aboard "SpoilSport" making daily multiple dives on the walls and reefs of this area. Daily we would encounter sharks. The species would range from reef white-tip, epaulette, gray whaler, silver-tip, oceanic white tip, and bull. None of the encounters were ever threatening. Of the species which we consider to be the … more aggressive shark(s), we had no negative encounters. The oceanic white tip would often come in from the deep blue while we were on wall dives and investigate the noise and continue back out, never spending more than just a few minutes checking us out.

In spite of the relatively congenial attitude demonstrated by the oceanic white tip in this encounter that took place in 1998, divers are better advised to steer as clear of these sharks as they possibly can.

The Least You Need to Know

- Great whites are the largest predators in the ocean and have the largest teeth of any shark.

- Bull sharks are aggressive predators, able to live in fresh water as well as the ocean.

- Tiger sharks are the second most dangerous species of shark after bull sharks and derive their name from the stripes on bodies of adults.

- Oceanic white tips, another aggressive shark, have been implicated in attacks on survivors of shipwrecks and crashes of airplanes at sea.

Chapter 8

Ocean Cruisers, Bottom Feeders, and Reef Dwellers

In This Chapter

- ◆ What makes the mako the fastest shark
- ◆ What makes the hammerhead's head so unusual
- ◆ Why blue sharks are such great travelers
- ◆ Why gray nurses were killed for the wrong reason
- ◆ How leopard sharks turn into protective coral
- ◆ How reef dwellers live and find prey

This chapter discusses three groups of sharks that are distinguished by their habitat. The first group includes makos, hammerheads, and blues. With the exception of hammerheads who prefer to stick close to the coasts, these are mostly pelagic sharks, who swim in the deep and travel astonishingly long distances in search of food and mates. Next, you'll take a closer look at two of the most prominent bottom feeders: gray nurses and leopards. Finally, you'll find out more about the best-known tip sharks, named for the white, black, and silver markings on their fins, who make their homes among coral reefs.

The Ocean and Coastal Cruisers

In this section, I discuss three species: a sprinter, a marathon swimmer, and an olfactory superstar. The sprinter is the mako, the fastest of all sharks. Makos are capable of reaching staggering speeds and performing stunning acrobatics. No angler who has ever tried to catch one will forget the experience. The marathon swimmer is the blue, who to date holds the record for long-distance shark migrations, traveling thousands of miles from one continent to another. The olfactory superstar is the hammerhead (of which there are several varieties). They are distinguished not only for their oddly shaped heads and sensitivity for scents, but for their social behavior. Scalloped hammerheads, unlike most sharks, are much more social than most species, hunting together at night and congregating around seamounts during the days.

Speedy Cruisers: Makos

Mako sharks are the fastest sharks and some of the fastest creatures in the ocean, registering average speeds of more than 20 miles per hour, although in short bursts they can attain speeds double or possibly triple that. The mako is capable of some extraordinary acrobatics, such as leaping high out of the water and turning somersaults; when threatened, the mako is capable of barreling through the sea in any and all directions. Like a gray ghost, the mako seems to appear out of nowhere or disappear before you realize he was there in the first place.

The International Game Fishing Association recognizes the mako as the only true sport-fishing shark. That's because the mako is the one shark that can give an angler a run for his money. In contrast, catching other sharks, in the words of writer Peter Benchley, is an experience more like taking in wet laundry or hauling a cow. Fighting a mako, Benchley says, is comparable to fighting a bull or wrestling a crocodile. (Admittedly, most readers have a difficult time relating to these comparisons from personal experience.)

Taste of the Bizarre

Mako sharks have been known to jump into boats and attack ship hulls.

Makos are the only shark considered a true "sport fish" by recreational sports fishing enthusiasts.

Speaking from a pure aesthetic viewpoint, I have to add that the mako has one of the ugliest faces imaginable. Mako sharks look sinister. (Some divers who have observed makos close up describe the look in their eyes as being like that of a menacing psychopath.) Their teeth are long, pointed, and snaggly. These teeth, which one writer terms "fanglike," are tailored for grabbing large fish, including mackerel and herrings. Makos have been known to pursue swordfish as well. Mako sharks also have conical snouts and long gill slits.

Makos do more than just look threatening. Like the great white, the bull, and the tiger sharks, mako sharks pick fights with humans and often win them. Incidents have been recorded where makos have attacked boats or jumped on board, demolishing the craft. Some anglers have chosen to jump overboard rather than risk being fatally struck by a thrashing tail. In one case recorded in 1988, a 10-foot mako smashed into a small fishing boat off western Australia, jumped on its deck, and then knocked the two anglers into the water. Before jumping, they somehow managed to radio for help. By the time a rescue vessel arrived an hour later, the dying shark had succeeded in destroying the boat.

> **Shark Lore**
>
> Some shark experts believe that makos show menacing behavior before they attack. In R. H. Johnson's book called *Sharks of Tropical and Temperate Seas*, he wrote that this behavior is characterized by "porpoising, followed by rapid figure eight swimming."

There are two species of mako shark: the shortfin (*Isurus oxyrinchus*) and the longfin (*Isurus paucus*); the longfin has longer pectoral fins and a blunter snout than the shortfin. Longfins are somewhat less common than shortfin makos, but in general, both are more common than great whites.

Like great whites, their closest relative, makos are warm-blooded, which gives them extra energy. Makos also have highly refined senses attuned even to very weak electrical fields. Makos eat just about anything that they set their sights on, but they have a particular taste for blue sharks.

Female makos reach a length of 10 feet; males measure more than 13 feet on average. These sharks breed off the coast of New South Wales in Australia around November (which is summer in Australia) and in southern California in July through October. Makos also bear their young live, giving birth to as many as 16 pups at a time, but the pups are not nourished through a placenta in the uterus.

A pelagic shark, the mako is equally at home in both cold and warm seas and prefers deep offshore water. The mako has frequently been spotted close to the shoreline in water depths averaging 600 to 1,200 feet deep. Experienced travelers, makos have been known to swim distances of more than 1,000 miles. One mako tracked by a radio device averaged speeds of about 15 miles an hour a day.

Olfactory Superstars: Hammerheads

No one can mistake a hammerhead for anything else. Viewed from the surface or by divers at depth, this shark's head is instantly recognizable. These sharks look as though someone squashed their heads, expanding and flattening them until they came to have the shape of a hammer or mallet. In addition to looking strange, their heads provide lift and make hammerheads agile swimmers. Of the five species of hammerheads, the best known is the scalloped hammerhead or kidney-headed shark (*Carcharhiniformes sphyrna lewini*). Most hammerheads are about five feet long.

A hammerhead's eyes are located at the tips of his head. Because their eyes are spaced far apart (sometimes up to 23 inches), hammerheads enjoy a spectacularly good view of their surroundings. The hammerhead also is "an olfactory superstar." Two nostrils occupy a prominent position in the front corners of the head. Because the nostrils are also spaced far apart, they give the shark the ability to detect changes in the concentration of a scent from one side to another. All that extra headroom also confers an advantage in that it is crammed full of the ampullae of Lorenzini, which are the sensitive, jelly-filled electroreceptors that pick up weak electric fields emitted by all living organisms. When hammerheads swim, they swing their heads back and forth, which researchers believe may increase the sharks' chances of detecting food.

> **Shark Facts and Stats**
>
> Hammerheads are camera-shy under the best of circumstances, but when surface water temperatures become warmer, they make themselves even scarcer and divers rarely see them.

Hammerheads are distinguished by their flattened hammerlike heads that are filled with sensitive electroreceptors.

Hammerheads are found in temperate and tropical seas. Unlike most other sharks, hammerheads are often known to travel in schools of a hundred or more. They can be found far offshore, but they usually prefer shallow waters in spring and summer. They feed on bony fishes, other sharks, cuttlefish, crabs, shrimps and other crustaceans, and *cephalopods* such as squid and octopus. They also can give birth to as many as 15 to 30 pups in a litter.

What Does It Mean?

Cephalopods are a class of predatory marine mollusks that includes the squid, the octopus, and the nautilus. Cephalopod comes from the Greek, meaning "head-footed animal," meaning the feet are attached to the head. These animals have a highly evolved structure and physiology.

Where humans are concerned, only the solitary hammerhead poses a danger. Most schools of hammerheads are timid, swiftly departing from any nearby divers at the first sound of regulator air bubbles.

Marathon Swimmers: Blues

Blue sharks (*Prionace glauca*) are the greatest wanderers of all sharks, showing no compunction about swimming 1,200 to 2,000 miles for food or a mate. (How they know a prospective match will be at their destination when they arrive is, of course, another question.) One blue shark was tracked swimming from Brazil to New York, a distance of 2,100 miles. Another was tracked from New York to Liberia on the west coast of Africa, where it was captured six years later. Like great whites and hammerheads, these pelagic sharks are warm-blooded, which offers them added energy for speed.

Blues live about 20 years and have litters of as many as 100 pups. This shark is a pack animal who rarely threatens humans, although on occasion blue sharks have killed people floating in the ocean. Actually, humans pose more of a menace to blues; overfishing has depleted large stocks of this species in recent years.

Taste of the Bizarre

A blue shark was found with 135 pups in her uterus—the largest litter recorded of all shark species.

Bottom Dwellers

Now I come to two prominent species that spend most of their lives contentedly living and feeding in the bottom of the ocean: the gray nurse shark (otherwise known as the sand tiger shark) and the leopard shark.

The Gray Nurse

Confusingly, gray nurse sharks—or *Eugomphodus taurus* to taxonomists—do not belong to the nurse shark family. They are also known as sand tigers in the United States (not to be mistaken for tiger sharks, which, as I noted in Chapter 7, can be very dangerous) and the ragged tooth shark in Africa.

Gray nurse sharks are well known to viewers of television nature shows; they are popular with underwater TV crews because they can always be counted on to display their large pointed teeth set in a narrow snout. (Curiously, these ragged-looking teeth aren't that strong, but they are well designed for grinding shellfish.) Relatively easy to identify, these sharks have thick bodies with whitish spots. Gray or brown in color, they have a pair of large dorsal fins and can grow to about 11 feet. This species also has nasal barbels, which are whiskerlike projections that enhance the shark's sense of smell and taste. Females have thicker skins than males because of biting behavior during mating, a behavior that often leaves females with a good many telltale scars on their bodies.

> **Taste of the Bizarre**
>
> Gray nurses produce eggs that are hatched inside the mother after a gestation period of about nine months. The first shark out is the luckiest—it then devours the other eggs for nutrition.

Nurse sharks are among the most common species of sharks who, though they are harmless to humans unless harassed, have often been confused for more aggressive sharks.

Unless gray nurses are frightened, they usually move quite slowly. The action of their gill pumps allows them to float virtually motionlessly in the water. They are commonly found in waters of about 60 feet deep or less, but have been sighted in waters as deep as 600 feet. When they are lazing about the sea floor, they're sometimes seen with their heads stuck in a cave or under a ledge. They subsist mainly on shellfish and are in the habit of feeding and migrating in groups. Their activity peaks at night.

In years past gray nurses have had to live down a bad reputation as man-eaters—which they most definitely are not. Gray nurse sharks are dangerous only if provoked. Many attacks on humans carried out by tigers and bulls were blamed on gray nurses. But before enough people realized that these sharks were basically harmless, large numbers of them were killed. In fact, so many were killed that Australia and many states in the United States have banned their killing.

> **Shark Facts and Stats**
>
> The photogenic gray nurses are a favorite of divers because they have a menacing appearance without posing any danger. They also are nocturnal hunters who hang out on the bottom of the sea, so they're easy to find. Gray nurses seem oblivious to divers, but if bothered, the sharks often wake up and speed out of their resting place to a new, more secluded location.

Leopard Sharks

Leopard sharks (*Triakis semifasciata*), who are also known as cat sharks, belong to the family *Triakidae* or hound sharks. They derive their name from the distinctive dark brown spots on their silvery gray skin. They are equipped with a large number of small, sharp, pointed teeth that are easily able to puncture the skin. The leopard shark is a slim shark with a narrow head and ranges in length from three to six feet. These sharks are not considered dangerous to humans unless they are provoked. However, there is one instance of a leopard shark's attacking a surfer with a nosebleed.

Leopards feed on *benthic* prey such as worms, clams, crabs, shrimp, octopus, and small fish. But because the sweet meat of leopard sharks is prized, they often find themselves turned into food. The leopard's reproduction is *ovoviviparous*, which means that eggs develop in the mother's body and are hatched. A leopard shark may have up to 30 pups in a litter.

> **What Does It Mean?**
>
> **Benthic** refers to the ocean floor. Benthic flora are vegetation that grows on the ocean floor; benthic fauna are animal life that lives on the ocean floor.

Leopard sharks live on the Pacific coast of North America and generally prefer bay environments near the shore. They are occasionally found in the open ocean as well.

During the summer months they migrate south to the vicinity of San Diego, particularly along the La Jolla shores. In the fall, they migrate north. Leopards prefer hiding beneath coral reefs where they are easily camouflaged and where they find a fruitful source of food. In death, leopards blend in even better with their environment, becoming part of the very coral that gave them shelter in life and making for a source of food for future generations of sharks and other fish. Off the coast of California, leopards snack on echiuran inkeeper worms, but to get at these worms they have to suck them up from their U-shaped burrows in the mud and swallow them whole. Leopard sharks sometimes mutilate their prey, too, consuming only a part of them—grabbing hold of the extended siphons of clams, for instance, and then ripping them off with a violent shaking of its head. Scientists have discovered dozens of fleshy bivalve siphons in the stomachs of these sharks, but not the bivalves from which they came.

The Reef Dwellers

The three reef sharks I talk about in this section are known collectively as the tips: black, white, and silver. Reef sharks are highly developed at birth, and they can be aggressive even before they're born. A pup once bit a scientist as he was trying to remove the pup from the dying mother's uterus. As potentially dangerous as reef sharks might be, they can be surprisingly tame. Some reef sharks have been trained to take fish from divers without biting them.

Reef sharks are opportunistic feeders that cruise reef walls displaying an indiscriminate appetite for shellfish, crabs, lobsters, cuttlefish, and occasionally sea lions. Like pelagic sharks, reef sharks have highly developed sensory detection systems that allow them to pick up weak electrical impulses from potential prey. In spite of their ravenous appetites, they can go for days without eating, relying on metabolic action to efficiently convert food to energy.

Reef sharks inhabit coral reefs and tropical waters where drop-offs are located. They also live in "reef flats," which are shallow, sandy lagoons dotted with coral formations. Instead of hatching eggs like so many other sharks and bony fish, reef sharks give birth to well-developed, live pups with only a few in each litter.

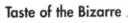

Taste of the Bizarre

In one of the rarest shark discoveries of recent times, a true albino leopard shark was found; it lacked all traces of the dark spots and saddles typical of this species and even had unusual pink irises.

The Reef Dwellers of Hawaii

There are about 40 species of sharks of the 450 species of fish indigenous to Hawaiian waters, ranging in size from the deep-water pygmy shark—about 8 inches in length—to the whale shark that can grow up to 50 feet or more. The most frequently encountered are the sandbar, reef white tip, scalloped hammerhead, and tiger. Of these, about eight species are commonly seen near shore, all of which are carnivores, feeding primarily on fishes. Although their importance to the coastal ecosystem is not well understood, it is believed that they improve fish populations by preying on the sick and injured fish, leaving the healthiest to reproduce. Only a few species of Hawaiian sharks are known to attack people— primarily the tiger and Galapagos. The gray reef and scalloped hammerhead appear to attack only when provoked.

Black Tips

Black tips (*Carcharhinus melanopterus*) derive their name from the large black blotch on their first dorsal fins and the black tips on their other fins. They can grow to about five feet.

Black tips are basically homebodies, sticking close to the reef flat where they were born. The small black-tip reef shark dwells mainly in shallower waters, searching for prey over the reef flat at high tide, his dorsal fin cutting the surface. Although they mainly feed on small fish, they have developed a fondness for land snakes that they probably snare from nearby mangroves. These sharks are reportedly able to jump over shallow coral and leap out of the water.

Attracted by splashing, reef sharks have been known to approach a snorkler's fins out of curiosity. Although these sharks are not dangerous, they have taken a bite out of snorklers' fins or the occasional diver's ankle.

Shark Lore

Australian Aborigines used to catch black tips by splashing the water to get them excited and then throwing in a baited hook.

White Tips

White tips (*Triaendon obesus*) are slightly larger than black tips and are about as common. They have long, thin bodies with nearly equal-size dorsal fins, which are tipped with white (as are their tail fins). They can grow to a length of nearly seven feet. Their small, narrow teeth are best suited to holding prey. Octopus is the preference of these bottom feeders, and they can prove very persistent, even going so far as to jam themselves into tight crevices to catch their prey. Researchers believe that these sharks can live up to 25 years.

White tips are partial to reef drop-offs, deep gullies, and caves. They sleep during the day, usually in waters about 75 feet deep, but sometimes they can be found snoozing in caves. If they were humans they would like pajama parties, they often sleep in groups of as many as eight at a time. They seldom deign to come to the surface. Like habitual late-night partygoers, they don't begin to get going until early in the evenings, which is the best time for divers to capture them on film.

Like black tips, white tips rarely bother people, putting up with intrusions unless they are harassed. It is wise not to chase to them. In an excited state, especially when a lot of people on board boats are throwing food to them at once, white tips can become overexcited and start biting the hands that feed them.

Silver Tips

Silver tips (*Carcharhinus albimarginatus*) have a reputation for curiosity. They are much larger than either the white or black tips. The silver tip has a high first dorsal fin and only a tiny second one. Silver tips are found in deeper water than the other two tips, around reef or island drop-offs at depths of about 60 feet (although they have been sighted in waters as deep as 1,200 feet). Silver tips feed at whatever depth they find themselves.

> **Shark Lore**
>
> In one incident that occurred off Papua New Guinea, a diver tried to feed a silver tip by holding out fish in her hand. The shark was completely docile until the tide lifted the diver's knee up into the shark's mouth. The resulting injury required 39 stitches to repair, but the diver expressed no regrets.

Silver tips' reputation for curiosity comes from their tendency to surface whenever they sense a commotion. They also like to follow divers around—sometimes as close as a few inches once they become accustomed to the divers' presence. Nonetheless, these sharks have not been known to pose any hazard to humans, although if they are provoked or scared, they will bite.

Gray Whalers

Another reef dweller, the gray whaler (*Carcharhinus amblyrhynchos*) is found in large numbers on Australia's Great Barrier Reef. The gray whaler (also known as the gray reef shark) can grow to six feet and, as its name suggests, is gray on top of its body with a whitish underbelly. Its upper teeth are slightly serrated and used for grasping and tearing; its lower teeth are long, narrow and nonserrated. Its hearing is keen—it can pick up a sound at a distance of about 600 feet. It favors reef drop-offs and a strong current, usually choosing waters on the leeward side of islands. Although the gray whaler will swim out to open waters it seldom dives any deeper than 300 feet. Given the choice, the shark would rather hang out at the bottom of the sea than cruise the surface. Intriguingly, gray whalers are never found in the same territory as black tips are and vice versa.

These sharks are not considered dangerous but if they sense that their territory is being invaded their mood can quickly darken. And it lets divers know, too—its pectoral fins slide down and it hunches its back. If at this point a diver continues to ignore the threatening posture, the shark is likely to take a quick warning bite to reinforce its message. In 1973, a time when little was known about these sharks, an underwater photographer named Bill Curtsinger encountered a gray whaler while diving in a lagoon in Micronesia in the South Pacific. "It was twenty feet away and closing. I saw it sweeping its head back and forth; its back arched like a cat's," he recalled. He had the feeling that the shark was speaking to him, only that he didn't know the words. What the shark was trying to tell him became clear soon enough when the shark took a bite out of his shoulder. There was a lot of blood but no lasting damage. In feeding frenzies—when the sharks become totally obsessed about getting food and will react violently if anything gets in their way—it is prudent to steer clear of them. Like most sharks, they can become unpredictable and their instinct is to attack. Several spearfishers have been bitten by gray whalers, with at least one fatality.

The gray whaler hunts at night, though it remains active during the daylight hours as well. Young sharks of this species are given to hunting in schools, but as adults they evidently have enough confidence to do their hunting alone. These sharks have also acquired a reputation for curiosity, especially the young ones. A sound can bring them to the surface; once their curiosity is satisfied, however, they generally swim off. Divers may spot several of them when he first enters the water and then not see them again even if he returns to the area over a succession of days.

The Least You Need to Know

- Mako sharks are the fastest shark of all, capable of attaining average speeds of more than 20 miles per hour. They are also are one of the few species that are known to attack humans.

- Hammerheads have distinctly shaped flattened heads with widely spaced eyes and nostrils that enhance their eyesight and sense of smell respectively.

- Blue sharks are the best traveled sharks of all, migrating up to 2,000 miles or more in search of food, mates, or warmer waters.

- Gray nurses and leopards are among the most prominent bottom-feeding sharks.

- Reef dwellers, including white tips, black tips and silver tips, are opportunistic feeders who consume a variety of prey.

The Slow, the Sleek, and the Ugly

In This Chapter

◆ Getting to the bottom of wobbegongs

◆ How bottom feeders camouflage themselves

◆ Why horn sharks have two types of teeth

◆ Shining a light on the mysterious goblin

The sharks I have discussed so far have mainly been the aristocrats of the shark empire: great whites, makos, tigers, blues, and hammerheads. These sharks are celebrated by the media and feared (whether justly or not) by divers, surfers, snorklers, swimmers, and armchair adventurers alike. The sharks that take center stage in this chapter are a different lot altogether.

The three species of sharks that I put under the microscope in this chapter are very unusual. If the world of sharks were a circus, they would be part of the sideshow. The first shark, the wobbegong, is a bottom feeder known for its exceptional camouflage. The second is called a horn shark because of its sharp spines. Finally, we investigate one of the most mysterious sharks of all, which is variously referred to as an imp and a piscine gargoyle but is known to baffled scientists and shark enthusiasts as the goblin.

Elegant Bottom Feeders: Wobbegongs

Wobbegongs are an unusual, but elegant, species of sharks with flattened bodies that nature seems to have designed specifically for camouflage. These bottom feeders have tough and variegated skin with a coloration that ranges from yellowish brown to grayish brown, with blotches of black over the back and bluish white patches elsewhere. This distinctive patterning allows the sharks to lie undetected among reeds or hollows of rocks waiting for prey such as crabs. Some types of wobbegongs even sport tassels or frills on their heads so that they look like beards of seaweed. (Not surprisingly, these sharks are called tasseled wobbegongs.)

What Does It Mean?

Spiracles are special gill slits located just behind the eyes of some sharks. The spiracles supply oxygen when the shark eats.

Shark Lore

The unique patterning of wobbegongs not only conceals them from their prey but also makes them difficult for divers to spot.

The mouth of this species juts out in front of the eyes behind which are well-developed *spiracles*. These spiracles are special gill slits that lie behind the eyes of most bottom feeders, allowing the absorption of oxygen whenever they eat. Spiracles also serve another function; by facilitating the movement of water over the gills, they give the wobbegong shark the ability to remain motionless at the bottom of the sea.

Wobbegongs also have nasal barbels (whiskerlike smellers and tasters) to help them in their search for food. These sharks come equipped with two rows of fanglike teeth in the upper jaw and three in the lower jaw to catch fish and invertebrates. Most of these sharks are on the smallish size; the largest reach a maximum of 10 feet. Like most bottom feeders, wobbegongs move sluggishly and seem to spread themselves on the bottom like a carpet, causing them to sometimes be mistaken for another species called the carpet shark.

Where Wobbegongs Live

Wobbegongs are one of the most common families of shark. Six species can be found in the western Pacific around Japan, the Philippines, Indonesia, Papua New Guinea, and all around Australia. One species, known as the ornate wobbegong, is frequently sighted in Australian waters. These inshore sharks happily inhabit shallow waters, but they can also be spotted swimming in depths of about 300 feet. During the day the sharks are often found lazing about on algae-covered rocks or coral reefs; sometimes they hunker down under piers or in caves. Come nighttime, though, they are ready to party and feed.

How Wobbegongs Feed and Breed

Wobbegongs are *benthic feeders*, preying on crabs, lobsters, octopus, fish, and whatever else they find along the bottom. Researchers believe that they serve an important ecological role by feeding on sick or weak specimens, which prevent these species from overpopulating.

Wobbegongs are *ovoviviparous*—that is to say, the mothers bear their pups live and do not hatch eggs. Female wobbegongs may have as many as 37 pups in a single litter. Males mature at three years old.

> **What Does It Mean?**
>
> **Benthic feeders** are sharks that feed on the sea bottom.

The Threats Wobbegongs Pose and Are Exposed To

Wobbegong sharks are usually harmless, but they can be potentially dangerous to humans because they are known to bite waders. Some wobbegongs (such as the ornate wobbegong and the tasseled wobbegong) have been known to attack divers who stumble upon them. In one incident in Australia, a wobbegong bit off the foot of a fisherman who apparently had stepped on it. Generally speaking, however, wobbegongs leave scuba divers and fishermen alone unless they are disturbed or provoked—or tempted. They are known to go after spear fishers who have just made a catch.

Compared to the relatively minor hazard we face from wobbegongs, the sharks face a far greater threat from us. They are a favorite dish in Japan, Korea, China, Vietnam, and the Philippines; their skin also is used to make sturdy and attractive leather goods.

Odd but Endearing: Horn Sharks

The horn shark (*Heterodonts francisci*) belongs to a family called *Heterodontoids*. The name is derived from the Latin, meaning "different teeth" and refers to the sharks' teeth, which are spiked in front and flat in back and are designed for crushing shellfish.

The members of this family, which are otherwise known as bullhead sharks, are unlikely to win any beauty prizes with their piglike snouts, their small puckered mouths, their cowlike browridges, or their chubby bodies that are covered with oversized scales. To observers, a bullhead's expression seems to be one of perpetual surprise.

Nor are bullheads likely to win any plaudits for athleticism. When they're on the sea floor they plod along on large, paddlelike pectoral fins. They swim with an exaggerated wriggling motion. Some bullheads rest with their heads lying under rock or coral ledges; you can tell because the denticles of their browridges have been worn smooth. Other bullheads, such as the horn shark, keep their heads exposed when they rest, and as a result their browridges remain as rough as ever. For many shark enthusiasts, bullheads have two qualities that the vast majority of sharks do not: They are cute and endearing.

Altogether there are eight varieties of horn sharks. Like other bullheads, horn sharks have blunt heads, snouts that look squashed-in, and big nostrils. As bottom feeders, they dwell on the seabed and feed on shellfish and small fish. White spines at the front of both dorsal fins give the sharks their name.

> **Shark Lore**
>
> The bullhead shark gets his name from the prominent browridge that recalls the head of a bull.

> **Shark Facts and Stats**
>
> Port Jackson sharks, the most common horn sharks, derive their name from a bay in eastern Australia where they have been found.

Most of these sharks have pointed and grasping teeth in the front with flat teeth in the rear that are well suited for crushing shellfish. Their eyes are very sensitive, and they tend to spend the days in dark places. The best-known and most common horn shark, the Port Jackson shark, is distinguished by dark stripes under the eyes. These stripes reduce glare when the shark swims over highly reflective bottoms. (For this same reason, soldiers often apply grease under their eyes when they conduct maneuvers on the battlefield.) Port Jackson sharks are usually gray with tints of brown or green and a black-banded pattern on the body. These brown and green spots give horn sharks protective cover so that they can lurk unseen among the coral and rocks of the bottom.

Where Horn Sharks Live

Some horn sharks are social animals. Divers have come on groups of 10 or 20 Port Jackson sharks sprawled out in sheltered caves or lying on shallow rocky reefs during the day. Others prefer a solitary lifestyle.

At nights, like so many bottom feeders, they mobilize and go to work in search of urchins and shells. They thrive in depths of 100 to 150 feet. Port Jackson sharks are found in southern Australian waters, especially in New South Wales. Horn sharks also make their home in kelp beds far off the California coast.

Another type of horn shark is found in the Galapagos Islands and other islands off Peru and is called—predictably—the Galapagos horn shark. Some sharks, notably the Port Jackson sharks, make annual migrations of up to 525 miles along the coast. Others prefer to stay put. One tagged horn shark was found in almost the exact same spot more than 11 years later.

How Horn Sharks Feed and Breed

Bullheads are nocturnal feeders whose diet consists of fish, sea urchins, crabs, worms, anemones, and other bottom-dwelling invertebrates. The bullheads show a special preference for blacksmith, or maybe it's just that blacksmith are so easy to catch. Blacksmith are fish who are active in the day and sleep at night in crevices on the reef, making them convenient pickings for the night-prowling horn sharks.

However, no treat is more delectable for horn sharks than purple sea urchins. They gobble so many of them down, spines and all, that many horn sharks have red-stained teeth. Horn sharks are hardly sticklers for etiquette, grinding up their food and swallowing it whole. If the shell is indigestible, well, they'll just get around to regurgitating it later on.

Horn sharks are *oviparous*, which means they lay eggs. These eggs take from 6 to 10 months to hatch. These eggs are enclosed in a case shaped like a spiral corkscrew; the pups' spines are sharp at birth and serve as protective armor against predators.

> **Taste of the Bizarre**
>
> Horn sharks have a proclivity for snacking on sea anemones by nipping off a mouthful of tentacles before the anemones can retract them.

> **Shark Lore**
>
> Fin spines were a common feature in many ancient sharks and are still found in bullheads and dogfish sharks.

Threats from Predators

The sluggish horn sharks pose no threat to people unless someone accidentally touches their sharp spine fins by mistake. However, horn sharks, because they are small (four to about six feet), are often in danger from larger predators. But those sharp spines on their fins serve to discourage any attack. According to one report from Australia, a wobbegong was spotted floating dead in the water with a Port

Jackson shark stuck in its mouth. This was one instance where a shark had truly bitten off more than he could chew.

Ugly and Rare: Goblins

One of the ugliest and rarest sharks to ever have been discovered, the goblin shark is also known as the elfin shark and imp shark (from the French *requin lutin*) and *tiburón duende* (Spanish for "hobgoblin shark"). One writer has termed this shark a "piscine gargoyle".

In many ways the goblin shark is the most mysterious shark of all those we have considered so far. Nearly everyone who writes about the goblin says the same thing: "Little is known about them …" What is known is this: The goblin shark has a long, daggerlike snout, protruding jaws when feeding, needle-sharp teeth, small beady eyes, and a flabby body. For all their fearsome appearance, goblins pose no threat to humans even in the rare event that someone stumbled on one of them.

Shark Facts and Stats

The goblin shark was first discovered in 1898 in the "Black Current," a region of very deep water off Yokohama. The specimen was a 42-inch juvenile male shark of a kind that the astonished fishermen had never seen before. They called him *tenguzame* or "goblin shark" in Japanese because he reminded them of depictions they'd seen of goblins.

Goblin sharks reach 10 to 12 feet at maturity and can weigh up to 450 pounds. (However, so few of these sharks have been found that it's difficult to know just what size they really grow to.) Their skin is soft, pale, and pink-gray—"bubble gum pink" as one writer put it. But that description doesn't begin to convey just how unusual their skin is. In some sense, goblins don't even have skin, not as we know it. Their "skin" is more like sandpaper in texture. It is rubbery in consistency and is translucent as well; the pinkish coloration is due to the oxygenated capillaries close to the surface of the "skin." There is no skin pigmentation as such.

For many years scientists used to think that the goblin's coloring was a drab grayish brown, but that was because they were relying on dead goblins for their evidence. In 1976, two Japanese ichthyologists published color photographs that showed the goblin's distinctive pink coloring for the first time, revealing as well translucent peacock-blue margins on the fins. The goblin they were using for their studies was dead, but because the shark was frozen shortly after he was caught, the original pigmentation was preserved.

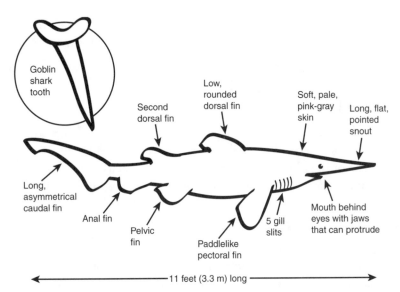

The rarely sighted goblin shark has a deceptively fierce appearance and a bubble-gum-pink body.

Goblin shark tooth

Second dorsal fin

Low, rounded dorsal fin

Soft, pale, pink-gray skin

Long, flat, pointed snout

Long, asymmetrical caudal fin

Anal fin

Pelvic fin

Paddlelike pectoral fin

5 gill slits

Mouth behind eyes with jaws that can protrude

11 feet (3.3 m) long

Goblins belong to the *Mitsukurinidae* family, and like other members of this family, they have two rounded dorsal fins, an anal fin, and a long, asymmetrical tail fin. Their mouths are located just behind the eyes and their snouts are greatly elongated, flattened and bladelike. Goblins are mainly found (when they are found at all) in deep waters.

The goblin's teeth are sharp and about an inch long. In addition, goblins have an unusual feature: a *basihynal* or tongue that some experts believe is used to produce a suctionlike effect, lapping up prey into the throat. The goblins' flexible jaws operate somewhat like forceps and bristle with teeth that are variously described as "fanglike" and "stiletto-shaped," causing the sharks to appear fierce (though they really are not) even in death. Their teeth are ideal for catching small fish, which the sharks pierce with a single bite. The sharks then swallow the fish whole.

The Purpose of the Unusual Snout

The goblin's bladelike snout is a subject of some speculation (just like most everything else about this shark). The snout looks as if it could serve as a prod to flush out small fish and crustaceans from crevices in which they've taken refuge. According to this theory, goblins use their retractable jaws "like a spring-loaded trap" to snap up prey. But once researchers examined the snout in question they had to conclude that this theory might be wrong: The snout is too soft and rubbery to function as a useful prod. However, the snout does serve as a bountiful repository of ampullae of Lorenzini, those electroreceptors we have mentioned so often. That suggested to scientists that the snout provides goblins with the means with which to locate prey rather than to shovel the prey into their mouths.

The Mystery of the "Many" Goblins

Goblins remain elusive. Since their discovery in 1898, only 45 sightings of the shark have been recorded. At one point researchers believed that several different species of goblin shark existed because of the observations they made of the sharks' bites after they were caught. Many of these sharks were ensnared by fishing nets and would try to bite their way out of them.

As we noted, these sharks have unusual retractable jaws that can push way out when feeding. When scientists examined the dead sharks caught in the nets, they noticed that the jaws had settled in different positions in their death throes. From this observation they concluded that because many of these goblins had different types of "bites" they must therefore represent different species. However, once the scientists figured out how the sharks' jaws worked they realized that they were probably dealing with only one species after all.

Where Goblins Live

Researchers believe that goblins can live in very deep water up to depths of 3,600 feet. Most evidence suggests, though, that they usually swim in depths of about 1,445 feet during the day and rise to about 985 feet at night.

Although rarely seen, goblins have been spotted in a surprising number of places around the world: off the coast of New South Wales and in the Bass Strait in Australia, on the southern tip of Africa, and off the northern coast of South America as well as in Japanese waters. The hard-to-find goblins pop up in such widely disparate places as Portugal, France, New Zealand, and Guinea on the west African coast. Over half of the specimens that have been studied were taken off the coast of Japan. Little is known about their mating habits, growth patterns, or their migration routes.

Some researchers believe that the goblin may not be so rare and may in fact be fairly abundant in some locations. These researchers reason that just because the goblins' presence goes unobserved or unreported doesn't mean that they aren't more prevalent than is currently thought.

How Goblins Feed

Not surprisingly, little is known about the goblin's feeding habits or prey, but given the large number of electroreceptors in a goblin's elongated snout, scientists believe that goblins probably hunt by picking up the electrical fields of their prey. This theory would seem to enjoy some support from reports that goblin shark teeth have been found in underwater electrical cables.

When goblin stomachs have been examined, they have revealed the remains of shrimp, fin rays, octopus, crab, and rockfish. But the evidence that scientists would like to have has so far been lacking. That's because stomach contents are recovered from these sharks only infrequently. That may be explained by the fact that many sharks regurgitate once they are caught and are being hauled up to the surface, depriving researchers of the knowledge they seek. In addition, stomach contents are often indistinguishable because by the time that scientists get around to examining them, the recently digested food has been turned into a thick, smelly mush by metabolic action.

A Look at Some Other Unusual Sharks

Cookie-cutter sharks. The cookie-cutter shark has a cigar-shaped body, a short, conical snout, and two low, spineless dorsal fins. A row of 19 huge teeth—proportionately the largest of any shark species—sits in its lower jaw. The placement of its large eyes (which have green pupils) may give the shark binocular vision. The largest of these sharks reach only about 20 inches in length. Found mainly in deep tropical ocean waters worldwide, it is also known as the cigar shark for its shape and brown color, the Brazilian shark and the Luminous shark because of a greenish bioluminescent patch on its belly. This patch is thought to lure fish to it in the dark, deep waters where the shark lives. Researchers theorize that because the patch is so much smaller than the shark itself, potential prey are deceived into thinking that they can make an easy catch, only to discover—too late—that they have made a serious mistake.

Cookie-cutter sharks will attack large fish, dolphins, and whales, attaching its lips to its victim with a suctionlike action to create a vacuum. Its sawlike teeth are capable of swiveling to take an oval-shaped bite of flesh. The shape of the bites gives the species its name. It reproduces via aplacental viviparity—eggs are hatched inside the mother, but little else is known about its reproduction.

continues

---

continued

Cats and dogs. Cat sharks typically have slanted and colorful patterns of spots or stripes just as cats do. Dogfish sharks range in size; some are tiny and others such as the sleeper dogfish can grow to 23 feet. Both are usually harmless to humans.

"Blind" sharks. The blind shark is a small bottom shark. These sharks get their name from their tendency to close their eyes when caught by fishermen. Its eyes are fairly close and located almost on the back of the shark rather than on the sides. It also has a couple of long barbels protruding from its mouth.

Izak sharks. The izak shark, also known as the shy eye shark, hides its eyes with its tail when it is caught. It has dark brown skin above, with lighter dots and lines and a much lighter belly and grows to be up to two feet long. It is oviparous, laying eggs that were internally fertilized.

The Least You Need to Know

- Wobbegongs are bottom feeders that are characterized by a distinct pattern on their skin consisting of lines and patches for camouflage.

- Horn sharks belong to a family called bullheads for the distinctive shape of their heads and have two types of teeth—one for grasping, one for piercing.

- Goblins, who are filter-feeders, are distinguished by their retractable jaws that bristle with sharp teeth, and their fierce appearance.

Part 3

The Evolution and Life Cycle of Sharks

Hundreds of millions of years ago, the ancestors of modern-day sharks were already swimming in tropical seas that then covered much of the planet. Sharks and their closest relatives, rays and chimaeras, are evolutionary success stories, yet it is only recently that scientists examining their behavior, habitats, and hunting strategies have begun to understand why.

Chapter 10

The Shark in Prehistory

In This Chapter

- ◆ Looking at the evolution of sharks
- ◆ Unearthing the shark's earliest ancestors
- ◆ Dating the appearance of modern sharks
- ◆ Sizing up the megalodon

Although scientists are aware that sharks have been swimming oceans for millions of years, their evolution is still a puzzle. Unlike bony fish, sharks rarely leave evidence of fossils, which makes it difficult for scientists to investigate the sharks' ancient ancestors. The cartilage that comprised most of their bodies quickly disintegrated, leaving researchers only the hard evidence of fossilized teeth, fins, and spines. Nonetheless, even working with such a paucity of evidence, scientists have begun to assemble some fascinating profiles of the bizarre creatures that would over the course of eons evolve into sharks as we know them today.

The Evolution of the Shark

The shark can trace its history so far back in time that by comparison humans are babes in the woods. Tracking the origin of any species for millions of years is a very technical, tricky, and controversial business for scholars and paleontologists who specialize in studying fossils. Nonetheless, evidence indicates that the earliest progenitor of the shark may have lived as long as 450 million years ago. Sharks in their present form emerged much later, yet they still appeared many millions of years before our earliest hominid ancestors first appeared in Africa. (The most generous estimate, based on recent anthropological finds in the western African nation of Chad, dates the earliest origins of our hominid ancestors back seven million years.)

> **Shark Facts and Stats**
>
> The earliest evidence of sharks comes from fossilized spines, teeth and scales that appeared about 430 million years ago in the Silurian Period, known as the "Age of Fishes."

Every discussion of evolutionary origins needs the following word of caution: There is a great deal that scientists still don't know about evolutionary history. Scientists haven't been able to piece together a seamless narrative, showing how succeeding generations of shark species evolved from earlier ones. The fossil record is spotty and sometimes contradictory. In some cases, species may not have evolved at all; some were simply wiped out due to some cataclysmic climactic or geological change or because they turned out to be unsuccessful environmental experiments. And even though we have acquired quite a bit of knowledge about the prehistoric origins of many species (including humans) through fossil evidence (and more recently genetic analysis), new discoveries are constantly throwing old theories into doubt. The origins of fish and sharks in particular are still not very well understood.

Researchers, for instance, were under the mistaken impression that sharks dated back to the middle Devonian period. (The Devonian period extends from 410 to 360 million years ago.) One slight problem: The researchers were searching in the wrong places for the wrong kind of evidence. They didn't realize that ancient shark teeth could be so small. It wasn't until 1986 that teeth belonging to the family of sharks called *Xenacanthids* were found in Spain. This remarkable discovery caused paleon-tologists to date the origin of sharks 50 million years earlier than previously thought. In addition, because of their cartilaginous structure and other traits, sharks were seen as "primitive vertebrates" or derisively regarded as "living fossils." However, further investigation has revealed that sharks are highly evolved with a complex biology comparable in many respects to that of birds and mammals.

One of the challenges confronting scientists trying to unravel the mystery of shark origins is the huge gap in fossil knowledge. Unlike the skeletons of bony fish, who have left an abundant record of fossils in rock formations, the skeletons of shark, which are composed of cartilage, are not preserved. This means that scientists have had to rely on the hard parts of a shark—principally their teeth, scales, and spines. The fossil record is scanty when it comes to soft tissue such as shark fins. Imagine trying to illustrate a full-bodied image of a person from head to toe using only that person's front molars and a few sections of their spinal cord as a guideline.

The First Finds

Fossils weren't considered serious evidence for a long time. Not until the seventeenth century did naturalists and scholars grasp that these fossils offered the potential to provide a crucial history of life on the planet. To some extent this reluctance to study fossils was due to the influence of religion. The Bible was considered the literal truth, and the book of Genesis stated that the universe was created in six days. To claim that it might have taken longer became little short of heresy.

Further, it was widely held that all the species that were present on Earth had always been present. So to find fossils of species that no longer existed posed a particularly thorny problem for scientists and scholars. Fossil remains (including those of sharks) were nothing new—people had been digging them up for thousands of years. It was just that these fossils weren't appreciated for what they represented. Shark teeth were often mistaken for birds' teeth or snake tongues. The larger fossil teeth called *glossopteris* (literally, tongue stones) were turned into amulets to ward off evil. The study and classification of fossils (called paleontology) did not become a science until the middle of the nineteenth century. Whatever we know about ancient sharks dates from that time.

The Mysterious Origin of Sharks

The origin of sharks is shrouded in mystery. One theory, based on similar appearances, maintains that cartilaginous fish (sharks, rays, and chimaeras) evolved from placoderms, bony-plated jawed fishes that were extinct long ago. Another theory states that placoderms and cartilaginous fishes share a common ancestry dating back almost 430 million years ago.

The third possibility suggests that cartilaginous fishes and *lodonts* (a group of primitive fishes) shared a common ancestor because of a similarity of scales. Extinct lodonts had bodies made of cartilage, but they had had no jaws or teeth. Like sharks, lodonts had paired fins and gills. They evolved quickly in the Tuva region of Siberia, a region where the oldest known shark scales have also been discovered. (The similarity of the lodonts to the earliest sharks makes it difficult for paleontologists to distinguish between the teeth found in rock formations. That in turn creates confusion when it comes to tracing the shark's earliest origins from the fossilized evidence.) The portrait of this possible ancestor is at best a conjectural one. No complete fossils of these long vanished lodonts have ever been found, which only compounds the problem. Some scientists believe that a lodont would look like a small fish with a long, slender body. It had one dorsal fin, paired pectoral fins, and no spine fins. Its scales varied in size and shape according to their position on the creature's body, and fork tailed fossils have been found.

Other superficial evidence suggests that shark lineage may have begun with the *Acanthodians*, who are very early fish identified as the first jawed vertebrates. *Acanthodians* lived from the Ordovician to the Carboniferous period. These geological epochs span a period from 535 million to 360 million years ago (the Ordovician) to 360 million to 290 million years ago (the Carboniferous). To put these time periods in another perspective, the earliest sharks were evolving 100 million years before dinosaurs set foot on Earth.

What Does It Mean?

The **Carboniferous period** (360 to 290 million years ago) derives its name from strata filled with coal in Wales and Britain. It literally means coal-bearing. This period was at a time when coal was forming, and peat swamps and lush forests covered much of present-day Europe and North America.

Most *Acanthodians* were small, only five or six inches long, but some grew to three feet in length, such as the one known as xylacanthus, who had huge jaws and may have been a primitive sharklike fish. (Xylacanthus, which I cited previously, was discovered from excavations in Spain carried out in the 1980s.) Most of the evidence that we have about these sharks comes from fossilized teeth and a few impressions of scales found in rock. Ancient teeth belonging to sharks were double-pointed and measured up to three feet long!

The Paleozoic Era

To appreciate the way in which today's sharks came of age, we need to go back to an era 400 million years ago. Earth looked nothing like it does today. The continents had yet to appear, and most of the planet's surface was covered with warm seas. This geological epoch is known as the *Paleozoic era*. During this era water governed evolution as ocean levels continued to rise. The only life consisted of animals and plants that could thrive in a marine environment.

What Does It Mean?

The **Paleozoic era** is the geological period that spans from 500 to 240 million years ago. This crucial period in the evolution of animal and plant life is marked by the emergence of landmasses that are still in existence today.

Primitive fish were already beginning to appear half a billion years ago. The earliest complete fossil of a fish was found in Australia. The creature appears to have been a mud grubber or filter feeder that inhabited coastal waters about 480 million years ago.

The next 100 million years saw the development of all the major fish groups that we see on Earth today—which isn't to say that scientists know how these species evolved or have even determined how they are related. In the Silurian period some 400 million years ago, most of these primitive fish were bony and had no jaws. But this period is also characterized by the evolution of a different kind of fish, one characterized by jaws and cartilage. The Silurian period is the first time that we have fossil evidence of the first advanced jawed fishes, so-called spiny sharks who sported large fin spines but aren't true sharks. (You might recall our discussion in Chapter 9 of horn sharks, named because of their prominent fin spines.)

What Does It Mean?

The **Devonian period** (the fourth division of the Paleozoic era) spans a period from 410 to 360 million years ago and derives its name from Devonshire, England, where fossils from this period were first uncovered in the 1830s.

Thirty million years later (a blink of the eye in geological terms), fish had diversified and spread throughout the world's waters. Twenty-five million years later, at the end of what is known as the *Devonian period*, evolutionary restlessness impelled some of these fish to risk trying life on land. These adventurous fish became the progenitors of spiders, amphibians, insects, reptiles such as dinosaurs, four-legged mammals, and ultimately us.

The Search for the Earliest Sharks

Scientists are determined to unravel the shark's ancient lineage and figure out how the primitive, often bizarre sharklike fish swimming the oceans hundreds of millions of years ago are related to the sharks we know today. A new class of fossil sharks called *iniopterygians* has recently come to light in rocks from the Carboniferous period in North America. These unusual fish, which lived 300 million years ago, have attracted interest because they might prove to be the "missing link" because they share certain features of both elasmobranchs (sharks, skates, and rays) and holocephalians (chimaeras). Studies made on tooth plates indicate that iniopterygians probably subsisted on a diet of shellfish, but little else can be deduced about them. For all the progress researchers are making, definitive answers about the origin of sharks remain elusive.

Cleveland, Ohio, may seem an improbable place to plumb the depths of prehistory, but that's where the first complete fossils of sharklike fish were discovered in mid-Devonian rocks. What were sharks doing in Cleveland, Ohio? Three hundred and seventy-five million years ago, when North America was covered by water, this region made a congenial habitat for these fish. The bacteria-free environment, which pre-served them to a remarkable degree, allowed scientists to examine their tissues. In one case, a shark was so well preserved in rock that his liver and kidney were still intact.

The earliest sharks predate both dinosaurs and humans.

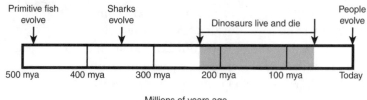

Cladoselache
==========

The most common form of these early sharklike fish is known as a cladoselache. This fish grew up to six feet in length, possessed pectoral and dorsal fins, had five pairs of gill slits, and also had a fin spine and a forked tail. Researchers believe that the cla-doselache was a fast swimmer, which was a critical asset for a creature frequently preyed upon by a giant 15-foot armored fish that swam in the same long-evaporated waters. Because scientists were able to sift through the contents of the fish's stomachs, they know that the cladoselache lived on small fish.

The good news is that we know so much about these early fish because their bodies were found in such miraculously good condition. The bad news is that we know enough to realize that this creature is probably not the ancestor of the sharks who swim in the seas today. That's because the cladoselache doesn't have claspers, those obvious sexual organs found in all modern male sharks. Given the importance of reproduction to any species, the absence of claspers suggests that the cladoselache was one evolutionary specimen that didn't survive.

In the meantime, the domination of marine life was nearing its demise. During the Devonian period, life was beginning to take formation on land. Seed ferns, scorpions, spiders, and insects made their first appearance on the evolutionary stage. Climactic conditions changed dramatically; the North and South Poles cooled, water levels dropped, and volcanic activity intensified, especially in the area that is now known as Siberia, Russia. These changes brought about wholesale extinctions of an untold numbers of species; the late Permian period (the last period in the Paleozoic era) is considered the greatest period of extinction in history. The Paleozoic era ended with a relatively small number of animal and plant species left to call Earth their home.

The cladoselache is the most common form of early shark-like fish.

The Paleozoic Era

The Paleozoic era is a geological term for the time that begins 570 million years before the present and ends 240 million years before the present. This era is sub-divided into several periods:

◆ Cambrian (570 million to 500 million years ago)

◆ Ordovician (500 million to 435 million years ago)

◆ Silurian (435 million to 410 million years ago)

◆ Devonian (410 million to 360 million years ago)

◆ Carboniferous (360 million to 290 million years ago)

◆ Permian (290 million to 240 million years ago)

Helicoprions

Another ancient fish who lays claim to being a forerunner of modern sharks is known as the *helicoprion*. This fish lived about 250 million years ago. Whether helicoprion is an ancestor of sharks or a shark himself is not clear. In contrast to cladoselache, we know very little about helicoprion. In the case of the cladoselache, the remains were well preserved; no helicoprion carcasses have ever been discovered.

The only evidence of helicoprions is fossilized teeth, which have turned up all over the world. Their teeth were arranged in an elaborate, expanding spiral: the smallest teeth were located in the center of the sharks' mouths, with larger replacement teeth surrounding them. Some scientists believe that the teeth were used for crushing shellfish and arthropods; others are of the opinion that these sharks used their teeth to stun larger prey until they got around to eating it. The portrait that scientists have drawn of the helicoprion is one of a fish measuring 7.5 to 10 feet in length and having a blunt snout and an elongated cartilaginous body (which probably accounts for why this fish hasn't left fossilized remains behind). Scientists know almost nothing about the helicoprion's habitats, diet, or behavior.

The Rise of Modern Sharks

Modern sharks, known as *Cneoselachkians*, did not rise to dominance until after the Jurassic period, which ended 138 million years ago. These modern sharks appeared only after the ancient sharklike fish disappeared. Why the sharklike fish became extinct is still not known. Skates and rays (close cartilaginous cousins of the sharks) can trace their origin back to the Jurassic period (which began 205 million years ago). But they began to flourish in the Tertiary period (between 65 and 2 million years ago) when stocks of bivalve shellfish increased exponentially, providing them with a plentiful source of food.

In the Cretaceous period (140 to 65 million years ago), the progression of shark lineage from ancient to modern becomes much clearer. During this time, ancestors of sharks we would recognize today including goblins, sand sharks, nurse sharks, and angel sharks populated the oceans. When we reach the Miocene epoch (25 to 5 million years ago), modern sharks as well as some sharks who are now extinct were already present in the oceans. Of the latter, none has captured as much attention or inspired such awe as the megalodon.

A True Sea Monster

No shark living today, not even the great white, could rival the megalodon in terms of size. If Steven Spielberg ever wished to combine the story lines of his movies *Jaws* and *Jurassic Park*, he would probably choose to give megalodon a starring role. According to some estimates, this mysterious behemoth was found in the oceans 25 to 1.6 million years ago during the Miocene and Pliocene epochs.

Some shark enthusiasts believe that megalodon might have existed as recently as 12,000 years ago, which was when mammoths became extinct and humans were beginning to populate the planet.

Whatever megalodon's history is, no one disputes that this shark was exceptionally huge, measuring from 40 and 50 feet with a weight of around 20 tons. (Some scientists believe that the monster might have grown up to 100 feet. In any case, megalodon would have been double or triple the size of the great white.) Because only teeth have been found, shark experts are reduced to speculating as to what megalodons looked like. The experts' best guess is that the sharks resembled streamlined great whites.

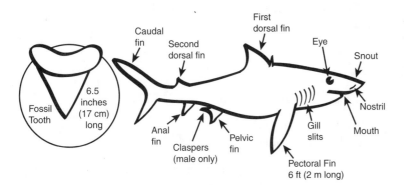

Although it has an anatomy similar to that of the great white, megalodon is still the largest shark known to have ever existed.

Daggers for Teeth

Megalodon teeth, although similar to those found in the great white, are much bigger, thicker, and have finer serrations. Fossilized megalodon teeth have been well studied and are found throughout the world from Europe to India and Oceania (Australia, New Zealand, and New Caledonia) as well as in North and South America. Some of the specimens measure more than six feet (!) in length, the size of daggers. Like most shark teeth, megalodon's teeth were probably located in rows. The front rows would have been used to catch prey; when the teeth broke or wore down, teeth from the back rows would rotate into the places where they were needed. Megalodon may have had hundreds of teeth at one time.

You would expect that the sizable teeth of megalodon's jaws would be a formidable (and intimidating) instrument. And you'd be right. This shark's jaws were capable of opening a gaping chasm six feet wide and seven feet high. Loosely attached by ligaments and muscles to the skull, these jaws could open so wide that a megalodon could easily swallow a large great white shark whole! But the megalodon's diet seems to have consisted principally of whales.

Tracing Megalodon's Ancestry

Shark experts are still at odds over whether megalodons represent an evolutionary dead end or whether they might be an ancestor of the great white shark. At one point megalodon was classified as *Carcharodon megalodon*, the same genus as the great white

(*Carcharodon carcharias*). Some scientists now believe that megalodon belongs to a separate genus and should be classified as *Carcharodon* ("giant tooth") *megalodon*.

No one is sure when the megalodon became extinct. There are those who against all scientific evidence still hold out hope that this monster might lurk in the ocean depths today, awaiting rediscovery.

The Least You Need to Know

- The origin of modern sharks extends back as far as 400 million years.

- The study of shark ancestors is hampered because shark cartilage does not survive for long (except under extraordinary circumstances).

- Scientists do not know whether sharks and their relatives, skates, rays, and chimaeras, developed separately or shared a common ancestor.

- Modern sharks began to dominate the seas in the Jurassic period (205 to 138 million years ago).

- The biggest shark of all, now extinct, was the megalodon, who lived between 25 and 1.6 million years ago.

Chapter 11

The Shark's Closest Relatives and Friends

In This Chapter

- ◆ Why rays appear to fly through the ocean
- ◆ How sharks and rays differ
- ◆ Why most rays aren't dangerous
- ◆ How some fish live off sharks

As mentioned in Chapter 1, sharks represent one species of cartilaginous fish. They do have a number of distantly related cousins, all of whom lack a true bone structure. No one knows whether they shared a common ancestor or tracked a different path of evolution. Scientists do say with some feeling of certainty that, like sharks, the other cartilaginous fish can trace their ancestry back as much as 400 to 450 million years. Together, all these cartilaginous fish are known as *Chondrichthyes*, which is just another way of saying "cartilaginous fish." In this chapter, you will find out about these close relatives of the sharks. Though they share many traits in common—their skeletal structure above all—they have many other attributes that make them very different.

The Other Cartilaginous Fish

There are nearly 1,000 species of cartilaginous fish, including a species called the chimaeras. This number tells us that there are approximately 600 species of cartilaginous fish that are *not* sharks, and new species of *Chrondrichthyes* are turning up all the time. Like sharks, these other cartilaginous fish have evolved into complex animals that have largely proven successful at mastering their marine environment for hundreds of millions of years.

According to the traditional classification system developed by taxonomists, *Chondrichthyes* are divided into two groups: the *Elasmobranchii*, which includes sharks, skates, rays, and some strange fossil relatives, and the *Bradyodonti*. *Elasmobranchii* have two distinguishing characteristics: hingelike upper jaws that are not fused to the braincase and separate slitlike gill openings.

The *Bradyodonti* differ from the *Elasmobranchii* in two respects. For one thing, they have an upper jaw fused to the braincase; for another, they have a flap of skin called the *operculum* that covers the gill slits. Among the *Bradyodonti* we find the chimaeras and ratfish, who are both relatively rare, deep-water fish that feed on mollusks.

Just like sharks, rays, chimaeras, and other cartilaginous fish show extremely varied behavior. Although most are predatory, others are scavengers. Some can be dangerous to humans, but the vast majority are not.

Shark Facts and Stats

The white sturgeon also has a cartilaginous body, a characteristic of sharks, as well as suckerlike barbels, spiny barbs bristling along the back of its torso. Its wide toothless mouth looks like it could use a set of dentures. The white sturgeon swallows its food whole and has great jaw strength, two more traits it has in common with sharks. The largest sturgeon caught in the 1950s by sport fishermen weighed more than 1,450 pounds. White sturgeons have no predators. They are prehistoric and date back more than 250 million years before the age of dinosaurs.

Getting to Know the Family

Rays, who are formally known as Rajiformes, belong to an order of cartilaginous fish who bear an eerie resemblance to a flying wing. They can vary in size from a few inches to more than 20 feet. Rays include guitarfish, sawfish, stingrays, electric rays, eagle rays, and skates. Some of the most popular rays are the largest: mantas and devilfish. Mantas can weigh more than 3,000 pounds.

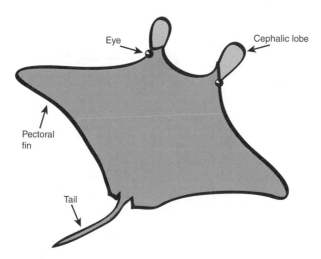

Eye

Cephalic lobe

Pectoral fin

Tail

Manta rays, also known as devilfish, can grow up to 23 feet from one tip of its pectoral fin to the other.

How Rays and Skates Differ from Sharks

The fins of a shark do not always play a crucial role in the shark's forward motion. For example, great whites use just their tail fins to speed through the water; their other fins serve primarily to maintain balance. For skates and rays, however, the fins, specifically the pectoral fins, play a crucial role in moving through water. When these fish swim, their pectoral fins, which are shaped like wings, undulate as they move forward. This movement gives rays and skates the appearance of flying through water. Giant manta rays have enormous wings and can measure up to 23 feet across. Tail fins are either small or nonexistent.

One of the most significant differences between sharks and cartilaginous fish such as rays is diet. The latter feed primarily on crustaceans and mollusks; thus, evolution has given skates and rays flattened bodies that are customized for

Shark Lore

Devilfish is a term applied to many rays, especially the Atlantic manta. However, octopus, cuttlefish, and squid have all been called devilfish because of their supposedly sinister appearance.

Shark Facts and Stats

The eagle ray is often found near shore in large schools. These rays fly through the upper waters on flapping pectoral fins, sometimes even leaping out of the water. They mainly subsist on mollusks near the bottom but they are also a popular treat for sharks.

their bottom dwelling existence. Their body shape allows them to glide slowly and gracefully over sandy and reef bottoms in search of prey. Not all skates and rays are bottom feeders, though; a few, such as the eagle ray and the manta ray, lead a free-swimming existence.

Rays also have fewer scales than sharks. Not surprisingly, their coloration and patterning reflects their feeding behavior. Many rays have bodies speckled with spots or blotches to camouflage them as they wait in ambush buried in the sand or lying among the rocks and coral. The color variation among rays is quite pronounced, and within some species this variation occurs between sexes, with males of one color and females of another.

Diet also explains the difference in teeth among sharks and rays. Many species of sharks have sharp, curved teeth. In contrast, rays have flat, platelike teeth. They don't need to capture prey with their teeth or rip out flesh or meat; all that's required for a tasty meal is the ability to crush shellfish.

The location of the eyes, mouth, and spiracles (those openings to allow the intake of oxygenated water) on rays can also be explained by their bottom-dwelling lifestyle. Instead of being found in the front of the head, as is the case with most sharks, the spiracles and eyes of rays are located on top of their heads, allowing them to see and keep water moving over their gills while they are partially buried in sand. A savvy diver might see only these eyes peering above the sand. Similarly, rays' mouths are located on underside of their heads, conveniently positioned for consuming prey on the seabed.

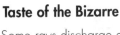

Taste of the Bizarre

Some rays discharge electric shocks to deter predators. They are one of three kinds of electric fish; there are also electric eels and electric catfish. Of these, the electric eel emits the most potent shock.

Like many species of sharks, some species of rays are viviparous, which means they deliver their young live. Most skates, on the other hand, are generally oviparous: They hatch eggs. (However, some skates do give birth to their young.)

Although rays might have a reputation for being dangerous because some have been known to deliver a powerful electric shock or a stinging blow, most rays and skates are docile and pose no threat to swimmers or divers.

How Skates and Rays Differ from Each Other

Although skates belong to the ray family, they differ in some respects from rays such as guitarfish, devilfish, and mantas. The principal difference is the way they reproduce:

Skates give birth by laying eggs, and rays give birth to live young. Otherwise, the differences are morphological—that is to say, the differences have to do with physical structure. Rays, for instance, have less mobility because of the way that their pelvis is constructed. Skates have one or two dorsal fins; in rays the dorsal fin is either absent or located near the pelvic fins or forms a long fold. Finally, rays have flat, plate-like teeth; skates have cusped teeth.

> **Shark Facts and Stats**
>
> The 200 species of rays can be regarded as sharks that have been flattened out and have adapted to living on the ocean floor.

Sharks vs. Rays and Skates

In a nutshell, these are the ways in which sharks and rays differ:

- Rays are bottom feeders; the majority of shark species are not.

- Rays have broad, flattened bodies; most sharks do not.

- Rays use their pectoral fins to flap in a "winglike" configuration for swimming; in many species of shark pectoral fins have less importance in moving through water.

- Rays have fewer scales than sharks.

- Rays have eyes and spiracles on the top of their heads and mouths on the underside of their heads. In sharks these features are usually found in the front or side of the head.

- Most rays nurture their eggs inside their bodies and give birth to live young except for skates which hatch eggs; in some shark species, by contrast, embryos develop in the mother and are born as fully formed pups.

- With few exceptions, most rays are harmless. Some species of shark, such as bulls and tigers, can pose a grave risk to swimmers and divers.

What the Fossil Record Shows

In Chapter 10, we talked about the origin of cartilaginous fish, but most of the primitive fish we cited are not thought to be related to the species of sharks, rays, or skates found in oceans today. Most of those ancient fish died off long ago.

Living sharks, rays, and skates belong to a group known as *Neoselachii*, most of which date to the Jurassic period (between 230 to 138 million years before the present). Keep in mind, though, that when we discuss eras so long ago, especially given the often spotty fossil evidence, much of what we say is, by necessity, purely speculative based on data that scientists have been able to piece together. However, we can say with a fair degree of certainty that most present-day species of sharks, rays, and skates had all evolved by the Cretaceous period (138 to 65 million years ago).

Where Rays Live and How They Breed

Like sharks, rays have adapted to a wide variety of environments. Some prefer relatively shallow waters; others prefer the open sea or tropical waters. A few species are even capable of thriving in lakes and rivers. Rays are social beings found in seas all over the world as well as in some estuaries. Unlike sharks, who, with few exceptions, tend to be loners, rays often congregate in schools of up to thousands of individuals. (However, some antisocial rays prefer to swim alone.) In general, rays grow slowly, mature late (at the age of 20 to 25 years for some species), and can live up to 70 years.

As we noted before, most rays are viviparous (bearing live young), and most skates are usually oviparous (laying eggs). Yet reproductive strategies for rays can range enormously. The female of the southern stingray, for instance, carries eggs internally but does not nurture the fetuses. Pups hatch while still in the mother's body. As many as three to five pups are born at a time, each about nine inches long. The pups are born with long, spiny tails and large fins; in this respect, they look like adults, but their bodies are somewhat slimmer. Most rays have relatively few young.

> **Shark Lore**
>
> Some skates lay their eggs encased in a protective rectangular case of hornlike material that is sometimes called a mermaid's purse.

What Extra Senses Do Rays Have?

Rays, like sharks, were among the first animals who were found to have electroreceptive organs such as the ampullae of Lorenzini, the jellylike network clustered in regions around the head but often extending in several directions over the entire body surface. The degree of distribution appears to depend on the species.

How Dangerous Are Rays?

Like sharks, rays have earned the unjust reputation for posing a threat to humans. But in most cases, the evolutionary weapon provided to rays is used primarily for defense, not for attack or predation. Rays are not known for their aggressiveness. Even stingrays are relatively defenseless because they are unable to direct their tails while swimming, making them vulnerable to their principal predator, the shark. (Kinship is no guarantee against being eaten for lunch.)

Taste of the Bizarre

The southern stingray, found mainly in Caribbean and South American waters, is potentially dangerous because of its ability to "sting" humans. If stepped on, the ray lashes its tail up and attempts to drive it into the intruder in self-defense. The spines on the tail cut and tear the flesh, inflicting a painful injury. The ray also injects a poison—while not life threatening, it can cause depressed respiration.

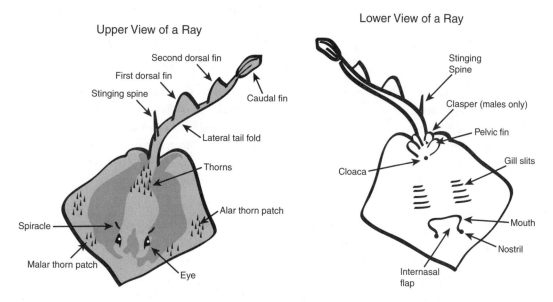

The anatomy of rays is similar to that of sharks, but they have a distinctive pancakelike shape.

All that said, rays still have an intriguing and often formidable arsenal at their disposal. Barbed spines located at the base of their long whiplike tails give stingrays their sting. Some rays have tail spines capable of delivering poison to their enemies. Other rays have bodies that bristle with thorns, making them an unpromising catch for any potential predator. If provoked, these rays can combine their spines and poison to inflict a wound and amplify the pain. In one chilling incident in Australian waters, a stingray drove his tail spine into the heart of an unsuspecting swimmer, killing him.

A Stinging Encounter

Over the years I've had a few close encounters that have given me an adrenaline rush. I've bopped a couple blues in the nose with my camera and scrambled out of the water when an oceanic white tip took too much of an interest of me. And I have never forgotten how a menacing Galapagos shark circled me and my buddy all the way to the surface. But I have never felt as though I were in serious danger of being attacked by a shark. The worse encounter I've experienced with a predator was a brief swipe by a jellyfish tentacle at Blue Corner, the famous shark-diving site in Palau, an island nation in the Western Pacific.

At the time I was wearing a T-shirt over my swimsuit. Even though I felt the sting on my tricep I didn't think it was serious enough to abort the dive. When I surfaced to the boat and told the crew that I had been stung by a jellyfish, they asked if I had trouble breathing. Needless to say, this was an alarming question. I was later to learn that box jellies in the South Pacific can kill a person in four minutes.

The crew on the boat poured vinegar over the area of the injury and other divers shared nonprescription pain medication. The pain was soon accompanied by swelling. One side of my body from the center of my left breast and down my arm puffed up like a balloon. Everyone searched through their first-aid kits. As the pain diminished (though it took six weeks before it was entirely gone), the itching began. I applied Hydrocortisone creme and Benydryl to the site of the sting.

The timing couldn't have been much worse; it was the third day of a 10-day trip and no one, including myself, wanted to return to port. I decided to make the best of it, sitting out only one dive. For the rest I ignored the pain and itching. Palau is too far from home and too great a dive destination to miss a single minute underwater. However, this unhappy encounter with the jellyfish did cause me to change one diving habit. Now I always wear a full-bodied Lycra suit for added protection. Just in case I do get stung, I carry an EpiPen, an auto-injector that administers epinephrine, in the event that another jellyfish sting causes an analeptic reaction.

If you happen to find yourself on the wrong side of certain types of rays, you might end up getting the shock of your life. Some rays defend themselves by administering electric shocks with organs on each side of their heads. One kind of ray can deliver a shock up to 200 volts, enough to be quite dangerous.

Taste of the Bizarre

The smooth stingray has razor-sharp serrated spines as long as 13 feet or more in length. The indigenous people of Polynesia, Malaysia, Central America (dating back to the Mayans), and Africa have used the spines of stingrays to make spears and knives. In some cases, the tails of the rays have been put to use as whips.

The Dangers Humans Pose to Sharks and Rays

The very survival of skates and rays is being threatened for many of the same reasons that sharks are in jeopardy. These species of cartilaginous fish mature slowly and produce only a few young at a time. Now fished in huge quantities, these species cannot sustain their population. And we are already seeing the effects as populations suffer serious declines. For instance, the largest ray found in European waters, who was once abundant in fisheries, has been drastically reduced in some areas and has completely disappeared in others.

Ironically, rays, skates, and sharks are often not the targets of commercial fishermen, but they are ensnared accidentally in their nets or long lines intended to catch highly edible fish such as salmon and tuna, a phenomenon known as bycatch. Estimates of the numbers of sharks caught in this manner range up to a staggering 100 million a year!

No one has yet documented the loss of rays or skates, though it is safe to say that the numbers are likely to be enormous. In Chapter 20, we will discuss the danger posed to sharks and their cartilaginous relatives from overfishing in more detail and examine what success conservation measures have served in alleviating the crisis.

Chimaeras

Chimaera is a common name for members of any of three families of deep-water cartilaginous fishes: the plownose, longnose, and shortnose. These fish are also known as the ratfish family. In ancient Greek mythology, a chimaera was described as a female monster with a lion's head, a goat's body, and a serpent's tail and breathed fire. This might give you some idea as to just how bizarre these creatures can appear.

The long, whiplike tail of the stingray has sharp, sometimes barbed spines at its base that can inflict grave injuries (often coupled with poison) and are responsible for the most common form of fish stings.

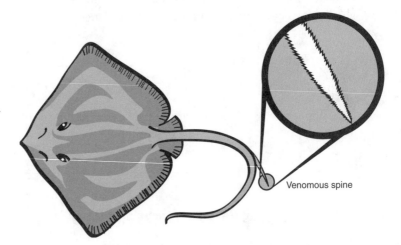

Venomous spine

Chimaeras, also known as the ratfish family, are related to sharks and rays, except that they are distinguished by a skin covering their gills and by the fact that they have a single opening instead of gill slits. They also lack the elongated and flattened body typical of skates and rays. Chimaeras can grow up to six feet. Instead of scales, they have smooth skin ranging in color from black to brownish gray, sometimes with markings. Their eyes are large. Ratfish have long tails and a poisonous spine in front of their dorsal fin.

Chimaeras' upper jaws are fully fused to their heads, which is in marked contrast to sharks where the upper jaws are only loosely connected. The chimaeras' teeth form flattened crushing plates for the consumption of shellfish, with two pairs located in the upper jaw and one pair in the lower jaw.

Where Chimaeras Live and How They Breed

Chimaeras are found in all oceans, mostly in the cool depths between 600 and 3,600 feet. As bottom feeders, they search for prey mainly on the soft muddy seabed of the deeper parts of the continental shelf or on the continental slope.

Just like male sharks and rays, male chimaeras have normal claspers near their pelvic fins, but they also have a second pair of flat, retractable claspers located in front of the pelvic fins. As far as scientists can make out, this extra set of claspers is probably used only to grip the female during mating.

All chimaeras are oviparous; they lay large eggs that are deposited on the bottom. These eggs are protected by a case of hornlike material, and the protection is desperately needed. Young chimaeras are not hatched until six months to a year after the eggs are laid.

Fellow Travelers: Swimming with the Sharks

Sharks may give the impression of being completely self-sufficient, but like most organisms on this planet, they can't go it alone. They need help from other species with whom they have formed a congenial and interdependent relationship. This kind of relationship is known as *symbiotic* (from the Greek *symbioun*, meaning "live together"). In this section we take a look at three types of fish that have developed a symbiotic relationship with sharks: pilot fish, remoras, and a fascinating creature called the cleaner wrasse.

First it may be useful to understand why symbiotic relationships are so vital in nature. Many of the interactions that take place between different species involve eating or avoiding being eaten. If one species helps another meet these two essential objectives over an extended period of time, we can call that relationship symbiotic. One requirement of a symbiotic relationship is that at least one member of the pair derives some benefit from it.

There are three types of *symbiosis:*

◆ Mutualism

◆ Commensalism

◆ Parasitism

Taste of the Bizarre

Fishermen have been known to attach a line to a remora and then release it. When the remora attaches itself to another fish, the fishermen haul in both the host and the remora—two for the price of one!

What Does It Mean?

In biology **symbiosis** refers to the interdependence of different species, often based on obtaining food or avoiding predation.

Mutualism is an association in which both species need each other to exist. They form such inextricable bonds that, in many cases, one species would not survive without the other. Some species of algae and fungi are involved in this kind of symbiosis.

In commensalism either one or both species benefit from the relationship, and neither is harmed. An underwater example of this relationship is the clownfish who lives among the tentacles of an anemone. In this kind of association the species can help each other out and then go their separate ways; they are not tied together as they are in mutualism.

In parasitism, however, one species exploits the other for nutrients or shelter. In a parasitic relationship, one species may be adversely affected. Mosquitoes who feed on blood, for instance, enjoy a parasitic relationship with humans, and all humans get in return is an irritating itch or, at least in certain parts of the world, a serious illness such as malaria.

Remoras

Remoras are bony fish found in abundance in warm coastal waters and in the vicinity of coral reefs. Their dorsal fins have been adapted to form a sucker. They use these suckers to attach themselves temporarily to a variety of hosts including sharks, rays, large fish, sea turtles, whales, and dolphins. They have even been known to attach themselves to ships and scuba divers' tanks.

When the shark feeds, the remora patiently gathers up the leftovers. Evidently sharks recognize the valuable service the remoras perform (though how they understand this is not understood) because they are not known to attack the bony fish. The relationship of remoras and sharks is commensal; both species derive benefit from a temporary and literal attachment.

Pilot Fish

Pilot fish are ocean-going bony fish found in subtropical waters who often travel in schools. Like remoras, pilot fish have entered into a commensal association with sharks. Although the exact nature of the relationship of these two species is not entirely clear, many researchers believe that pilot fish conserve energy by hitching a ride on the hydrodynamic bow wake of the shark. And like remoras, pilot fish are happy to hang around to collect whatever scraps they can after the shark feeds. What benefit do the sharks derive? Well, pilot fish are pretty indiscriminate feeders and also dine on the shark's parasites (and excrement), possibly helping the shark ward off disease.

> **Shark Lore**
>
> Many species of sharks seek out specific sites where cleaner wrasses and other fish enjoying a symbiotic relationship with them will clean them of parasites. These sites are known as cleaning stations.

Cleaner Wasse

The cleaner wasse is a most unusual fish; his sole purpose in life, as his name suggests, is to clean! Scientifically known as *Wrasse labroides dimidiatus*, the cleaner wasse is a common coral reef fish about as long as your finger. A cleaner wasse has no compunction about swimming up to fish many times his size and going to work plucking parasites off the fish's body, which to the rest of the world looks like grooming. Far from objecting, bigger fish (both bony and cartilaginous) virtually plead for these cleaners to come and rid them of their pests and dead scar tissue by opening their gills and mouths and spreading their gills in almost a kind of begging behavior.

Investigators have discovered that the main component of the cleaners' diet was a particularly nasty parasite that fed off the blood of the host fish. Scientists believe that the cleaners may play an instrumental role in preventing diseases from being transmitted by the parasites that they find to be such a delicacy.

The Least You Need to Know

- Sharks, rays, and chimaeras are all cartilaginous fish known as *Chondrichthyes*.

- Rays have an anatomical structure similar to sharks but they have distinctive flat, elongated bodies.

- One group of rays is called skates; they differ in their physical structure and, in some cases, in their method of reproduction.

- Chimaeras are related to sharks and rays, but they have no scales on their bodies. Like rays, they are bottom feeders.

Chapter 12

Sex and the Sea

In This Chapter

- ◆ How sharks mate
- ◆ Why shark embryos practice cannibalism
- ◆ How sharks give birth
- ◆ Where nurses and lemons breed

Sharks develop slowly, reaching sexual maturity relatively late in life and producing relatively few young each year. Their slow development is key to understanding their mating and reproductive behavior. Mating among sharks—a messy, often brutal business—has to be understood in the context of genetic diversity. Or to put it simply: Females must pick their partners to ensure that the shark population has sufficient genetic diversity to keep it healthy.

Sharks give birth in several distinctive ways. Many species give birth to their young live; others lay eggs. But whatever the method of reproduction, the aim is the same: preserving the pup or the egg against predators. As you'll learn in this chapter, evolution has contrived some ingenious and fascinating solutions for pup protection.

Sharkadelic Mating Rituals

Where the mating habits of sharks are concerned, scientists still have much to learn because few people have actually observed sharks having sex. Marine biologists do know that the mating season usually lasts only a few weeks once a year. For some species mating seasons may occur only once every two or three years. (Except for mating, the two sexes generally remain segregated the rest of the time.) However often it occurs, shark sex is not for the fainthearted; it's a rough and aggressive busi-

> ### Shark Facts and Stats
>
> Unlike most sharks, who are loners, basking sharks gather in "mating circles," though the exact relationship of these circles and reproductive behavior is unknown.

ness. Females emerge from the experience with bruises and lacerations and males drop (literally) from exhaustion. And once it's over the couples immediately split up and go their separate ways. All the same, there is some evidence to suggest that sharks, especially the females, do discriminate among potential mates.

Before we get into the tawdry details, a little anatomy lesson might be helpful.

Sharks are considered sexually *dimorphic*, which means you can tell them apart visually. For one thing, females when they reach maturity are larger than males. For another, male sharks have specialized sexual organs called *claspers*, which are extensions of the pelvic fins that are used to deliver sperm to the female and fertilize her eggs. Claspers are rolls of cartilage that in adults stiffen with calcium. These organs are what makes it possible to differentiate between the sexes.

The male sexual organs (left), called claspers, are used to grasp the female during mating; sperm is transferred into the female sexual organ, the cloaca (right).

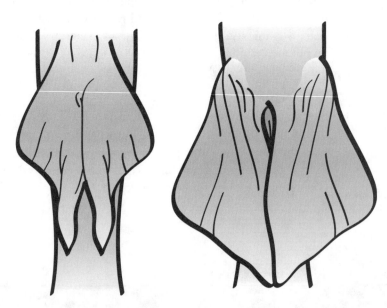

Males also have paired testes, which produce sperm; the right one is always more developed than the left, which is either smaller or absent altogether. The testes are internal (unlike in humans, for example). The urinary and reproductive tracts are joined to form the urogenital sinus; this is where the sperm is released into a groove of the claspers, from where they are conveyed into the female cloaca. The cloaca, located between the pelvic fins, is a cavity that functions in both reproduction and digestion. The internal ovaries are in pairs, but the one on the left is smaller and in some species doesn't even carry any eggs. Some female sharks have been known to carry the sperm for a month before fertilization takes place.

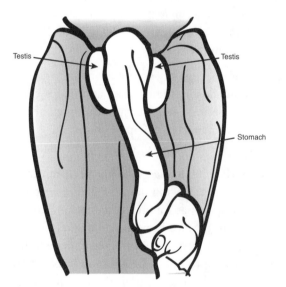

Testis

Testis

Stomach

Sharks have internally paired testes—the right always larger than the left—which produce sperm.

Although different species of sharks have different mating behavior, we can make a few generalizations:

- Sharks mate infrequently.

- Males of smaller, more flexible species wrap themselves around the females.

- Males of larger species with less flexibility position themselves either parallel or head-to-head with the female.

- During the mating ritual, the males of many species have a tendency to bite their partners on the pectoral fins or the middle of the back. They do this to keep the females from slipping away. Scientists believe that basking sharks retained small teeth (which they don't use to chew food because they subsist on plankton) because they wanted to hold females during copulation.

The evidence of these deep-sea liaisons is plain to see; the bites leave the females strewn with scars or telltale marks (produced, researchers have found, by the teeth from the male's upper jaw). In some species nature has compensated females for the injuries they sustain; in blue sharks, for instance, females have skin twice as thick as that of the males. At any rate, most of the wounds left by these mating bites quickly heal.

While mating behavior is fairly predictable from one species to another, some differences between sharks have been observed. In nurse sharks, for instance, mating begins with an aquatic dance, and the male leads by signaling his acceptance or rejection of a potential mate. As many as six males may gang up on one female, but that's as far as the collaboration goes. Then it's every male shark for himself. The winner is the one who secures the tightest grip on the female.

However, the female does not necessarily accept every suitor; female sharks are known to be pretty particular when choosing their mates, and males may have to contend with tough competition. This competition helps ensure that the babies will be healthy by receiving the strongest genetic material. A female shark can show her disdain by arching her body, keeping her fins from being grabbed by the male.

Once the male gets hold of the female, he grabs her pectoral fin in his mouth—literally inhaling her fins—and then begins towing her into deeper waters without even suggesting a nightcap. Once the male has found a place to his liking, he rolls the female over, flicks her tail underneath to brace himself and inserts his clasper into her cloaca. Only one of two claspers is employed to deliver sperm, depending on which side of the female the male has managed to grasp. Copulation lasts for only a minute or two. Then the male drops from exhaustion, falling to the bottom of the sea to recover. This exhaustion is due to the fact that he has had less oxygen for the entire time he's been grasping hold of the female's fins.

Sex Among the Hammerheads

Scalloped hammerheads are one the most sociable species of sharks. They cruise up and down the vertical walls of reefs or in open seas in schools of hundreds. These enormous schools seem to play a pivotal role in mating. Females fight to secure positions in the middle of the school, and the biggest female makes sure she occupies the center. Her prominent position makes her more attractive to the males. At night the action really begins. The schools break up as hammerheads pair up. (Not all hammerheads are so lucky; the rejected ones are left to go hunt for food instead.) At daytime the sharks return to the school, and the ritual is repeated. The scars on the larger females leave little doubt as to their success.

Sex Among the Reef Sharks

Some species of reef sharks breed in summer. Males rely on scents to select their mates. They pursue a female's scent trail through the water until they catch up to her. The male grips her body or fin with his teeth, inserting his claspers into her cloaca. The sperm is transferred into a special sac within the female where it's stored for several months before her eggs are fertilized the following spring.

Reproduction

In contrast to most bony fish, shark's eggs are fertilized inside the female's body. Sharks give birth in a number of ways. Most of them give birth to live young, but others lay eggs that hatch later. For bony fish, eggs are expendable; they lay thousands of eggs at a time, the vast majority of which are gobbled up by predators. Sharks, in marked contrast, don't need to produce such a surplus because they hold their eggs inside their bodies. Pups, as baby sharks are known, are self-sufficient at birth, which is a good thing because their mothers abandon them right away.

Shark Facts and Stats
Female sharks have two uteruses.

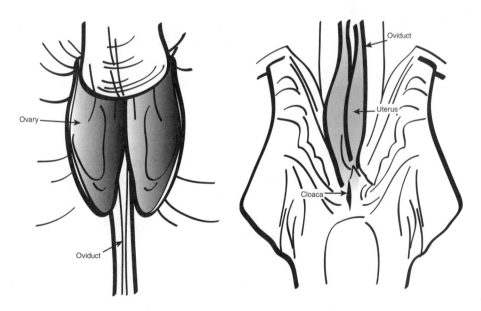

Sperm enters through the cloaca; fertilization takes place in the ovaries—female sharks have two—and the fertilized egg is then propelled up the oviduct to the uterus where gestation occurs.

Sharks who lay eggs outside their bodies (up to 25 at a time) are usually smaller species, such as dog, cat, carpet, and horn sharks. These eggs are concealed in a leathery shell or hornlike case that is attached by dangling tendrils to seaweed or otherwise camouflaged. Pups survive by feeding off the yolk and may have to wait up to 10 months before they are ready to eat their way out of the case and swim off.

The three types of embryonic development in sharks are: oviparous, ovoviviparous, and viviparous. About 40 percent of shark species lay eggs, and 60 percent bear live young, either by means of ovoviparous or placental viviparous reproduction.

- **Oviparous reproduction.** In oviparous sharks such as the horn shark, a protective shell or case (secreted by a special gland) protects the egg as it passes through the oviduct. (In higher mammals, including humans, this oviduct is known as the fallopian tube.) The mother subsequently deposits the egg cases in the sea.

  Initially the egg case is soft and pale, hardening into a tough leathery membrane and darkening after a few hours. They vary in shape from pouchlike (the California horn) to screw-shaped (the Port Jackson shark). Some eggs (such as those of cat sharks) come equipped with tendrils that attach the egg to objects on the seabed. The embryo obtains its nutrients from the egg yolk.

- **Ovoviviparity.** Ovoviviparity refers to a method of giving birth in which the shark eggs first develop inside the mother and are then hatched. The mako, pygmy, nurse, great white, and tiger sharks reproduce in this manner. No placenta is attached to the embryos. The shell is often just a thin membrane, and in some cases the membrane may shield two or more eggs. This group of eggs is called a *candle*. The embryo doesn't take long to slough off the membrane and continue developing in the mother's uterus.

> **Shark Lore**
>
> Egg cases are sometimes called mermaid's purses.

- **Viviparous reproduction.** In placental viviparous sharks, such as whales, blues, bulls, hammerheads, lemon sharks, and white, black, and silver tips, the eggs hatch inside the mother's body, and the embryos develop in the uterus. The embryos are attached to the uterine wall by a placenta, which is connected to the baby shark behind the pectoral fins. Nutrients and oxygen from the mother's bloodstream are delivered to the embryo through the placenta. Meanwhile waste products from the embryo are transferred back to the mother for elimination. Viviparous sharks give birth to live young. The number of pups in a litter ranges from 2 to 20 or more. One exception to this rule is the whale shark. Whale sharks are viviparous and can give birth to hundreds of pups in a litter.

Baby Brother for Lunch

Sharks are famously competitive, especially where food is concerned. In some species, the competitive frenzy starts even before birth. In these cases, rather than relying on the yolk of the egg for sustenance, pups either receive their nourishment from the placenta or absorb nutritive fluids secreted by the mother's uterus. These fluids are known as uterine milk.

Once the uterine milk is gone, embryos devour other eggs. This phenomenon is called *ovophagy*. If a smaller embryo is in the uterus, so much the worse for the smaller embryo. In such cases, only one embryo survives in each uterus, nourished by one of its brothers or sisters.

> **What Does It Mean?**
>
> Ovophagy (literally "egg eating") refers to a phenomenon in which embryos practice cannibalism in the uterus of a shark mother.

The Case of the Bullhead Shark

Bullhead sharks are known to produce egg cases that are among the most bizarre in all of nature. They are mostly conical and are surrounded by two broad spiral flanges. This shape proves convenient for wedging the egg cases into crevices where they are safe from predators. The egg case of the crested bullhead has a pair of tendrils that wrap around kelp so the egg case doesn't float away. But the problem is that, given the unusual shape of these egg cases, the bullhead has difficulty expelling them. The female bullhead spends hours laboring to rotate the case from her cloaca. Depending on the species, bullhead eggs hatch after a gestation period of 5 to 12 months.

> **Shark Facts and Stats**
>
> Eggs in a whale shark can grow up to 14 inches long—the largest egg ever found in the world. It was discovered in the Gulf of Mexico in 1953. Whale eggs are usually hatched inside the mother's body.

The Whale Shark: Oviparous or Viviparous?

The discovery in 1953 of a shark egg case containing a 14.5-inch whale shark embryo in the Gulf of Mexico triggered a controversy that lasted for 42 years. According to some scientists, the egg case meant that whale sharks were oviparous (egg-laying sharks). Others heatedly contended that whale sharks were viviparous (live-bearing sharks), and the egg case's discovery was accountable to premature birth. In 1995, Taiwanese fishermen harpooned a pregnant whale shark, which resolved the debate.

When National Taiwan Ocean University scientists dissected the shark, they found twin uteruses filled with 300 embryos ranging in size from 16 to 25 inches in length. Now they had definitive proof that the whale shark hatched eggs inside her body and bore her young live. Remarkably, of the 300 embryos, 15 were still alive and ready to be born.

Fast Attackers, Slow Breeders

Sharks, who develop slowly, usually have much longer *gestation periods* than most bony fish. However, gestation periods vary among shark species and between individuals within a species. Because most sharks are cold-blooded, there is no precise gestation time; the rate at which the embryo develops depends on the surrounding water temperature. Most shark embryos develop somewhere in the range of several months up to two years for the spiny dogfish shark, who appears to hold the record for sharks in gestation time.

> **What Does It Mean?**
>
> **Gestation period** is the time it takes an embryo to develop inside a female.

The Virgin Birth

Is it possible that sharks have a fourth reproductive strategy—one that dispenses entirely with males? Virgin births, known as *parthogenesis*, actually do occur in nature, although they are very rare. For example, some female aphids, water fleas, and snails can fertilize themselves and reproduce without males. Until 2002, marine biologists seldom considered the possibility that some sharks, too, could also reproduce asexually. They had to reassess their opinion when a female whitespotted bamboo shark at Detroit's Belle Isle Aquarium laid three eggs that hatched with no evidence that it had had any sexual relations with a male. Female sharks are known to lay infertile eggs without having mated, but not to have given birth. Or at least the aquarists used to believe that the eggs were infertile because in the past they would discard these eggs.

However, the aquarist at Belle Isle left these eggs alone in the tank after they'd hatched in the winter because he had heard about another case in which a hammerhead had given a virgin birth. In the summer three of the eggs, subsequently transferred into another tank, hatched. Aquarists discount the possibility that the shark, which is about two feet long, might have been impregnated prior to her arrival at Belle Isle. An even more unlikely possibility is that the Detroit shark was *hermaphoriditic*—having both male and female reproductive organs, which does occasionally occur in nature. But the consensus among scientists is that somehow the shark succeeded in stimulating the eggs without sperm.

Scientists hoped that genetic testing might be able to shed more light on the mystery. But shark experts recognize that so little is known about reproduction among the 400 or so species of sharks that parthogenesis among bamboo sharks—and possibly others—might be happening all the time in nature without anyone being the wiser.

Pups

The number of pups a shark gives birth to depends on the species. Some have more than 130 pups; blues and whales give birth to about 100 pups in a litter. Most species, however, have fewer than 30. The sand tiger has only two.

Pups are born with a full set of teeth and are immediately ready to adapt to life at sea. If their mothers haven't already deserted them, pups are likely to swim off anyway—and this is a wise choice. If they hang around, their mother might eat them—female sharks are not known for their maternal instincts!

Nurseries of the Young and Restless

Sharks do not give birth just anywhere. Even if the mother is going to desert her pups immediately after birth, she wants to make certain that conditions are conducive for their survival (that is, if she doesn't decide to eat her young herself). Some mothers give birth in warm waters because such waters are more likely to be free from predators and have a greater chance of containing an abundance of small fish for food. Female basking sharks, for instance, appear to give birth before migrating to shallower coastal waters, or they move offshore into deeper waters where the pups have a better chance of surviving.

Breeding Grounds of Nurses

An example of just such a nursery is located off the remote islands of the Florida Keys, which are favored by nurse sharks. Researchers have been studying sharks in this area for several years because these sharks are easy to track (which is not always the case with many other species). Nurses are reliable; they keep coming back to the same breeding ground year after year. Through this study, scientists hope to discover more about shark mating

Shark Lore

Nurse sharks have been reported in the same Florida Keys breeding ground as early as 1860, and they may have been there long before that.

habits and their relationship with the environment. Why a certain species of sharks (even the same individuals) prefers a particular site remains a tantalizing mystery to scientists studying these animals.

What makes the mystery even more baffling is the fact that the shallow waters that make up the Keys breeding ground make it difficult for male sharks to initiate mating. That finding suggested to researchers that the breeding ground was the choice of the females so they could more easily select the male partners they found desirable from those who weren't up to grade.

Spring Break for Lemon Sharks

Another favorite shark breeding ground of interest for researchers is a lagoon in Bimini, Bahamas. Each year, late spring attracts hundreds of juvenile lemon sharks to the lagoon (kind of like spring break). Female lemon sharks breed on a two-year cycle and give birth every other year. The researchers observed that the females were the ones who could be counted on to return every year to Bimini; the males tended to be ocean rovers. That meant that a relatively small pool of sharks were in the lagoon during breeding time. That raised concern that a good deal of inbreeding might be going on between these sharks, who would therefore lack genetic diversity. Genetic diversity (having a lot of genes in the pool) makes for a healthier population. That's because the greater number of genes there are, the more likely the chances of having beneficial genes that can help the species survive in varying environmental conditions. But to guarantee genetic diversity, you need to have a number of potential partners available to contribute their genes.

Shark Facts and Stats
Lemon sharks are large coastal sharks found in the western Atlantic from New Jersey to Brazil. They are also found along the West African coast and in the Pacific from Baja California to Colombia. They are members of the family *Carcharhinidae*, which includes more than 50 species of large, active sharks.

So how were the lemon sharks able to resolve the dilemma? How could they ensure genetic diversity even though there were only so many females and males to mate with one another? Using genetic sampling, the Bimini researchers made a startling discovery. Females were found to have litters of 10 to 12 pups with up to four different fathers. The researchers suspect that multiple paternity may be the case with other large species of sharks as well. In this way genetic diversity could be maintained for the population as a whole.

Because of their odd-shaped heads, hammerhead sharks can sense move-ment all around them and enjoy an extraordinary peripheral sensitivity. This hammerhead was photographed in the Galapagos Islands.
(© Marc Bernardi, 2000)

Hammerheads are among the most social of sharks and often travel in schools, as shown by this school of scalloped hammerheads in the Galapagos Islands.
(© Marc Bernardi, 2000)

The whale shark is the largest fish known to modern man. Note the size of the shark in relation to the divers.
(© Marc Bernardi, 2000)

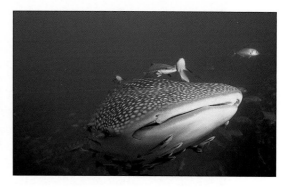

A whale shark in waters off Thailand.
(© Marc Bernardi, 2000)

Nurse shark with divers. The nurse shark is one of the smaller shark species.
(© Marc Bernardi, 2000)

A nurse shark feeds at the bottom of the ocean.
(© Marc Bernardi, 2000)

A blue shark swims through chum off San Diego. Blue sharks are an endangered species.
(Mary L. Peachin)

Note the long, thin body and needlelike profile of this blue shark as opposed to its wide, flat, blunt nose.
(Mary L. Peachin)

A large gray reef shark.
(Carl Roessler)

The silver markings on its fins and tail give the silvertip
shark its name.
(Carl Roessler)

A silvertip shark swims over a coral reef. Coral is an active ecosystem where many sharks
are at the top of the food chain.
(© Marc Bernardi, 2000)

Contrary to popular belief, great white sharks are not the largest or most dangerous sharks in the ocean. This one's nose shows the battle scars of age.
(Carl Roessler)

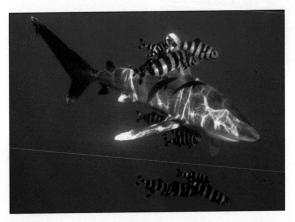

Larger sharks like this oceanic white tip are often followed by pilot fish who feed off the organisms on the shark's skin.
(Carl Roessler)

A leopard shark lies in the sand on the ocean floor.
(Carl Roessler)

This great white shark prepares to feed. Many sharks' jaws unhinge so they can swallow large prey whole.

(Carl Roessler)

Great white sharks typically avoid humans when possible.

(Carl Roessler)

This great white prepares to bite the shark diving cage. Notice the multiple rows of teeth typical to sharks. Sharks often lose teeth, but the teeth are quickly replaced from rows inside their jaw.

(Carl Roessler)

A cousin to the great white shark, mako sharks can grow to 500 pounds and often swim with less-aggressive shark species such as blue sharks.
(Mary L. Peachin)

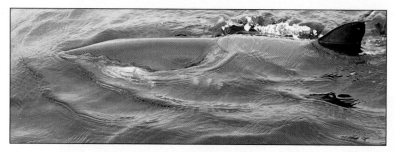

Mako sharks are considered one of the fastest and most aggressive shark species.
(Mary L. Peachin)

Mako fly-fishing is becoming a popular sport. Makos often jump while they swim, and many anglers release the fish if they catch them.
(© Doug Oleander, World Publications)

The markings on this tiger shark give it the name.
(Carl Roessler)

Can you see the family resemblance between this large guitar ray and a shark? These rays have the tail and body of sharks and the fins and heads of rays.
(Carl Roessler)

Under this cow-nosed ray are remoras, or suckerfish, eating parasites on the ray's underbelly.
(Carl Roessler)

Sharks are more active feeders during evening hours. Rarer species, such as these sand tiger sharks, are not always seen schooling, although they are sometimes seen feeding together.
(Carl Roessler)

The author, Mary L. Peachin.

San Diego shark expedition cages for blue shark diving. These square cages are most often used for blue and mako shark diving. They can hold three divers, and divers usually enter the cages from the water. Great white shark diving cages are round or cylindrical and hold only one diver. The diver enters the cage from the boat.

(Mary L. Peachin)

The Least You Need to Know

◆ During mating, male sharks use their claspers (extensions of their pelvic fins) to guide the sperm into the female cloaca, a cavity used for reproduction and digestion.

◆ The three different types of shark reproduction are oviparous (laying eggs), ovoviviparity (eggs developing in the mother), or viviparous (giving birth to live pups).

◆ Shark eggs are protected from predators by their design, camouflage, or by a hardened egg case.

◆ Gestation periods for sharks can range from several months up to two years.

◆ Baby sharks are called pups and are self-sufficient at birth.

◆ Many species of sharks return year after year to the same waters to breed.

The Life Cycle of Sharks

In This Chapter

- ◆ How long sharks live
- ◆ How sharks sleep (or do they?)
- ◆ How sharks hunt
- ◆ Whether sharks feel pain
- ◆ Sharks and their parasites

Although in recent years, scientists have uncovered a great deal of new information about shark anatomy and behavior, the day-to-day life of sharks is still shrouded in mystery. Our knowledge of sharks is based primarily on the observation of sharks in the wild or postmortem examinations of captured or dead sharks.

Sharks have been identified and tagged in New York, for instance, and sighted several months (or years) later in Brazil or on the west coast of Africa, but how they lived and their whereabouts between sightings is unknown. Sharks are notoriously elusive, especially those who prefer depths where divers seldom venture. Nonetheless, scientists are gradually discovering more about shark behavior, and in the process they are giving us a more complete and complex picture of these extraordinary creatures. In this chapter, you learn the latest discoveries about how sharks live their lives.

The Times and Lives of Sharks

Mysteries abound where sharks are concerned. Consider the subject of shark age. Life spans of sharks vary widely. Although the average age of sharks is about 15 to 17 years, some species of sharks live to a ripe old age even in human terms. Because so many different species exist, researchers are still uncertain how long many of the species live.

The longevity of sharks is not just a matter of incidental interest. Like all fish, sharks continue to grow larger throughout their lives, even after they reach maturity (though at a slower rate). Different species of shark grow at different rates. In general, the longer a shark lives, the later in life it matures. The spiny dogfish shark, for instance, has one of the longest life spans; it also has the longest gestation period, nearly two years. Some evidence indicates that male whale sharks can live for 100 years, but by the same token they are not able to breed until they are 20 or possibly 30 years old. That has profound implications. Before whale sharks are even in a position to reproduce they have spent a minimum of a fifth of their lives just avoiding predators. And no species poses a greater danger to sharks of all species than human beings.

Shark Lore

Want to know a shark's age? Count the growth rings of his vertebrae (his spine), and you'll know the answer. This method is similar to counting the rings on a tree.

The spiny dogfish shark has one of the longest gestation periods of any shark—up to two years.

The whale shark—the largest shark of all—can grow to forty feet in length, dwarfing a human as shown in this figure.

Getting Forty Winks

Do sharks sleep? That question has vexed shark experts and enthusiasts for years. In the past it was assumed that they do not: Sharks, as we noted earlier, need to keep moving forward in order to force oxygenated water through their gills—a phenomenon known as ram jet ventilation. (Not all species must keep moving, however; some species, such as the nurse shark, suck water through their mouths while remaining motionless.) So the answer would seem to be that sharks couldn't possibly sleep because they have to keep swimming. But some scientists questioned this assumption, raising the possibility that at least some species of shark doze off from time to time.

Some sharks, even if they don't necessarily sleep, spend their time in a virtually motionless state, lying on the bottom of the seabed. Of course, these sharks are the bottom feeders: nurses, wobbegongs, and angel sharks. In spite of the absence of movement, water continues to pump over their gills. In addition, many bottom feeders have spiracles (openings behind the eyes) that act as an auxiliary respiratory system. But on the other hand, these sharks have strong, well-developed gills that allow them to breathe without difficulty even when they remain frozen in place.

Although they may not sleep, nurse sharks can rest in a motionless state on the ocean floor for long periods of time.

But what about the streamlined sharks, such as hammerheads, and other sharks with weak gill muscles? They have little choice but to keep moving if they want to keep breathing. On the other hand, some of these streamlined sharks have contrived a way of taking a break and kicking back for a stretch. In 1969, a diver exploring a cave off the Yucatan peninsula observed several reef sharks that, to his eyes anyway, looked as if they were sound asleep. How could that be? For one thing, the water in the cave had an unusually high oxygen content; for another, it had reduced salinity. Because the water had more oxygen in it, sharks could more easily stay in a dormant state for hours at a time without exerting any apparent effort. Researchers even speculated that not only were these sharks taking a snooze, but also that they might even be getting high! The rich oxygen content may produce a narcotic effect.

Some evidence, gathered from research on the long-lived spiny dogfish, suggests that at least some species of shark move and sleep simultaneously. In dogfish sharks the motor coordinator responsible for swimming movements is not located in the brain, but in the spinal chord. That raises the possibility that dogfish could shut down different parts of their brains in sequence while continuing to swim (and, thus, continuing to breathe). Which is to say that dogfish (and perhaps other species of shark) might actually sleepwalk or, in their case, sleepswim!

Taste of the Bizarre

In contrast to sharks, dolphins are known to take two- to three-minute catnaps, shutting down one hemisphere of their brain at a time.

Staying Cool in the Deep Blue

We all know the popular image of a shark "knifing" through the water with his dorsal fin raised menacingly and weaving above the water's surface. Although this ominous fin is the one most frequently observed by fishermen and other boaters, sharks rarely swim with their dorsal fins exposed in this manner. Most sharks spend their lives in the middle or the bottom of the sea and seldom brave the surface unless they are enticed by prey such as schooling fishes and sea turtles in shallow waters.

Biologists have discovered that sharks have a good reason not to expose their backs or dorsal fins—they get sunburned! Ultraviolet radiation can penetrate water to a depth of about three feet, which can prove damaging to the shark (just as it can to humans). In a series of experiments, young scalloped hammerheads were placed in shallow pools and exposed to sunlight; they showed signs of being suntanned within only a matter of days.

Hunting Alone and Together

From the moment sharks are born, they usually lead solitary lives. Their mothers don't hang around (unless they decide to eat their newborns), so even pups know how to fend for themselves. They evidently have no expectation of receiving assistance from other sharks. In most species, sharks are interested in other sharks only for mating (if the other sharks are the opposite sex and the same species) and for eating (if the other sharks are smaller).

There are, however, some notable exceptions to this pattern. Scalloped hammerheads, for instance, often travel in large schools. Exactly why hammerheads are so sociable is a puzzle for researchers. Sharks do not need to rely on other sharks to protect them from predators or to help them find food, after all. The hammerheads' social behavior must have some evolutionary function, even though scientists cannot be certain what it is. Basking sharks, too, show a tendency to gather together in groups during migration and mating, unlike most sharks that prefer to swim, hunt and search for mates by themselves.

Surviving on Their Own

Sharks usually hunt for prey alone. Most hunting strategies rely on the element of surprise. Bottom feeders can get away without doing much of anything except waiting in ambuscade, relying on their camouflaged bodies to deceive approaching prey. All the sharks have to do is keep their mouths open for the unsuspecting fish and crustaceans who come their way.

The eating—and by extension hunting—patterns of sharks varies from one species to another. Small sharks usually have several meals every day if they can find the food. For larger, pelagic sharks, though, hunting requires more energy and more stealth—and they may go for long periods without a meal. Bigger sharks do not usually attack right away; they first need to scope out their prey, circling it to get a sense as to whether it will make a tasty meal. When sharks decide to move in for the kill, they do so with a lightning burst of speed. Often one bite is enough; the wound is fatal. All the shark needs to do is wait until the prey dies of blood loss. Disabling prey first before eating it is practiced mainly by great white sharks, but is not true of all pelagics. Species such as the blue and mako, for instance, catch and consume their prey all at once. Larger prey sustains a shark for weeks, and if the prey is especially rich in protein, it lasts even longer.

Great Whites on the Prowl

I've talked about great whites earlier, noting, for example, that they generally found humans unpalatable and that the evidence suggests that an attack on a human is likely to be a mistake on the shark's part. In this section, I examine the way that great whites hunt in more detail to try to understand why they go after some prey and leave other prey alone.

Great whites are 10 times larger than the average shark; they grow up to 23 feet long and weigh 2 tons. This large size means that their energy needs are enormous. Moreover, they are warm-blooded, giving them the ability to accelerate to 20 miles an hour in short bursts.

> **Shark Facts and Stats**
>
> The great white's muscle temperature is about 5 degrees Fahrenheit warmer than the seawater around it.

However, that ability also requires a cost in energy that cold-blooded sharks don't have. Given these energy needs, great whites have to be very choosy about what they eat, and in fact, they eat relatively infrequently. They can't afford to spend extra energy on hunting and eating.

Some scientists speculate that the hormonal system of sharks (which regulates many activities of the body, including muscle contraction) is only capable of functioning well in waters with a narrow temperature range. Large, endothermic (warm-blooded) sharks that spend prolonged periods in warm water may actually suffer from problems with overheating. Generally speaking, the larger the animal the slower its metabolic rate. That appears to hold true in sharks as well; the larger sharks are more sluggish while the smaller ones have a higher metabolic rate.

Great whites can grow up to 23 feet or longer—three to four times the size of an average adult male.

Hunting Strategies of the Great White

Scientists have learned that great whites have excellent color vision. These sharks seem to rely on their vision to pick out a search image of a potential target when they hunt pinnipeds such as sea lions or seals. The sharks swim along the bottom and then strike upward, adapting their strategy depending on the type of pinniped.

Take, for example, northern elephant seals. These large animals are powerful swimmers and superb divers, but they move with far less agility on the surface of the water—and that is when they become the most vulnerable. The Great White strikes the seal from below and behind. One bite on the hindquarters is usually all that is necessary; the seal bleeds to death, and then the shark takes the juiciest morsels and consumes them at lower depths.

However, that attack strategy is modified for smaller seals such as the harbor seal. Harbor seals present a tempting delicacy for the great white because they swim slower and are usually found in large colonies. The shark simply plucks them from the surface, drags them down, and swallows them whole without any formality.

The California sea lion, on the other hand, presents a different kind of challenge. Sea lions are more proficient swimmers than harbor seals, so the shark strikes the sea lions in the middle of their bodies, dragging them below the surface and gripping them in their jaws until any struggling is over. The shark then eats the sea lion at the bottom of the sea.

Curiously, great whites attack humans in their midsection, which may indicate that the sharks confuse humans (who they do not find very tasty) with California sea lions. Humans, as I noted, are rejected as food two out of three times they're bitten; they're more trouble—and represent less fat—for the shark than they're worth.

The Great White's Eating Habits

These three different hunting strategies all require different expenditures of energy. Great whites choose the most economical method of attacking and killing their prey, expending only as much energy as required to gain their objective. For the great white, pursuing larger prey with lots of nutritional value or even chewing on a whale carcass is easier than picking off smaller creatures day after day.

Researchers at the Woods Hole Oceanographic Institute, Massachusetts, attached a sonic tag to a great white feeding on a whale carcass, and then tracked him for three and a half days as he ranged almost 120 miles. On the basis of the data the researchers collected, they estimated that the great white could sustain himself on this blubbery feast as long as two months without another meal. Unfortunately for the shark, whale carcasses are difficult to come by (and great whites are not known to take on live healthy whales, though some live whales have been observed with wounds from shark bites), so the shark needs to keep plying the waters in search of seals and sea lions.

Conserving Energy on the Hunt

Conserving energy is crucial to all animals, including sharks and humans. Animals run on calories; every expenditure of energy costs something in calories, so the only enterprise worth undertaking is one in which the gain in calories more than makes up for the calories lost in achieving the goal. This sort of cost-benefit calculation takes place before an animal decides to pursue a prey. Lest we fall into the trap of anthropomorphizing, we need to recognize that the animal isn't using reason to make these calculations. Hunting behavior is either instinctual or results from past experience. A certain fish might have tasted bad or caused injury in the past, for instance; so the shark will avoid it in the future.

Hunting in Packs

As mentioned in Chapter 12, sharks are loners except when they gather to mate (and even then they aren't exactly social beasts). But from time to time shark watchers have observed collective behavior in some species. It doesn't happen often, but it happens. Dating back as long ago as 1915, sand tiger sharks (not to be confused with tiger sharks) were sighted hunting in a school off Cape Lookout, North Carolina. A school of a hundred or more sand tigers joined in a team effort to systematically surround a school of bluefish. They then herded the bluefish into shallow water like ranchers on a roundup corralling their livestock. Once the bluefish were trapped, the sand tigers struck simultaneously. More recently, in New South Wales, Australia, a diver observed sand tigers herding a small school of juvenile yellowtail kingfish by using their tails to produce sharp underwater pressure waves.

> **Shark Lore**
>
> Sand tigers use "whip crack-ing" (moving their tails to create waves) not only to herd prey but also as a kind of defensive ritual-istic behavior to keep potential predators at bay.

Run Silent, Run Deep

Sharks have a reputation as silent predators. Are they truly silent though? To all intents and purposes, the answer is yes. Whales sing, dolphins click, shrimp crackle, and a few fish can grumble and grunt. So why are sharks so mute? In short, they lack an organ that can produce sound. Even the construction of their scales is designed so that they can swim through the water without mak-ing much noise at all.

> **Shark Lore**
>
> Sharks may not be able to generate sounds, but they can hear them very well. The lowest note a shark can hear is 10 hertz. (The lowest note a human can hear is 25 hertz.) The high-est note a shark can hear is 800 hertz (or G above high C on the piano). Humans can hear higher notes than sharks.

However, some observers contend that the draughts-board shark, who is found in New Zealand waters, barks like a large dog. Curiously, this shark makes these unusual sounds only when it is in a net or has been hooked and being rapidly hauled to the surface. Scientists speculate that the barking sounds originate when instead of filling with water the stomach bal-loons out with air. When the cardiac sphincter mus-cle relaxes, trapped air is expelled—and that's the cause of the "bark." In essence, the shark is simply belching.

Are Sharks Unpredictable?

Some sharks demonstrate patterns of defensive behavior that make them, at least to some degree, occasionally predictable. There is even evidence that certain species of shark engage in what could be considered ritualistic behavior. For instance, gray reef sharks signal an imminent attack by first raising their snouts and depressing their pectoral fins. They then arch their backs while flexing and extending their tails sideways. At the same time they swim in an exaggerated figure-eight pattern. The sharks exhibit this kind of rolling behavior if they feel threatened, an observation reported by several divers. If the sharks sense their escape route has been cut off, they will intensify this display—and if that doesn't work, they will launch a fast, slashing attack, followed by an instant retreat. Several other shark species demonstrate similar ritualistic behavior, though each species has a particular variation that distinguishes it from the others.

The Healthy and Sick Shark

Sharks are generally free from many of the afflictions that bedevil humankind, such as heart disease (contrary to popular opinion, they do get cancerous tumors, though the incidence seems relatively rare). (We examine the implications of this finding in Chapter 16.) Sharks may occupy the apex of marine life, but even their superior position doesn't immunize them from being preyed on by other creatures or even from suffering from deformities. In this section we take a brief look at some recent discoveries offering more insight into the health of sharks and what ills can befall them.

Why Sharks Recover Quickly from Injury

Although researchers have long been aware that sharks' wounds heal quickly, they never investigated the phenomenon. This was in marked contrast to the interest they paid to the shark's (now disproven) resistance to cancerous tumors and their ability to fend off bacteria and environmental toxins. Now some researchers are trying to address that gap, most notably at the University of Tuebingen in Germany.

These researchers theorize that sharks heal so quickly because of the nature of their dermal denticles, the toothlike scales that compose their skin. Denticles are continually being replaced in the course of the shark's lifetime even in the absence of injury. Studies of nurse and leopard sharks showed that when pieces of skin were removed, the healing process went through three phases over a period of two weeks. First the area around the wound secreted mucus; then it contracted; and finally the epidermis or outer skin layer regenerated. Within four months most of the scarred tissue was covered with denticles.

Rapid healing has been observed in the wild, too, among blackfin reef sharks. Even after being severely injured in combat, these sharks begin to heal rapidly. The area around the wounds appears whitish after two months, black after four months, and completely vanish after six months. Ugly wounds produced in adult gray reef female sharks after mating frequently healed in as little as two weeks. Similarly, wounds sustained mainly in mating by female bluntnose sixgill sharks disappear within the course of a single season or about four months.

Two other factors, aside from the repair capacity of denticles, may also be involved in rapid healing. There is some speculation that immersion in saltwater may hasten healing. In addition, bacteria that normally inhabit the mucus coating the mouth, gums, and lips of some types of sharks may also play a role. (Remember that many types of bacteria perform beneficial functions, assisting in the digestive process in humans, for example.) Other factors, however cannot be ruled out, including the sharks' success in finding food, their social rank and the kind of bacteria that enters the wounds.

The Stressed Shark

Sharks are notoriously difficult to maintain in aquariums. Many species become ill or die soon after being captured and placed in confined spaces. The reason shouldn't be difficult for overworked humans to understand—it's stress.

Stress can be induced by many factors, depression among them, and if the stress persists for any length of time the body begins to react. A lowered immune response, for instance, is one consequence of protracted stress. Captive sharks have also been studied—specifically adult horn sharks—to assess their response to stress. Scientists intentionally placed the sharks under stress by removing them from the water and injecting them with a saline solution that otherwise had no physiological effect. Blood samples taken from the sharks at various intervals over the next several hours showed in all cases a rapid rise in the acidic content of various biochemical byproducts, not unlike humans who under stress resort to antacids to calm roiling stomachs. But it wasn't necessary to analyze the sharks' chemical response to realize that stress can have an adverse impact on captive sharks; for example, they often demonstrate a loss of coordination and equilibrium, when the size and/or shape of the tank constrains their movements. They also develop infections as well as chronic injuries to the tip of their snout from repeatedly colliding with the walls of the tank.

Do Sharks Feel Pain?

When sharks gather to feed, the sight is not pretty. The feeding frenzy that ensues is a terrifying spectacle, a bloody bacchanalia. What has especially struck longtime shark observers is the apparent imperviousness of sharks to pain during these episodes. Some of the most astonishing reports come from whalers seeking to protect the carcasses of recently caught whales from shark depredations. The whalers would inflict deadly wounds on the sharks without succeeding in diverting the sharks from their goal of eating the whales. During feeding frenzies sharks bite one another to get at the food, but the bitten sharks seemingly do not register the pain. (It should be noted, however, that if a situation is too threatening sharks swim away even though food is still around.) So it's no wonder that scientists came to the conclusion that sharks cannot feel pain. (We should point out that even human pain is not yet well understood; the study of pain is only in its infancy.)

In 1993, a team of Australian neurophysiologists (scientists who study the connection between the nervous system and the body) examined the sensory neurons of three species of elasmobranchs. All three species, the researchers determined, lack the neuronal machinery considered essential for the perception of pain.

This finding brings up a more fundamental question: what is the purpose of pain anyway? The answer is that for many species, humans included, pain is crucial to survival. If you could put your hand over a flame without feeling pain, you might never have the sense to take it away. But for rays and sharks, pain doesn't appear to play such a crucial role as it does in, say, mammals. This conclusion about pain does not suggest that sharks aren't sensitive to other stimuli. After all, they have highly refined detection systems for hearing, seeing, and picking up faint electric signals. The fact that they have survived for so many millions of years strongly suggests that they are able to avoid serious injury. However, their perception of pain does not seem to offer them any benefit.

Deformities

Like humans, sharks are subject to deformities. Scientists have recorded a range of deformities among various species of sharks including abnormal coloration or fin shape. And scientists in Sarasota, Florida, have observed sharks who appear to be hunchbacks with abnormal curves in their bodies. Such deformities have appeared in sharks belonging to several species, but at this point scientists have no idea about their cause or whether they impede the shark's survival.

Playing Reluctant Host to Parasites

In Chapter 11, I talked about how pilot fish, remoras, and cleaner wrasses contribute to the sharks' well-being by cleansing them of parasites. Now it's time to take a closer look (though, one hopes, not too close) at the parasites who find sharks so appealing. These parasites look upon sharks as their source of food and shelter. The best educated guesses put the number of shark parasites far higher than the number of sharks. Even though most sharks are loners, we can't think of a shark as an independent animal because they are, in the words of one shark expert, "a mobile community of organisms." Wherever sharks go they take their parasites with them. These parasites don't just thrive on the skin; they also feed on tissues, consume the mucus between the shark's lips, and dine on the food in shark's gut. There are parasites who specialize in the nitrogen-rich shark excrement, and some parasites even feed on other shark parasites!

A Mobile Community of Organisms

These parasites make sharks their home:

- Crustaceans (copepods, aquatic invertebrates such as crabs and shrimp, and barnacles)

- Nematodes (roundworms)

- Platyhelminths (various types of worms that attack the digestive tract and other internal organs and cause several types of parasitical disease)

- Hirudinoideans (leeches)

- Mollusks (bivalves such as clams or oysters)

- Protozoans (the collective name given to one-celled organisms that form colonies in animal or plant hosts)

- Bacteria

The Copepod Threat

Among the most common parasites are *copepods*, who are tiny crustaceans. They are *exoparasites* because they are found on the body of their host and not inside it. One group of copepods called the *siphonostomes* has been particularly successful colonizing fishes, including sharks. They have a relatively long mouth tube with two saw-toothed mandibles that are used while feeding. Enlarged a few hundred times, these creatures would make for a very terrifying presence. These copepods inhabit nearly all sharks in the northwestern Atlantic Ocean. The blue shark may hold the record for hosting the greatest variety and total number of copepods: up to 3,000 of five different species, each specializing in a particular region of the shark's body. One attaches itself to the pectoral fins, another to the nose, another two to the gills, and another is happy to feed indiscriminately on all parts of the shark body.

What Does It Mean?

Exoparasites are parasites that live outside (or on the exterior) of the host body.

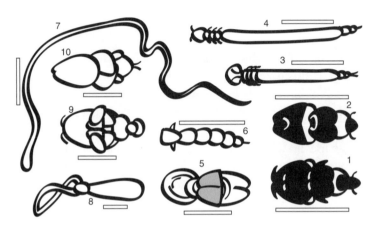

Copepods (a family that includes crustaceans such as shrimp, lobster, and many other tiny acquatic arthopod invertebrates) are common parasites found in sharks.

Parasitic copepods:

1. Pandarus satyrus
2. Pandarus smithii
3. Kroyeria carchariaeglauci
4. Kroeyerina elongata
5. Echthrogaleus coleoptratus
6. Nemesis lamna
7. Kroyeri caseyi
8. Ommatokoita elongata
9. Phyllothyreus cornutus
10. Anthosoma crassum

Scale bars beside each copepod = 0.25"
Figures modified from several sources

Alone, a copepod does little harm to the shark. But collectively, these parasites can cause a good deal of damage to their host. In the shortfin mako, for instance, a copepod can modify the gill filaments it infects in detrimental ways, disrupting water flow. In effect, these parasites clog the gill openings, impeding the ability of the mako to oxygenate his blood. This condition would have a debilitating impact on the shark's growth and possibly his survival.

Shark eyes provide another tempting target to a group of tiny pinkish-white copepods known as *Ommatokoita elongata*, who permanently attach themselves to the eyes of the Greenland shark. This shark subsists on a diet of small fish and seals. Although only one of these copepods attaches itself to an eye, the parasite is capable of doing significant damage to the corneas, producing round scars that are responsible for partially blinding the shark.

That raises the question: How do these partially blind sharks survive? Researchers believe that Greenland sharks compensate by using their sense of smell to ferret out prey as they swim above the ocean floor sucking up small fishes and invertebrates.

Mercury in Sharks

Manmade pollution also seems to be having an impact on sharks, though to what extent is impossible to judge at this point. Recent studies of five species of sharks in Brazilian waters have turned up high levels of mercury which vary according to the shark's diet, age, and sex (males have higher concentrations than females). While the risk to sharks is unknown (and it is possible that there is no adverse impact) the risk to humans who consume sharks may be considerable. Other studies found that the excessive contamination of mercury was present in all parts of the shark's body and that neither frying nor baking in a regular oven and in a microwave removed the metal.

Shark Cartilage Linked to Fatal Asthma

Humans may face another danger from sharks—but not in the water. A recent study carried out by the Institute for Occupational Safety and Health, a unit of the Atlanta-based Centers for Disease Control and Prevention, found that dust from shark cartilage may be a serious hazard in the workplace. A 38-year-old employee of a facility that granulated and powdered various substances (including shark cartilage) for types of plastics began to experience chest symptoms after 10 months of exposure to the cartilage. He was diagnosed with asthma. Six months after the diagnosis, he complained of shortness of breath at work and died. An autopsy confirmed asthma as the cause of death. What was so disturbing to health officials was that the fatal attack occurred so soon after the asthma was first diagnosed, underscoring the gravity of the danger that even relatively brief exposure to ground-up shark cartilage posed to workers' health.

The Least You Need to Know

- Most shark species live an average 17 to 20 years, though some may live as long as 100 or more.

- Most species of shark are loners (except when they mate), though a few species are known to hunt in packs.

- Sharks cannot produce sounds.

- Sharks conserve energy by choosing only prey that has the caloric value to make attacking it worth the cost in energy.

- Thousands of different parasites infect every part of the shark and in some cases can cause significant damage to their host.

Part 4

Researching Sharks

Sharks are found in waters all over the world—in open seas and in lagoons, even in rivers and lakes. But only with modern technology have researchers begun to learn how far they travel, how deep they dive, and where they feed. Modern aquariums are also contributing to our knowledge of these predators. At the same time, scientists in the lab are revealing what it is about the shark's immune system that protects them so well from bacteria, viruses, and pollution.

Chapter 14

Diversity, Distribution, and Migration

In This Chapter

- Why sharks of different species choose similar habitat
- Why the shark's daily routine mystifies researchers
- How scientists track shark migrations
- How sharks navigate without landmarks
- Why pelagic sharks have a window on top of their heads

Suppose you have just returned from a long journey and a friend asks you where you went. You say, "Well, I began my trip in Chicago, and here I am in Miami." Although this statement sums up the trip succinctly, your friend would no doubt wonder why you were leaving out everything related to what you did from the day you left and how and when you arrived at your final destination. Scientists who study sharks have the same sorts of questions about their journeys. Through tagging, scientists can track shark movements to the extent that they know where the sharks were caught and tagged and where they were recaptured, but where they swam between the two locations remains a mystery.

And although we have a rough idea of how many species of sharks exist (about 400), we are only beginning to learn how these species are distributed throughout the oceans (and in some cases freshwater bodies). Sharks have no roadmaps, no AAA to call upon if they get into trouble. Yet with few exceptions sharks are able to find their way year after year, often across distances stretching thousands of miles. The question is how do they do it?

Identifying Shark Hangouts

Sharks belonging to several different species are known to converge on the same habitat. Like vacationers on package tours coming from a variety of countries, different species are attracted to a particular habitat, such as tropical waters or a mangrove-lined lagoon, because they all have a great deal in common, according to researchers. For one, these sharks are morphologically similar (their body structures are very much alike), and they exhibit similar patterns of behavior. That understanding led to a new classification of sharks based on their morphology, the environment they prefer, and the habits they display. This classification is called *ecomorphotype*.

The greatest diversity of shark ecomorphotypes is found on continental and island shelves. The region of water above the *continental shelf* is divided into several zones. The waters closest to shore is called the intertidal zone which is rich in algae. The open water is known as the neritic zone (or simply as the oceanic zone) and is the most productive area of the ocean. Immediately below this zone is the epipelagic zone (the uppermost zone), which is filled with phytoplankton and zooplankton, the plentiful supply of food that is so vital to the marine food chain. At a depth of 3,300 feet is the mesopelagic or twilight zone, where most fish, invertebrates, and marine mammals feed; below that is the bathypelagic and then the abyssopelagic zone, also known as the abyssal plain. Light never penetrates these frigid regions, which are suited only to highly specialized types of marine life.

What Does It Mean?

Ecomorphotyping is a method of classifying animals on the basis of their structure, environmental preference, and behavior patterns.

The **continental shelf** is defined as the shallow body of water above the edge of a continent.

The habitats that various species of sharks prefer range from shallow temperate waters to the darker colder waters at the ocean bottom. Naturally, the availability of food sources plays a crucial part in where a given species will likely be found. But keep in mind that many species often move between one zone and another—some species, for instance, will coast along the ocean bottom during the day and ascend at night to waters closer to the surface in search of food.

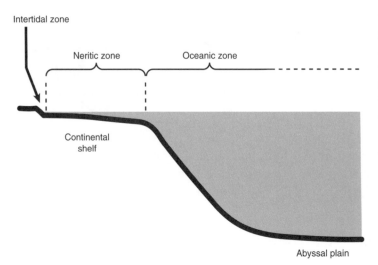

The ocean is divided into several regions or zones, based on their distinctive environmental conditions, ranging from the open waters (or neritic or oceanic zone) to the ocean bottom— the abyssal plain.

Close to Shore

The littoral zone is defined as the area between the highest and lowest tide marks on a seashore. Here is a list of the different littoral zones where sharks that prefer shallow water are likely to be found. The littoral zone is in turn divided into smaller zones, each of which has certain types of food sources.

- ◆ **Mesotrophic littoral.** This is a zone that offers a wide range of prey, including fish, crustaceans, and mollusks. Sharks found in this zone include some types of nurse sharks, spiny dogfish, sand tigers, silver tips, black tips, gray reef sharks, Galapagos sharks, and hammerheads.

- ◆ **Tueuthotrophic littoral.** This zone is rich in octopuses, squid, and cuttlefishes, prey that is especially appealing to active coastal sharks that are soft-bodied, fast swimmers such as the tawny nurse shark.

- ◆ **Cancritrophic littoral.** This is a zone where crustaceans are plentiful and attract zebra and some types of nurse sharks.

- ◆ **Durotrophic littoral.** This zone is filled with clams, oysters, and sea urchins and attracts sharks with a preference for hard-shelled prey. They have short, thick-muscled jaws with blunt teeth ideally tailored for this prey. This group includes adult bullhead sharks.

- ◆ **Microtrophic littoral.** This zone is characterized by plankton and small fish, which makes it attractive for filter feeders including megamouths, whale sharks, and some species of basking sharks.

Basking sharks prefer to swim close to the shore but undertake seasonal migrations to deeper waters.

♦ **Eurytrophic littoral.** In this zone, you can find large coastal sharks feeding on a wide variety of marine animals such as sea lions and seals. They have large jaws and large, broad, serrated teeth. The broadnose sevengill is among this group.

Types of Oceanic Sharks

The open ocean is a more difficult habitat for most sharks than closer in shore—that's because, given the vast expanse of the ocean, there are fewer food resources and the climactic conditions are often less favorable. That means that in these vast tracts of ocean, shark diversity is relatively low. All the same, a number of species of sharks, such as great whites and other pelagic species, prefer to stay in deep ocean waters most of the year.

♦ **Macropelagic.** These are large oceanic sharks that cruise slowly but are capable of rapid bursts of acceleration; active swimmers, they range from 10 to almost 20 feet in length, they typically have a streamlined body and large jaws with relatively large serrated teeth. They prey on fish and squid—whatever comes easy and fast. The species includes longfin makos, oceanic white tips, and blues.

♦ **Micropelagic.** These are tiny to small oceanic sharks—about four feet or less in length or less—most of which spend their daylight hours in deep waters and migrate at night up towards the surface. They typically have a long, cylindrical body, large eyes, a bulbous snout, a large oily liver and relatively small fins. Some are luminescent and certain females even squirt a bluish glowing goo from their cloaca, probably to startle predators. Such sharks include spined pygmies, cookie-cutters, and crocodile sharks.

♦ **Tachypelagic.** These sharks are large, fast-swimming oceanic sharks that have adapted to a high-energy lifestyle (sounds like New Yorkers) because of their ability to maintain high body temperatures. They range in length form 10 to 13 feet when they reach adulthood, have highly streamlined bodies, conical snouts, and a large mouth bristling with large, unserrated, knifelike teeth. They include such high-speed cruisers as the shortfin mako.

Tracking Shark Diversity

Every 10 years the U.S. Census Bureau is required by law to survey the nation's population. In spite of the bureau's best efforts, millions of Americans fall through the cracks. They go uncounted because they fail to return their census forms or just prove too difficult to locate. So you can imagine how hard it must be to conduct a census of animals living in the wild, especially the marine world.

Scientists have long been eager to know more about shark populations. How many species exist? So far 375 to 400 have been identified. Of course, others may have evaded detection so far. Some species are more common than others: nurse sharks, for example. But how many nurse sharks exist in the world's oceans? How healthy is the population? Are goblin sharks as rare as we suspect on the basis of the number of goblins sighted, or are they rather numerous, but just too difficult to locate? The answer to all these questions is: We don't know.

The Mystery of the Great Whites

For all their fame, great whites are very mysterious creatures. For years no one was certain how long they live, where they go to breed, how many there are, how often they reproduce, or how deep they dive. But the advent of satellite technology may at last give us answers to some of these questions.

In the past researchers were stymied by technological limitations. While they knew that the sharks left San Francisco every year at the same time they had no idea where they went. They speculated that the sharks traveled to Baja, Mexico. The new findings show that instead they travel West—and much farther than previously estimated. One shark, for instance, traveled 2,360 miles to waters off the coast of Hawaii while three others traveled to waters in the subtropical eastern Pacific—a long way from Baja!

Tagging per se was never a problem. Researchers waited for a great white to attack a seal and then set out in a boat to the area. All they had to do was wait for the sharks to oblige them by circling around the boat. The real problem was getting the tag off. But researchers were given new tags that had the added benefit of detaching at a designated time. Once the tag reaches the surface of the water, the data collected in the tag is transmitted to the scientists via satellite. From the data, scientists can determine where sharks went, how deep they dove, and what the water temperature is at any particular depth.

continues

---

continued

Researchers were able to track the range of the shark travels by attaching data-recording tags to the six sharks off the coast of San Francisco and then following their movements. After tagging the great whites, a team of California-based researchers tracked their movements in hope of learning more about these sharks' habitats and behavior. The data emerging from these studies may prove pivotal to developing effective conservation measures. Because the great white is considered among the most endangered sharks worldwide, the need to take action to protect them is more urgent than ever.

Among other discoveries researchers made is that great whites travel farther and dive deeper than previously thought. The new findings also reveal that contrary to what experts used to believe, these sharks also spend nearly half of their time in deep ocean waters—about five months of the year. Great whites, it turns out, mostly inhabit waters between the surface of the ocean down to about 100 feet deep. The sharks moved back and forth between two depths—either from the ocean surface to 16 feet deep, or in depths from 985 to 1,640 feet. The range of water temperatures the sharks found congenial also surprised researchers—from 68 to 79 degrees Fahrenheit closer to the surface and about 40 degrees Fahrenheit in the deepest dives of 2,130 to 2,230 feet. Until recently scientists thought that the sharks tended to spend their time in temperate waters close to the coastline along the continental shelf. That put them in proximity to swimmers, the reasoning went, with a greater incidence of attacks on humans. (Chapter 18 includes a discussion on whether these attacks are intentional or a result of the shark mistaking humans for a more palatable prey such as a sea lion.)

Why these sharks spend so long offshore and in deep waters is thought to be related to feeding or breeding migrations, but scientists still need to learn more before they can say for certain.

For all their size and the terror they inspire, great whites are considered vulnerable throughout the world; their total population is low. It has a low reproductive rate, which makes the population more vulnerable to human predation in the form of overfishing. For example, scientists have found that the females return only every other year to their breeding grounds, meaning that they only breed once every two years. Based on these new findings, conservationists will be in a better position to come up with effective strategies to protect these endangered sharks.

Learning from Shark Captures

For years scientists had to rely solely on records of shark captures as a criteria for establishing a pattern of shark distribution. This method of tracking sharks left much to be desired. More attention was lavished on large and unusual specimens than smaller, less exotic sharks. And because sharks were being caught by commercial fishermen and not by researchers, many specimens were misidentified, casting the accuracy of the records into further doubt.

What conclusions can scientists draw from a shark capture? When several sharks of a particular species are found in particular marine habitat, this finding does not necessarily mean that the species populates these waters in abundant numbers. The sharks may have been straying far from their home turf at the time they were caught. A capture did not provide any information about the geographical range of a species, such as whether the sharks remained close to the coast, for instance, or migrated thousands of miles across the ocean.

The expansion of commercial shark fishing helped advance scientific understanding of shark distribution patterns. In order to figure out where to find commercially valuable sharks, fishermen began to keep much better records, noting capture date, location, and depth.

From this data certain patterns began to emerge. Some species of sharks, for instance, returned to particular waters on a seasonal basis. Some sharks segregated themselves by size, sex, and age. Some forms of segregation made sense: Juveniles steered clear of their mothers most likely to avoid being eaten. Why males and females of certain species should remain apart, though, was more puzzling, especially because at some point they had to mate in order to perpetuate the species.

Commercial shark fishing also revealed another important bit of information about sharks: Concentrated fishing was wiping out the targeted populations. If fishing continued in a particular location, eventually few if any sharks were available to catch. This process didn't take long to happen; two to five years of intensive fishing was usually sufficient to deplete stocks below the point where it made any economic sense to operate in the area. The explanation for these boom and bust cycles is not difficult to understand: sharks, as we've noted before, reach sexual maturity later in life (in some species, only at age 20). Obviously, if enough immature sharks are killed the population is not going to be replenished at a rate necessary to sustain itself.

Additional opportunities to learn about sharks came from dissecting the sharks and examining their stomach contents. These dissections gave researchers a clearer idea about the diets of various species. Certainly these findings confirmed sharks' long-standing reputation as unparalleled scavengers.

Where problems arose was in determining which depths certain species of sharks favored. Just because the sharks were caught at a certain depth did not necessarily mean that they usually swam at that depth. Many species swim closer to the ocean surface in search of prey and then retire hundreds of feet down to consume it.

Tracking Changes in Sharks over Time

Complicating the problem of studying sharks is a phenomenon known as *allometry*. We all grow and change. Allometry refers to tracking those changes to get a more complete portrait of the animal being studied. It's the difference between a snapshot and a video. One offers us a glimpse of the subject at a particular moment in time; the other provides a sense of the subject *over* time.

Examining a shark who has been caught and killed tells us a lot about the shark, but it says little or nothing about how a shark matures or changes in response to the environment. Individual sharks change over time, but if you were not aware of these changes, you might draw the erroneous conclusion that you are seeing a different species of shark. You may recall our example about the mysterious goblin shark in Chapter 9. For a long time researchers mistakenly believed that they had found several different species of goblins because of the differences in the positioning of the jaw seen in a number of specimens. But the jaw just happened to be more tractable than the researchers first realized; all the specimens belonged to the same species.

Using mathematical formulas, marine biologists can calculate the average consumption of food compared to body size; the bigger the shark the larger the consumption.

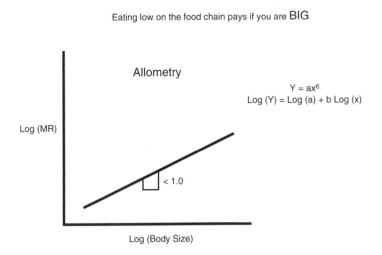

Eating low on the food chain pays if you are BIG

Allometry

$Y = ax^6$
$Log (Y) = Log (a) + b \, Log (x)$

Log (MR)

< 1.0

Log (Body Size)

Tagging Sharks

Fortunately, we now have other ways of learning about the movements and habits of sharks without having any adverse impact. Researchers are able to track sharks by *tagging*. (Other species, such as birds, are tagged for the same reason.) Tags may be in the form of bands or collars; they may be a simple label or a sophisticated device that communicates electronically to satellites.

In order to tag as many sharks as possible, researchers have enlisted the help of anglers. Fishing for sharks used to be a pastime for the wealthy, but its popularity is spreading among younger generations, too. And where once no one went fishing for sharks without intending to kill them, a number of anglers who are interested only in the thrill of the chase are now quite happy to return their catch to the sea. Seizing on the new respect that angling enthusiasts are according the shark, marine biologists have asked them to tag sharks and to record the date, location, length, and sex of sharks before releasing them. Tens of thousands of anglers have responded enthusiastically to this idea.

The U.S. National Marine Fisheries Service (NMFS) has mounted one of the largest-scale studies involving tagging in the northwestern Atlantic. In this study, begun in 1962, fishermen have tagged more than 100,000 sharks belonging to 33 species. Of this number, 4,600 sharks of 29 species have been recaptured. Most of these recaptured sharks, though, belong to just eight species including blues, tigers, shortfin makos, black tips, and scalloped hammerheads. Not surprisingly, members of these species are some of the most well-traveled sharks. Many of these sharks are known to migrate hundreds or even thousands of miles.

This collaborative effort between researchers and fishermen, as ambitious as it is, has a built-in limitation: The tagging reveals only the starting point and recapture point, but it gives little information about the shark's movements in the interim.

Shark Lore

The blue shark holds the long-distance record for sharks. One individual, tagged off California, was recaptured 2 years later 560 nautical miles off the Japanese coast.

Monitoring by Telemetry

A more advanced surveillance technique known as *telemetry* may provide the solution to the dilemma posed by tagging. Telemetry is a system of electronic communication; the data is collected by sensors at one site and then relayed (often by satellite) to another site where the data is recorded and analyzed. In telemetry's simplest form, sonic telemetry, an electronic pinger is attached to a shark by bolting it to the dorsal fin, inserting it into the body cavity, or hiding it in bait for the shark to swallow.

What Does It Mean?

Telemetry is a technique that relies on electrical or electronic equipment to collect and process physical data from one location and transmit the data to a second site where the information is recorded and analyzed.

The use of telemetry has begun to generate a wide range of sensor data about sharks: their location, the depth at which they swim, their preferred water temperature, their body temperature, and so on. Already telemetry has revealed new findings about the extent of shark home ranges and their daily movements. In the future, telemetry may reveal a great many surprising answers to questions about sharks that have kept scientists guessing until now.

Sonic vs. Archival Tagging

The simplest kind of telemetry is called *sonic telemetry*. An electronic pinger is attached to a shark by placing it directly on the dorsal fin or inserted into the shark by concealing it in bait. Data is relayed from the pinger to a receiver in the form of encoded sound pulses. With advanced electronic components and long-lasting energy cells, many of these devices can transmit for several months. Their drawback is a very limited broadcast range—usually less than two miles. This means that a manned boat often has to follow the tagged shark. In any case, human intervention may alter the behavior of the sharks being tracked.

A new technique called *archival tagging* is increasingly being used to overcome the limitations of sonic telemetry. Instead of transmitting their data in real time, these tags store the information until they are recovered. Many archival tags are programmed to detach and float to the surface at a specified time, then broadcast a signal to pinpoint their whereabouts. These tags are also known as pop-up tags for this reason. These tags have several advantages over sonic tags:

- They are smaller because they do not have to transmit data continuously.
- They are less obtrusive.
- They are longer lasting.
- They do not need to be tracked by boat.

To supplement archival tagging, researchers are planting a series of stationary monitors on the seafloor in areas frequented by shark populations. Whenever an archival-tagged shark swims past these monitors, the tags emit a continuous, low-energy signal. The monitor records the individual shark and the time and dates it passed by. In the future video cameras may be attached to these monitors, installed inside clear, acrylic domes. When the monitors are activated the camera will record what the shark is doing, providing researchers with an intimate glimpse of sharks behaving unselfconsciously in their natural habitats.

Living in Frigid Waters: Arctic Sharks

One can make few generalizations about where sharks live, but at least some species can thrive in practically any body of water, including rivers and lakes. (Recall that bull sharks have been sighted far up the Mississippi and in Lake Nicaragua.) Although the majority of sharks live in warmer waters, a few species have adapted quite nicely to the frigid waters surrounding the Arctic Circle. Eight species have been recorded in the Arctic, including blue sharks, basking sharks, spiny dogfish, and the Greenland shark.

The Greenland shark is of special interest to shark observers; in size and dimension it's similar to the great white, measuring almost 20 feet in length, but that's where the similarity ends. Unlike the warm-blooded, fast-swimming great white, the Greenland shark is slow and sluggish. Greenland sharks are so sluggish that Inuit fishermen in Canada's far north have caught them by simply scooping them up with their hands.

These sharks can pick up the pace when they're hungry, though, feeding on such fast prey as salmon and Arctic seals. Scientists have speculated as to how these reputedly sluggish creatures can suddenly attain such speeds. They have figured out that the sharks' short, broad tails give them the capability to accelerate at an instant's notice. And although these sharks pose no threat to humans (as underscored by the example of the Inuit fishermen), they can prove deadly to caribou. Sharks on Baffin Island, for instance, have grabbed unwitting caribou by their heads and necks as they drink obliviously by the river mouth.

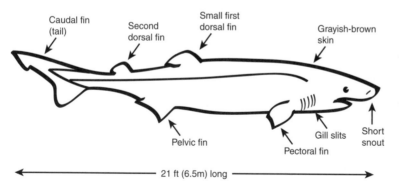

Caudal fin (tail) · Second dorsal fin · Small first dorsal fin · Grayish-brown skin · Pelvic fin · Pectoral fin · Gill slits · Short snout

21 ft (6.5m) long

The Greenland shark is one of the few shark species capable of living in frigid waters; ordinarily a sluggish creature, it displays great speed when necessary to catch prey.

Migrating by Magnetism

Magnetism and electricity are closely related. Electric current, whether in the form of a burst of lightning or the movement of a muscle in your body, produces a magnetic field.

The outer core of Earth is about 3,600 feet thick and flows between the mantle and the solid inner core. Because this core consists of a circulating mass of nickel-iron alloy, it is not magnetic—the reason being that the temperature of the inner core is too hot. Rather the circulation of electric charges in the molten mass generates Earth's magnetic field.

As we have noted before, sharks, like all elasmobranchs, have special sensory organs (such as the ampullae of Lorenzini) that allow them to detect magnetic fields. In 1982, a researcher at the renowned oceanography center at Woods Hole, Massachusetts, conducted a series of tests in an aquarium to see how a stingray would orient itself to magnetic fields. He set up weak magnetic fields meant to simulate Earth's magnetic field and trained the rays to feed in both the magnetic and geographic east. Then he pulled a trick on the stingray and rotated the magnetic field, so that, in effect, east wasn't east anymore. It didn't matter to the rays, though; they went looking for food in the newly defined "east," responding not to precedent (the old "east") but to the magnetic field emitted by the new east, wherever it ended up.

In a more ambitious experiment conducted in 1987, the same researcher set up a ring of electromagnets in the shallow waters off the coastline of Bimini, a popular breeding ground for lemon sharks. First he observed how the sharks behaved when he turned the electromagnets off. Then on the following day he turned on a pair of electromagnets that aligned with Earth's magnetic field at that location. In other words, the magnets were sending the same signal to the shark that Earth's own magnetic field was. Not surprisingly, the sharks behaved exactly as if nothing had changed.

The third day, though, the researcher rotated the artificial field 90 degrees to the natural field. But the artificial field was stronger, and it was this field, not Earth's magnetic field, that the sharks responded to by altering their course by 90 degrees! This experiment offered compelling evidence that sharks do in fact navigate by means of Earth's magnetic field (unless humans place an artificial magnetic field in the sharks' path).

What Does It Mean?

A **tesla** is a unit of measurement of magnetic flux density, which is the force that a magnet or electromagnet exerts on other magnets or charged particles, such as electrons. It is named after Nicholas Tesla, inventor of the first practical electrical motor.

The ocean doesn't usually have landmarks or lines of sight to aid navigation. And marine life is not known to navigate by the stars. Scientists reason that many fish, especially elasmobranchs with their highly sensitive electroreceptors, rely on magnetic landmarks to make their way safely from one location to another.

Earth's magnetic field produces an electric current that flows through any organism passing across it. Geomagnetic fields vary in intensity, which provides yet another navigational aid. These fields, for instance, increase with latitude from 30,000 *nanoteslas* at the equator to less than 70,000 nanoteslas at the poles. The field intensity decreases the further away you travel from Earth's surface. Moreover, geomagnetism can vary slightly from one locality to another. Magnetic hills and valleys stretch for huge distances across the ocean floor, forming the equivalent of "magnetic freeways," which often, but not always, follow the continental shelf. Altogether these various geomagnetic features allow fish to form a fairly accurate map of their route through water.

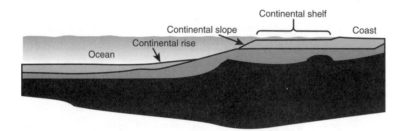

Magnetic pathways that sharks appear to rely on for navigation usually follow the direction of the continental shelf shown here.

Strandings

In the summer of 2002, nearly 60 pilot whales became beached on Cape Cod, Massachusetts, having lost their way. In spite of heroic efforts by local rescuers, practically all the whales in the school perished. Although the reasons for these strandings, as they are known, are not well understood, many researchers believe that they occur because of a malfunction of the whales' navigational system. Cape Cod is especially treacherous for whales in that the shoreline is constantly shifting because of storms and other environmental changes. The same magnetic roadmap that guided the pilot whales in the past with perfect accuracy turns into a deadly trap because of abrupt alterations of the coastline. The whales may be following magnetic roads straight to their doom.

Sharks, too, beach themselves, possibly because of a failure to read their magnetic roadmap correctly. However, they do so far less frequently than whales for reasons that are not entirely clear. In British Columbia, Canada, for instance, there have been six shark strandings in the last 40 years. Recently, scientists have observed a spate of strandings by a small number of salmon sharks that occur each spring in central and southern California.

Scientists suspect that whales and perhaps sharks, too, rely on a certain pattern of

Shark Lore

Porpoises and dolphins rarely beach themselves, possibly because they do not travel widely and are very familiar with the anomalous features of their home territories.

variation in the total geomagnetic field, presumably from past experience. This pattern provides the whales with a kind of day calendar, which can be disrupted by several different factors, such as a change in the coastline or even unusual solar activity, such as sunspots. Some researchers even contend that these strandings are basically the "magnetic equivalent of traffic accidents."

Window on the World

Some pelagic sharks have a window on the world in the form of a thin, translucent "window" in the skin and skull underneath that regulates their response to light and darkness. This window is known as the *pineal gland*. (In humans the pineal gland is located deep within the brain.)

The unusual pineal organ was first discovered in pelagic sharks by a team led by shark biologist Samuel Gruber. He proved its existence by placing a flashlight in the mouth of a lemon shark. The glow radiated out from the top of the shark's head. Until recently, the function of this gland was poorly understood, though we know now that it is photosensitive and is involved in the regulation of the body's internal clock.

This pineal window is designed so that sunlight can filter through the skin and skull and stimulate the brain directly. The pineal gland responds to gradations of light by producing two hormones: *melatonin* and *serotonin*. Melatonin is produced in periods of darkness, and serotonin is produced mainly during periods of light. These hormones vary in inverse proportion to one another—that is to say, if there are greater levels of melatonin, the levels of serotonin are diminished and vice versa. How these levels change depends on the duration and intensity of daylight.

In humans, these hormones are both involved in mood and orientation. Melatonin has been recommended, for instance, to alleviate the effects of jet lag, and an excess of serotonin in the brain cells appears to be a factor in causing depression. In winter months, when periods of daylight diminish significantly, some people are more at risk for a milder form of depression called SAD (seasonal affective disorder). The recommended therapy is regular exposure to powerful artificial lights.

Like humans, sharks respond to the fluctuation of light over the course of the year. In pelagic sharks, such as the great white, the pineal gland may allow the shark to track seasonal changes in terms of the duration of each day. Or to put it another way, the pineal gland in the sharks functions as a calendar, providing important clues as to when it's time to mate and migrate.

The Least You Need to Know

♦ Sharks of different species who gravitate to the same habitat have similar body structures and patterns of behavior.

♦ Until recently, most data about shark distribution and diversity came from commercial fishing.

♦ Sophisticated surveillance techniques, such as telemetry, have given scientists a greater understanding of shark migratory and behavioral patterns.

♦ Sharks appear to rely on sensory organs to detect changes in Earth's electromagnetic fields to navigate across great distances.

♦ Pelagic sharks have a translucent organ called a pineal gland that serves as a calendar, regulating behavior according to fluctuations and intensity of daylight.

Chapter 15

Sharks in Captivity

In This Chapter

- ◆ Why aquarium shark exhibits are such a big draw
- ◆ How aquariums contribute to shark conservation
- ◆ Why sharks do not live long in captivity
- ◆ Why raising sharks at home is a bad idea

The closest most people come to sharks is in an aquarium. Maintaining sharks in captivity—especially large pelagic sharks—is an extraordinary challenge. All the same, aquarists, as they're known, are designing aquariums to immerse visitors (as much as possible without their actually getting wet) in the sharks' habitat. At some aquariums visitors can view sharks from above and below. However, aquariums have another crucial function apart from satisfying curiosity or providing a memorable experience. Most major aquariums are now actively engaged in educational efforts, dispelling misconceptions about sharks. In the process, they hope to instill in their visitors an appreciation for sharks and enlist them in an urgent mission to conserve these creatures from extermination.

The Role of Aquariums

Sharks have attracted excited and enthralled people from all over the world, regardless of their culture, language, or nationality. Because most people are never going to experience sharks in the wild, aquariums have come to serve an essential need. But aquariums must do more than put sharks in a tank and expect that to satisfy people with so many demands on their leisure time.

Competing for audiences with theme parks (not to mention movies, the Internet, and video games), aquarium officials are pulling out all stops to provide their visitors with an experience that is as entertaining as it is informative. Natural habitats are duplicated as much as possible. Aquariums now feature innovative acrylic tanks and tunnels that put visitors in a privileged position where they feel as if they are in the deep, watching sharks swim all around them without getting so much as a drop of water on them. Aquariums have a not-so-hidden agenda: to convince the public that sharks, far from being "killing machines," are a miraculous evolutionary achievement in danger of being exterminated by human greed and carelessness unless we take measures to conserve them now.

Shark Lore

Sharks are a proven draw for the public. At the National Aquarium in Baltimore, a special shark exhibit proved one of the most popular exhibits in the entire history of the aquarium. Most institutions that have sharks on display undoubtedly have the same experience. That popularity can be used to mobilize people to support the cause of shark conservation.

The fact that humans are deeply fascinated by and often intimidated by sharks goes without saying. But how many opportunities do most people get to see sharks up close? Divers, of course, have a chance to visit sharks in their native habitat, and boaters and fishermen sometimes encounter them on the ocean surface. To be sure, modern technology such as submersibles and underwater cinematography gives us a more vivid impression of sharks in the wild than ever before, but that's still not the same as having a personal experience with a shark. For most people, aquariums offer the best way to observe sharks in an environment designed to resemble their native habitats.

Modern aquariums view their role as having three basic components: education, conservation, and research. By emphasizing the importance of sharks in the ecosystem and showing how sharks are becoming endangered, aquariums offer a needed corrective to the lurid picture of bloodthirsty sharks sometimes served up by the media. Moreover, the best aquariums actively work to foster "the planned management of a natural resource to prevent exploitation, destruction, or neglect," which is the mandate of conservationists. In other words, aquariums are carrying on a lobbying effort on behalf of the marine life that they are exhibiting. The potential for reaching a large public is enormous; an estimated 100 million people in North America throng to aquariums in the United States and Canada each year.

Shark Lore

The first popular aquarium was opened in the London Zoological Gardens in 1853; it closed shortly afterward, reopening only in 1924. Other large European aquariums sprang up in Paris, Nice, Naples, and Berlin, all but the last of which survived World War II.

In exhibiting sharks, aquariums seek to erase the impression that all sharks are large man-eaters by displaying smaller, more exotic, and more benign-looking sharks. The idea is to inform the public that of the hundreds of species of shark, fewer than a dozen pose any threat to humans.

The National Aquarium in Baltimore, for instance, divides all presentations on sharks into three parts. The first part of the aquarium's presentation is intended to dispel the negative image of the shark. Visitors are informed that relatively few humans suffer shark attacks each year in contrast to the danger posed by other animals. Saltwater crocodiles, elephants, pigs, and even bees kill more people every year. Part two underscores the importance of sharks to maintaining the environmental balance. The third part focuses on the conservation needs of the shark. So far this strategy appears to be working well for the Baltimore aquarium: The shark exhibit has proven one of the most popular draws.

Aquariums are also actively involved in promoting research, especially in terms of shark breeding in captivity. Getting wild animals to breed in captivity can be a difficult problem; pandas provide a good example of this difficulty. Aquarium officials hope that if they can succeed they won't have to take sharks from the wild in the same numbers they do now.

Shark Facts and Stats

Bullheads and horn sharks, who both belong to the order of sharks called *heterodontoids*, do very well in captivity. Bullheads are bottom feeders who swim at depths of about 300 feet in the wild. The horn shark holds the breeding and longevity record in captivity, living up to 25 years.

The research effort extends beyond the limits of the aquarium itself. Much of the research is carried out in the sharks' habitat. The Baltimore aquarium, for instance, has participated in a National Marine Fisheries Service (NMFS) shark tagging survey, tagging and releasing hundreds of sharks over several years. One aim is to put together a population index of juvenile sandbar sharks in the Delaware Bay. The Delaware Bay is of special interest because it serves as an important nursery ground for these sharks as well as for sand tiger sharks. It's premature at this point, however, to say just how successful these efforts will be in terms of their impact on saving sharks in the wild.

Dropping in on the Sharks

In August 2002, some 23 sharks in an exhibition at Audubon Aquarium of the Americas in New Orleans were surprised when 10 intruders—of the human kind—dropped unexpectedly into their midst. The adults and children who dropped in on the sharks were on a fiberglass walkway over the shark exhibition when it suddenly collapsed, dropping the visitors into a 400,000 gallon tank. Fortunately, aquarium employees were near at hand when the accident occurred and responded quickly. The visitors, who sustained only minor bruises and scrapes, were quickly pulled from the water. According to all accounts, the sharks—nurses and sand tigers, neither of which are prone to attacking humans—left their guests alone. The sharks' indifference to their uninvited guests accords with what many divers have experienced in the wild—when sharks are well-fed and not provoked, they generally have no interest in humans (with the exception of a few aggressive species such as bulls, perhaps). Investigators suspect that the weight on the walkway exceeded the recommended limit.

From start to finish, the $40 million Aquarium of the Americas took less than four years, a record unmatched by any other facility of its kind in the country. The aquarium and nearby park are situated on 16 acres of riverfront property on the crescent of the Mississippi River. The design of the three-story 110,000 square foot aquarium was intended to give visitors of experiencing the entire habitat of the species they are viewing—from both above and below, but not in, the water.

The Challenge of Keeping Sharks in Aquariums

As you might suspect, taking care of a shark is no simple matter. For one thing, you have to have a place to put them. Sharks take up a good deal of room, even the smaller species. Most sharks grow to at least 36 inches and require a 200-gallon tank at a minimum. Of course, many sharks can get a good deal bigger. The leopard shark, for example, can grow as large as 6.5 feet. They require a minimum 400-gallon tank. Consider the challenge involved in trying to care for a great white that reaches 20 feet or more!

In his 2002 book, *Close to Shore* (Broadway Books, 2001), Michael Capuzzo states:

> The great white, at nearly 20 feet, 3,000 pounds will not submit to dental examination, and will not accept confinement. The fish is too big, too violent, beyond control. Man has never been able to keep the great white in captivity. When this has been attempted, the giant shark batters its head against its prison, unable to accept boundaries, hammering at the metal stays in the concrete that it senses electromagnetically.

In spite of the nearly insurmountable difficulties, several aquariums have tried to exhibit great whites in recent years. But the success rate is dismal: they rarely lived for more than a few days. It should be noted that many of these sharks were already sick before they were brought to the aquarium.

The Steinhart Aquarium in San Francisco is especially designed to hold and exhibit pelagic sharks. Sharks swim in a donut-shaped pool that featured an artificially induced current. Just as they do in the wild, most of the sharks swim against the current while visitors watch from a central viewing area in the center of the donut. According to many shark experts, this kind of environment is considered a fairly healthy one for young pelagic sharks. But could a great white survive here?

Sandy's Story

In 1980, aquarium officials had a chance to find out when a 7.5-foot young great white was delivered to them. Unlike other specimens of the great white held in captivity, this shark, nicknamed Sandy, was in good condition. Sandy, the aquarium director said, was an "aquarium's dream." She became an aquarium nightmare. The first problem, the staff discovered, was that Sandy was very sensitive to light. The lighting was toned down. But then when the lights were turned off at night, Sandy became irritable, too. So the aquarium obligingly left some lights on all night to keep her happy.

Divers ventured into the tank to videotape her. She ignored them. Other fish failed to evoke her interest, either—even when they were offered to her for food. At the same time, though, she seemed to acclimate herself to her new home. She soon began to swim faster around the perimeter of the tank, suggesting that she was becoming more confident about mastering her environment. Observers noticed that she was bumping her nose hard against some metal seams in the tank that protruded a few inches into the tank. The problem was quickly remedied.

After only a few days in captivity, Sandy showed signs of a more serious problem; every time she came to a particular point in the tank she began banging her head into the wall. Experts finally realized that she was responding to a faint change in electrical activity behind the tank wall. The change was just 0.125 of a millivolt, which was so small of an amount, in fact, that other sharks and fish never appeared to register it at all.

Once the experts realized the problem, they confronted a grave dilemma: they couldn't allow Sandy to continue bumping her head because she would eventually die from the repeated blows. Already her sluggish behavior was weighing heavily on them. On the other hand, they couldn't fix the problem without emptying the whole tank. The decision was made to release her in an area known to be frequented by great whites. As soon as she was free Sandy responded by showing renewed vigor and slipped happily back into the sea.

A Whale's Tale

In spite of the difficulties in maintaining large sharks in captivity some aquariums have actually succeeded in keeping the world's largest shark, the whale, in an exhibition. The first to do so was the Okinawa Expo Aquarium in Japan in 1980. Subsequently the feat was duplicated at the Ring of Fire Aquarium in Osaka, Japan. In 1992, the Osaka institution put two of these enormous sharks on display—a male and a female, both more than 20 feet long. The Okinawa aquarium accounts its success to its proximity to the sea; aquarists used a special barge to capture the sharks in an area not far offshore. The barge, with openings at both ends, was submerged to a depth just about even with the water's surface. Swimmers then guided the whale shark into an opening; after it was inside, the openings were immediately closed, trapping the shark. The barge was then towed back to the pier where a hammocklike sling was placed beneath the shark. The shark was then hauled up into a large tank of water on a flatbed truck which transported it to the aquarium.

Needless to say, the tank had to be large—and it is: 88 feet long, 39 feet wide and 11 feet deep. It holds 290,000 gallons of water. Over the past decade, the tank has been home to four whale sharks (though only one at a time). The sharks have done remarkably well.

A Tiger's Tale

Like great whites, tiger sharks have also proved too troublesome for aquariums to maintain for any length of time. In one case in April 1935, a 14-foot tiger shark was caught in the Pacific when he became tangled in a fishing net. He was delivered to the Coogee Aquarium in Australia, but he managed to survive for only a week. However, in that short time he acquired instant notoriety by suddenly regurgitating most of the contents of his stomach. Researchers found the remains of a rat, a dead seabird, and a human arm with a piece of rope round the wrist. The limb bore a tattoo of two boxers. The police had no difficulty identifying where it came from: the arm had come from a Sydney mobster who had mysteriously disappeared not long before. The shark had apparently swallowed the arm after it had been severed, providing macabre evidence of a gangland slaying.

Aquariums in America

Great aquariums are found all over the United States: the Steinhart Aquarium in San Francisco, the Shedd Aquarium in Chicago, the New England Aquarium in Boston, Scripts Aquarium in La Jolla, the Monterrey Bay Aquarium, the Oregon Coast Aquarium, the Aquarium for Wildlife Conservation in Coney Island, Brooklyn, New York, and the National Aquarium in Baltimore, Maryland, location of the Osborne Laboratories of Marine Sciences. Several aquariums offer special exhibitions about sharks:

♦ **SeaWorld (Florida, California, and Texas).** SeaWorld seeks to bring "visitors face to face" with sharks through the use of underwater tunnels. SeaWorld in Florida offers an exhibit featuring other "Terrors of the Deep" such as barracuda and lionfish in addition to sharks. Visitors to the Texas aquarium can view what is billed as the "biggest display of hammerhead sharks in North America." California's SeaWorld boasts of having "the largest exhibit of sharks in the world."

> **Shark Facts and Stats**
>
> In 2000, researchers at the National Aquarium in Baltimore began a study on the hormonal levels of sand tiger sharks in the hope that they would reveal correlations between reproductive hormone levels and behavior that have never been previously documented in this species.

♦ **National Aquarium (Baltimore, Maryland).** The seven-level National Aquarium occupies a prominent location on Baltimore's restored waterfront district. It features a special 225,000-gallon tank filled with sand tiger, lemon, nurse, and sandbar sharks. Smaller sharks are displayed in a smaller tank along with stingrays. A popular tourist destination, the aquarium is frequently sold out. Best times to visit are before 11 A.M. and after 3 P.M. in summers and in the fall and winter. The National Aquarium also serves as the location of the Osborne Laboratories of Marine Sciences.

- **Underwater World (Bloomington, Minnesota and Fisherman's Wharf in San Francisco).** Underwater World has two locations: in the Mall of America in Minnesota and at Fisherman's Wharf in San Francisco. Its design is meant to give visitors a sense of what it's like to dive underwater without getting wet. Visitors move along a moving walkway through a 300-foot-long curved tunnel, which allows them to view sandbar, nurse, and black tip reef sharks among others, which are all species found in the Gulf of Mexico. Shark feedings take place on Tuesday, Thursday, and Saturday at 11 A.M.

- **Monterey Bay Aquarium (Monterey Bay, California).** The Monterey Bay Aquarium, founded in 1984, features a re-created kelp forest where divers feed sharks by hand twice daily at 1:30 P.M. and 4 P.M. Exhibits are designed to replicate as much as possible the natural habitats of sharks. Raw seawater is pumped into tanks directly from the neighboring bay. Visitors proceed along "the habitats path" that takes them past a variety of bay ecosystems where they can watch large sharks swimming among schooling fish.

- **Oceanic Adventures Newport Aquarium (Newport, Kentucky).** Located on the banks of the Ohio River across from Cincinnati, the Oceanic Adventures Newport Aquarium features a shark exhibit that offers visitors a simulated diving experience, using a series of underwater tunnels. Over 25 species of sharks can be viewed, and there is a shark feeding ground as well.

Shark Lore

In September 2001, staff members of Vancouver Aquarium noticed a fin protruding from the vent of a female black tip, which was the first sign that she was pregnant. She gave birth to two pups—a rare event in aquariums. Unfortunately, only one pup survived.

- **The Aquarium of Niagara (Niagara, New York).** This aquarium is one of many that celebrates sharks during summer months with a Shark Week. During this event visitors are given the opportunity to witness shark feedings, experience close-up (but entirely safe) encounters, attend special discussions, and enjoy presentations about sharks.

- **Vancouver Aquarium Marine Science Centre (Vancouver, British Columbia, Canada).** Some of the aquarium's most popular features are the daily noon shark dive by staff members and the twice-weekly feedings on Thursdays and Sundays.

An Aquarist's View

According to Vancouver Aquarium Marine Science Centre aquarist, Takuji Oyama, Vancouver currently has six adult black tip reef sharks (two females and four males) and one juvenile (male). "It looks like the largest female is the strongest one, but I don't think (as some people do) she is the dominant animal in the six of them." Oyama doubts that the sharks have any organized social structure at all. Do black tips have a social structure in the wild? "That's what I would really like to know," Oyama says. "If they make an exclusive group as a pack or are they just bunch of individuals are hanging around in the same area?"

In his comments to me, made by e-mail, Oyama is candid about how much aquarists have yet to learn about the behavior of sharks in captivity. "We did have a chance to observe their mating behavior and a birth; however, we do not know what triggers their mating. So far, we don't know how often do they reproduce either." He adds: "Oh yeah, we don't even know their longevity."

Oyama has hit upon a fairly reliable method of identifying the sharks in the aquarium's care: "I found that the shape of the bottom edge of the dorsal black tip varied by individual. I'm not sure if this could be generalized for this species, though. It works for my seven sharks." He admits that after diving with them for the last four years, he can recognize them by the coloring of their tips. And although he has no scientific basis for his opinion, he senses that "each of them has their own character/personality." Their personalities express themselves, he adds, by different ways each shark has of feeding and approaching him.

Home Sweet Home Aquariums

About 90 percent of home aquariums in the United States are primarily goldfish bowls or similarly rudimentary systems. The remaining 10 percent have tanks equipped with filtration, but only a minority of these tanks, perhaps only 1 percent of the total, specializes in marine life as opposed to freshwater life. You wouldn't think that sharks would make ideal candidates for even the most sophisticated home aquarium systems owing to their size and needs. And they don't. Yet some enthusiasts are raising sharks in the privacy of their own homes.

In spite of the difficulties inherent in establishing home aquariums for sharks and the dangers of doing so (for the shark, not to the hobbyist), young, small sharks are still being sold in the United States. Presumably the people who are buying these sharks have no idea how big they can get or how hard they are to care for. Some of the sharks that are being sold include black tips (who can grow to be 6 feet long), nurses (who can grow to 14 feet), and the cat shark (who can grow to more than 7 feet). Horned and bamboo sharks are also popular with hobbyists.

On a website called the Conscientious Marine Aquarist, home aquarium expert, Robert Fenne candidly discusses the challenges involved. "Except for the smallest species (while they're small) that have sedentary (bottom sitting) behavior," he writes, "the vast majority of sharks are poor candidates for aquarium specimens. They're just too active, too big, too messy for all but the largest of systems."

For those aquatic hobbyists who refuse to be discouraged, a few tips are in order. Even though in a feeding frenzy sharks will attack one another, they seem to display better etiquette in captivity. Unless sharks of vastly different sizes are put in the tank with one another (or unless they have gone unfed for too long) they generally seem to eat the foods they've been trained on and not each other. Typically, feeding sharks two or three times a week is considered perfectly adequate. Because they are cold-blooded, sharks don't eat frequently in the wild. Hobbyists who give them too much food, run the risk of dirtying the water and producing a shark much bigger than the one initially purchased

> **Shark Facts and Stats**
>
> Recommended food for sharks in home aquariums includes all kinds of meaty foods, live or prepared, such as fish, squid, shrimp, and the occasional live goldfish—in short, anything that sharks can eat with one bite.

> **Shark Lore**
>
> Anecdotal evidence suggests that the average life of a shark in a home aquarium is less than a month. Most succumb from the effects of being housed in too small an aquarium, mishandling, or poisoning from filtration chemicals.

Of course, keeping sharks does not make much sense without a large enough system and few systems exist that are large enough to accommodate more than one shark. Almost any invertebrate placed in the tank with them—even sea cucumbers, bivalve mollusks, and hermit crabs—will be turned into shark food. Remember: Sharks need a great deal of room, they can't change direction or move from one depth to another with much ease—and they hate systems with square corners.

Any hobbyist who wants to give a home to a shark has many other thorny problems to work out as well: lighting, filtration, water temperature, environmental risks that might impair the shark's health, and the danger of getting bitten.

However, even under the best conditions, home aquariums are not substitutes for a natural habitat. The bottom line is that most sharks should be left in the sea. If you like to spend time close to sharks, don some diving gear and enjoy them in their natural habitat.

The Least You Need to Know

- Aquariums have three basic roles in exhibiting sharks: education, conservation, and research.

- Large pelagic sharks do not ordinarily do well or live for very long in captivity, though some whale sharks have flourished in aquariums.

- Several new aquariums in the United States and Canada now feature sharks in environments that simulate their natural habitats and give visitors the experience of coming face-to-face with them.

- Keeping sharks of any size in a home aquarium is inadvisable because of their size and the risks to the sharks' well-being due to mishandling, poisoning, and lack of space.

Observing Sharks in the Lab

In This Chapter

- What makes the shark's immune system so unique
- Why the shark's immune system may be a midpoint in evolutionary development
- How the shark's immune system compares with the mammals' immune system
- Why shark cartilage extract does not help fight cancer

In recent years, as Americans become more health-conscious (even if they still eat too much and don't exercise enough), sharks have begun to receive greater attention. That's because of the supposed therapeutic value attributed to shark cartilage, now available in a variety of forms. Sharks, it is thought, don't get cancer and so therefore it follows that their cartilage must have some kind of cancer-fighting agent. However, the fact is that sharks do get cancer (though perhaps not very often) and that there is no proof whatsoever that shark cartilage can prevent or fight cancer.

There is no doubt, though, that sharks are remarkably resilient creatures, evolutionary triumphs, able to flourish in seas teeming with bacteria, viruses, and human-generated pollution. They possess an immune system that they somehow acquired hundreds of millions of years ago, possibly through microbes. How they acquired this immune system (while such other jawless vertebrates, such as sponges, did not) is a mystery that scientists are still trying to unravel. Their discoveries may help us understand how mammals developed their extraordinary immune system. The results, it is hoped, may benefit us all—humans and sharks alike.

How do Sharks Resist Disease?

The venerable history of sharks has created some interesting and intensive scrutiny by scientists in recent years. Scientists are especially interested in understanding why sharks, skates, and rays have managed to survive for hundreds of millions of years in oceans teeming with bacteria, viruses, and, more recently, cancer-inducing pollutants.

Sharks have a highly efficient ability to resist disease. Sharks do get sick, but they succumb to disease at a much lower rate than bony fish, even though the species of cartilaginous fish are exposed to the same hazards. Scientists are investigating the shark's unique immune system in their attempt to account for the ability of sharks to maintain their healthy lifestyles as long as 70 years or more. In the process, scientists are making some astonishing finds.

Dr. John Marchalonis, an immunologist and molecular biologist at the University of Arizona, describes why this line of research is so important: "The study of the immune system of sharks has major implications for understanding how the immune system works in human health and disease, as well as helping understand the origins of the immune system."

The Evolution of the Shark's Immune System

Research on the shark immune system didn't begin in earnest until relatively recently. That's because there weren't enough live specimens to study. According to Dr. John Marchalonis, researchers had to wait until aquariums collected sharks in significant numbers. Even now only three major research institutions located in Arizona, Florida, and California are studying shark immunology. Nonetheless, the science of shark immunology has accelerated in the last few years because of the development of DNA recombinant technology, which is a technique of cloning genetic material. The same technology has received more attention in solving criminal cases and tracing paternity. Using this genetic technology means that scientists don't need to study live sharks for most of their studies because a sample of DNA does perfectly well.

In their efforts to investigate the shark's immune system for clues as to why cartilaginous fish resist disease, scientists are also learning more about the evolution of the immune system in mammals. They have discovered that the immune systems of cartilaginous fish and mammals are similar in many ways.

Sharks evolved more than 400 million years ago while the earliest mammals only began to appear about 100 million years ago. That means that the immune systems of sharks (and rays and skates) have had many more years to develop than those of mammals. That is not to suggest that sharks have better immune systems. In fact, their immune systems are not as well developed or responsive as humans, but they seem to work just fine for sharks.

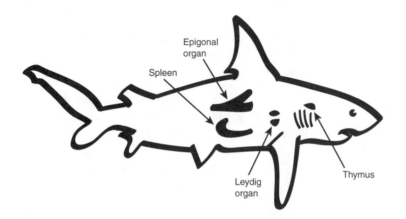

Epigonal organ

Spleen

Leydig organ

Thymus

The shark's immune system is primitive compared to a mammal's but remarkably effective in fighting off disease.

The Differences Between Shark and Mammalian Immune Systems

The immune systems of sharks and mammals typically consist of two main parts: an innate immune response and an adaptive or combinational immune response. The innate immune response is based on *macrophages* (white blood cells) that engulf and destroy foreign invaders such as bacteria. Primitive beings such as lamprey eels and starfish also have innate immune responses.

Adaptive or combinational immune response is present in all jawed vertebrates of which cartilaginous are the earliest examples. The adaptive immune response reacts to each attack by foreign invaders such as viruses or bacteria by creating "memory" cells that reject the same invader each time the threat recurs. This type of adaptive system can be stimulated by vaccination. The animal's immune system is tricked into responding to a harmless form of the virus, tagged by identifying protein

What Does It Mean?

Macrophages are white blood cells that surround, ingest, and destroy bacteria and other foreign organisms in a process called phagocytosis (literally cell-eating) that produces an inflammatory response.

fragments, as though it were the real thing. If the animal is ever exposed to the actual virus, the adaptive immune system mobilizes the specific cells that are designed to fight the infection.

Mammals have very specialized immune systems. By contrast, the shark immune system, although it is very effective, is still considered more primitive. Many of the shark's immune cells have the same function as those found in mammals, but shark cells are produced and stimulated differently. Mammalian immune systems produce *antibodies* in response to an invader. Researchers believe that the shark immune system is always in a state of alert, ready to defend against invading organisms at all times. However, sharks can be immunized by purposeful injection and respond well to most *antigens* by producing high levels of antibodies.

> ### What Does It Mean?
>
> **Antibodies** are proteins in blood that are generated to fight invaders called **antigens**. Antibodies are also known as immunoglobulins.

> ### Shark Facts and Stats
>
> At some point, about 400 to 450 million years ago, sharks split off from the jawless vertebrates such as lampreys, sponges, and hagfish and went on to develop an adaptive immune system; so far, all evidence indicates that the jawless vertebrates did not. (Insects, too, have no adaptive immune system.) Sharks are the lowest form of vertebrates to have this more advanced immune system.

Mammals have a variety of antibodies in their immune systems. Humans, for instance, can produce up to 100 million distinct antibodies that bind to specific antigens. Sharks, on the other hand, have only one type of antibodies. However, these antibodies circulate in the shark's blood at high levels. (Nobody knows how many antibodies a shark can make, but the number is likely to be high.) In spite of the high amount of antibodies in their systems, sharks do not appear to get autoimmune diseases such as lupus or rheumatoid arthritis the way humans do. Autoimmune diseases are caused when the body, in effect, turns against itself and mistakes the normal components of the body for foreign invaders and then produces antibodies to fight them. That was why scientists were so surprised to find such a high number of antibodies in sharks, which might otherwise indicate an autoimmune disease.

In mammals, bone marrow (along with other sites) serves as the factory where immune cells are produced and mature; they are later pressed into service in the bloodstream to combat invaders. But sharks, skates, and rays have no bone structure and thus no bone marrow. Instead, shark immune cells are produced in the spleen, thymus, and unique tissues associated with the gonads and esophagus. There's another difference, too: Researchers have recently discovered that rather than maturing elsewhere, many immune cells in sharks mature as they circulate in the bloodstream. This fact means that, in contrast to mammals, sharks have no lag between the manufacture of immune cells and their use against invaders.

The Shark's Immune Arsenal

Sharks have four immune proteins that are not found in any pre-shark creature: antibodies, T cell receptors, MHC proteins, and RAG proteins. The puzzle is how and when these proteins evolved in sharks. There are other mysteries as well. For example, although a shark's immune system and a mammal's immune system share many similarities, there are also some significant differences. For one thing, the arrangement of genes is not the same. For another, the immune systems of sharks and mammals respond in different ways.

In 1965, Dr. John Marchalonis (then a graduate student) and Dr. Gerald M. Edelman, who received a Nobel Prize for his work with human antibodies, found that sharks make antibodies similar in structure to those of humans. Specifically, they resembled the immune IgM antibodies that are the first to appear developmentally in humans and mice. "Thus, in the first place, it was striking that the most primitive jawed vertebrate—sharks—had antibodies that were structurally similar to ours," Marchalonis says. Interestingly, only "the most primitive form of antibodies" found in humans were also found in the shark.

> **Shark Facts and Stats**
>
> In 1985, scientists reported the first cloning of a shark gene responsible for making antibodies. Several shark genes have since been cloned, thus making it easier to study shark immune systems.

Take the T cells, for example. T cells recognize millions of different antigens thanks to proteins in their membranes called T cell receptors. The receptors react to the invaders like a lock-and-key system. The receptors bind to unusual protein fragments on the surface of invaders that they recognize, setting off a cascade of events leading to the invader's destruction.

In sharks, T cells behave very sluggishly—unlike in mammals where T cells respond robustly to any outside threat. Some scientists theorize that in sharks T cells are simply not as important as other types of infection-fighting molecules, such as the shark steroid *squalamine*, which are responsible for fighting bacteria and also seem to fight viral infections. Other scientists take another view: T cell response in sharks, they say, is quite robust so long as it isn't being compared to the T cell response in mammals. The response is perfectly adequate for the shark's needs.

> **What Does It Mean?**
>
> Squalamine, a shark steroid, is being investigated for its potential to fight bacteria and viral infections.

Immune cells are specifically tailored to fight specific types of infectious cells. The immune cells (T cells) "lock on" to the infectious cell and destroy them.

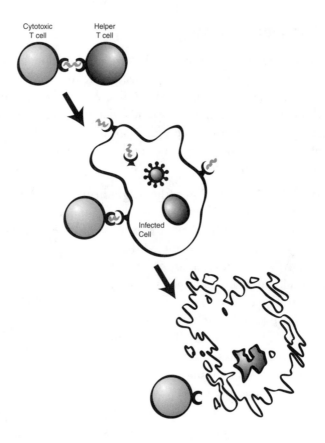

A Substandard Immune System

Speaking in evolutionary terms, sharks have substandard immune systems. For instance, they reject grafts slowly. Unless the grafts are compatible, humans reject grafts quickly, an indication of immune efficiency. (This is a major problem in finding organ donors; if a tissue type of the donor doesn't match that of the recipient, rejection is a likely outcome.)

In addition, the shark immune system seems to have no built-in memory for previous invasions. Although the shark responds to invaders by producing antibodies, the response remains the same regardless of how many times the same kind of foreign invader attacks. In humans and other mammals, by contrast, the immune response improves with each recurrence of the attack by the same invader.

Shark Facts and Stats
Sharks are the oldest existing species with immune systems.

The Evolutionary Big Bang

One question that has long puzzled scientists is the origin of shark antibodies. How did T cells and the genes involved in immune function get into the shark in the first place?

Some scientists believe that sharks acquired their adaptive immune system in an evolutionary "big bang." In cosmology, the term "big bang" refers to the creation of the universe 15 to 20 billion years ago. In evolution, the term refers to a period of about half a billion years ago that saw a tremendous upsurge in the creation of life forms that took place for more than 10 million years (a relatively brief span given the context).

So that brings us back to the puzzle: Where did cartilaginous fish get their immune system? Scientists believe that they may have found the answer: microbes. Microbes possess the pieces of genetic information that make up a major component of the adaptive immune system. At some point in the distant past, these scientists theorize, primitive microbes may have infected the sharks and transmitted this genetic information to them in the process. Genes can duplicate themselves, and they can recombine in different formations in ways that are sometimes positive and sometimes negative or in ways that have no discernible impact on the organism at all. So according to this theory, once this transmission took place, the genes then became incorporated into the shark's genetic makeup and subsequently passed onto the shark's progeny.

This same phenomenon might also explain how higher vertebrates, including amphibians, reptiles, birds, and mammals, obtained their adaptive immune systems. If microbes were responsible, then they saved the vertebrates the trouble of developing an immune system slowly through trial and error, in effect bypassing millions of years of evolution. This extraordinary genetic windfall essentially meant that the higher vertebrates all received a vaccination against a multiplicity of invaders. This theory of horizontal transfer from microbes to higher vertebrates may go far in accounting for the appearance of so many diverse life forms that took place during the evolutionary big bang.

The Development of the Shark Immune System

But even if the microbe theory is correct, it still leaves the question of how sharks developed their immune system. Did they get it all in rapid succession with its full repertoire of immune cells and lymphocytes? We don't know. But what is certain is that the shark system responds that the same way that ours does when an infected, although the antibody and T cell responses of the shark are "low tech" compared with the kind of rapid response we find in the mammal's far more sophisticated immune system. However, low tech is not essentially bad, because simple systems are easier to fix than complex ones. Just think about how difficult it is to repair the computerized modular automobiles of today compared with those of 30 years ago that could be fixed by virtually any kid hanging around a gas station.

One possibility is that the genetic transfer from microbes may not have happened directly; some other species, an ancestor of cartilaginous fish who has since become extinct, may have been involved. Some researchers wonder whether the shark's immune system, which is so like that of the higher vertebrates and yet so different in organization and responsiveness, may represent an evolutionary midpoint, a state of development halfway between jawless vertebrates and mammals.

As investigators continue to travel back in time in search of clues to the origin of the shark's immune system (and by extension our own), we can expect many more mysteries to emerge—and no doubt many more theories to explain them. As researcher Gary Litman of All Children's Hospital in St. Petersburg, Florida, puts it, "Little we've ever done in the cartilaginous fish system has been predicted accurately by us—it's almost always been a surprise. But that's been the most exciting thing about it."

Sharks and Cancer

Sharks do get cancer. The evidence that sharks develop malignant and benign cancerous tumors comes as a rude shock to many people who bought into the myth that sharks are immune to cancer and, as a result, believed shark cartilage had an important therapeutic role to play as a cancer-fighting agent in humans. But sharks develop cancer relatively rarely, and scientists are trying to discover why that is the case. They hope that the results of their research may turn out to benefit humans as well.

Tracking the Incidence of Cancer in Sharks

What we know about cancer in sharks is largely derived from an enormous database maintained by the Smithsonian Institution in Washington, D.C., called the Registry of Tumors in Lower Animals. The tumors classified by the registry include cancers from all possible sources throughout the world. Although most of the tumors come from bony fish, about 40 come from sharks, rays, and chimaeras. Most of these are not cancerous tumors; instead they are classified as fibrous responses to wounds, parasites, or goiters. For instance, sharks occasionally develop enlarged

> **Shark Facts and Stats**
>
> A shark's immune system resembles that of a human fetus; but as human babies develop, their immune systems grow more complicated and less like a shark's.

thyroid glands in captivity. The remaining few are cancerous tumors, including one kidney cancer in a dogfish shark and lymphoma blood cancer in a sandbar shark. No one, however, has ever done a systematic study to see how susceptible sharks are to cancer or whether bony fish get cancer more often than sharks do.

Even allowing for the possibility that the proportion of cancers in the wild is higher, the registry's statistics do suggest that something interesting is going on. Why is there such a low incidence of tumors among the sharks and their relatives? The question has prompted biochemists and immunologists at Mote Marine Laboratory (MML) to look for mechanisms that may explain the unusual disease resistance. Sharks and skates are now being studied at MML under controlled conditions similar to those for lab mice and guinea pigs.

Exposing Sharks to Carcinogens

The MML team, under Dr. Carl Lauer, carried out experiments to see whether sharks and skates would develop cancerous tumors when exposed to potent carcinogenic (cancer-causing) chemicals. Then scientists examined how the animals metabolized (and/or detoxified) the chemicals. They noticed a number of similarities and differences in metabolic activity compared with mammals, but in no case did they observe any changes in the tissues or genetic material that might result in tumor formation in the sharks or skates.

Why cartilaginous fish do not respond to toxins in the same way that mammals do is still unclear. According to some scientists, the better resistance in sharks may be due to differences between mammals and sharks in the regulation of immune cells. Other researchers feel that one reason for the shark's increased resistance stems from the fact that shark DNA does not mutate easily compared to mammalian genes. (Genetic mutations are implicated in many cancers from prolonged exposure to toxins or radiation.) Scientists are hopeful that someday their research will find applications in boosting human immune response to cancer.

Exposing the Myth of Shark Cartilage's Therapeutic Value

Sharks, who are often reviled and feared in the wild while alive, hold a revered place in the hearts of many people once they are dead. That's because sharks have long been seen as water-borne repositories of a therapeutic treasure—a cure for cancer, arthritis, and other afflictions. Shark cartilage has been promoted in a variety of forms: freeze-dried pills, powders, and as nutritional supplements (a classification that puts them beyond the authority of the U.S. Food and Drug Administration).

The belief in the therapeutic properties of shark cartilage has a long tradition. For centuries the Chinese have prized shark cartilage for its supposed medicinal and aphrodisiac properties. In 1993, shark cartilage enjoyed a surge in popularity thanks to a *60 Minutes* segment that reported on a Cuban study in which cancer patients went into remission after having taken shark cartilage. The study, while highly questionable, was nonetheless taken as proof that shark cartilage could cure, or at least arrest the spread of, cancer. There was even a popular 1992 book called *Sharks Don't Get Cancer* by Dr. William Lane about the benefits of shark cartilage. The book enjoyed enough of a success that the author followed it up in 1997 with *Sharks Still Don't Get Cancer: The Continuing Story of Shark Cartilage Therapy*. Saying it twice, though, still doesn't make it correct.

The idea that shark cartilage had special cancer-fighting properties can be traced back to studies conducted during the 1980s at the Massachusetts Institute of Technology and at Mote Marine Laboratory in Florida. These studies looked at cow and shark cartilage to understand how cartilage is naturally able to resist penetration by blood capillaries. (Cartilage bears a closer resemblance to teeth in its composition than it does to skin.)

Scientists studying cancer have focused on the way in which cancerous tumors are produced. Tumors grow because they develop new blood vessels. If some agent could block the growth of blood vessels, it was reasoned, then it might be possible to starve the tumor and destroy it. Similarly, an inhibitory factor that blocked the proliferation of blood vessels might reduce the inflammation associated with arthritis.

To obtain the inhibitory agent, though, scientists had to first obtain large amounts of raw cartilage, and then put it through several weeks of harsh chemical procedures to extract and concentrate the active ingredients. But once the concentrated extract was obtained, the scientists showed that it could in fact prove effective in curtailing the growth of blood vessels in lab animals.

But the extract had to be applied to the targeted area; it could not be injected, say, and then be carried in the bloodstream to the tumor. So there was no apparent reason to believe that taking cartilage orally in freeze-dried pill form, for instance, would have any effect on a tumor elsewhere in the body. Somehow adherents of shark cartilage feel that once the cartilage is absorbed the active ingredient is able to find its way to the tumor site. There is not a shred of evidence to support this assertion.

Nor is there any reason to think that shark cartilage possesses some extraordinary advantage over cartilage from other animals. What distinguishes sharks is the fact that they have much more cartilage in their bodies than other animals and make for a more abundant source of the material. In addition, there is no proof that cartilage of any kind, regardless of its source, contains an active ingredient in promoting disease resistance in any animal.

All this should not suggest that it would be a mistake to continue research to understand the chemical basis for cartilage resistance to blood vessels. And as we have tried to show in this chapter, there is good reason to expect that the research into the shark's unique immune system may yield new drugs. But grinding up shark cartilage as a panacea for serious illnesses, such as cancer and arthritis, cannot be justified on any scientific or moral basis. People who are swayed by the promotional efforts of shark cartilage advocates may shun the treatments they should be getting. For sharks, too, the fad poses a danger because it encourages overfishing of sharks for the purpose of obtaining more cartilage.

The Least You Need to Know

- Sharks are remarkably disease-resistant although they do develop cancer and other illnesses.

- Unlike jawless vertebrates, such as lampreys and other eels, sharks have a relatively developed immune system.

- The shark immune system is still primitive compared to that of mammals.

- There is no evidence that shark cartilage, promoted as a tumor-fighting agent, can cure or arrest the spread of cancer.

- Promising avenues of research being conducted on the shark's unique immune system may lead to drugs that benefit humans.

Part 5

Humans and Sharks

Despite the image of sharks as menacing man-eaters, an estimated quarter of a million people sign up with tour operators to dive with sharks each year. Although shark attacks on humans get all the attention, there are many other kinds of marine life that are equally threatening, possibly more so. If anything, because of commercial fishing practices, humans pose more of a threat to sharks. Without urgent conservation measures, several species of sharks—the apex predator of the ocean—may be driven to extinction before too long.

Chapter 17

A Diver's Thrill

In This Chapter

◆ Why shark diving is becoming so popular

◆ What makes shark diving so exhilarating

◆ How to find shark diving sites

◆ What diving with hammerheads and blues is like

The history of human-shark relations hasn't been a very happy one. For centuries sharks were considered terrifying predators with no distinction made between the hundreds of species that present no threat to humans at all and the few that demonstrate aggressive behavior. One of the principal reasons humans were so terrified of sharks was because they didn't know anything about them. Chances were that, if they didn't go deep-water fishing, they would never see a shark close up in their lives. That ignorance persists to this very day.

However, the situation is gradually changing. We are beginning to understand the important environmental role played by sharks, and visitors to aquariums now have the opportunity to view them in exhibits that duplicate as much as possible their natural habitats. Others—such as myself—want to experience sharks in the wild. Recently, diving with sharks—once thought of as lunacy or sheer folly—has been growing in popularity. If you don't believe me, check on the web and see for yourself how many diving operators now offer special shark diving tours. But more than an adventure, shark diving is also teaching us to appreciate these marvelous creatures. Those who have experienced sharks in their own world have become emissaries in their cause, eagerly spreading the word to all who will listen that sharks are worth saving—for their sake and ours.

Where to Dive with Sharks

Although sharks can be found in almost any sea in the world, they can often make themselves scarce. Finding them is tricky and getting close to them is more difficult still. Every dive site is different—and that means that every diving experience is different as well. If you go to the Cocos Islands in Costa Rica, for instance, you are likely to encounter schooling hammerheads, who gather in the same area day after day. In the Galapagos you may have a chance—if you're fortunate—to encounter a whale shark. Or you may wait for days before you catch a glimpse of any shark at all.

At the time of this writing, there are about 200 prime shark diving sites around the world, which can be visited through the auspices of organized tours. But new ones are being added all the time as the popularity of shark diving continues to grow. Some of these sites are fairly accessible, requiring a boat trip of a couple of hours or less; other locations are far off the beaten track, putting them beyond the reach of all but the most intrepid (and often the most well-heeled) divers.

Shark Diving Sites around the World

There are hundreds of diving "hotspots" with more being added all the time. Some are served by organized tour groups, others are not. To reach many, an extended boat trip may be necessary, while others are easily accessible from shore. Divers planning for a shark dive need to keep in mind that some sites are frequented by sharks only at certain times of the year.

The following list gives you an idea of where you can go shark diving in the United States, Canada, and Mexico. It is by no means exhaustive.

- **Canada.** You can see sixgill sharks in Barkley Sound and Hornby Island near Vancouver Island, British Columbia.

- **United States.** For blue and mako sharks, visit San Clemente Island and La Jolla Bight (San Diego, California), Wilson Rock (San Miguel Island, California), Fisherman's Cove (Catalina Island, California), Montauk Point (Long Island, New York), and Papoose wreck (Cape Lookout, North Carolina).

Papoose wreck is also a good place to view sand tigers. You can see leopard, horn, and whale sharks off of Kona Coast (Big Island, Hawaii). Boca Raton, Florida, is the place to be to see Caribbean reef and nurse sharks.

- **Mexico.** Whale sharks and hammerheads swim in the Sea of Cortez by Baja California as well as near Isla Las Animas and El Bajo Seamount (near La Paz). You can catch sight of an angel shark near Whale Island (Baja California, Sea of Cortez).

- **Caribbean.** Reef nurse sharks can be seen on Grand Bahama Island; if you're interested in bulls, black tips, lemon, and occasionally silky sharks the place to go is Walker's Cay. New Providence Island offers divers Caribbean reef, bull, and occasionally oceanic white tips.

- **Central America.** Nurse and Caribbean reef sharks are found in Lighthouse Reef, Belize, and the Bay Islands of Honduras. Scalloped hammerheads, great hammerheads, and (occasionally) whale sharks swim in Dirty Rock or Roca Sucia (Cocos Island, Costa Rica).

- **South America.** Scalloped hammerheads, reef sharks, whale sharks, and, of course, Galapagos sharks swim in the Galapagos Islands of Ecuador.

- **Europe.** Basking sharks off Cornwall, Wales, and Scotland are about the only species you will see in dive sites on the continent.

- **Africa.** Great whites, whales, makos, dusky sharks, and hammerheads all swim in a variety of sites in South African waters—Mossel Bay and Seal Island in Cape Province and Protea Banks in Natal; Zambezi, silver tips, hammerheads, and tigers in The Pinacles in Mozambique; gray reef, silvertip, silky, and oceanic white tips in Madagascar.

- **Asia.** White tip, black tip, and leopard sharks in Sabah, Malaysia; leopards and occasionally whales off Phuket, Thailand; silver tips, gray reef, white tips, and juvenile whales off Richelieu Rocks and in Burma Banks in Thailand.

- **Australia and New Zealand.** Blues and makos off South Island, New Zealand; whales off Ningaloo Reef in Western Australia; tigers and whales in Rowley Shoals in Western Australia; tigers off Raine Island in northern Queensland, Australia; gray reef, white tip, silver tip, and occasionally hammerhead off Great Detached Reef in northern Queensland.

- **Micronesia (South Pacific).** Gray reef and white tips in Truk Lagoon, Pizion Reef and Pohnpei.

- ◆ **Palau (South Pacific).** Gray reef and white tip in New Drop Off and gray reef and oceanic white tips in Peliu Corner.

- ◆ **Solomon Islands (South Pacific).** Gray reef, white tip, and nurse in Florida Islands, Russell Islands, Mary Island, and Uepi Island.

- ◆ **Fiji (South Pacific).** Gray reef and silver tips in Nigali Pass, bronze whaler and nurse in Koro Sea, and nurse and hammerheads in Viti Levu.

Where Are the Great Whites?

Over the last hundred years commercial fishermen and whalers reported sightings of great white sharks up and down the east and west coasts of America and Mexico, though their presence was never firmly established. Indeed, many diving enthusiasts were under the impression that the only places to find these sharks was in the waters off Australia and South Africa. However, attacks by sharks on surfers in California waters that took place in the 1970s convinced the public that a predatory shark must be at large even if no one could prove it. Then in the early 1980s, researchers discovered that adult great whites were returning annually to the Farallon Islands and Ano Nuevo Island, off San Francisco and Santa Cruz to feed on Northern Elephant Seals. (Some evidence indicates that they may migrate as far away as Hawaii.) This discovery paved the way for caged shark diving in the Farallon Islands. Several years later, another population of great whites was found off the coast of Mexico near Isla de Guadalupe, 200 miles southwest of San Diego, a prime location for catching game fish as well as sea lions and elephant seals, favorite prey of great whites. Researchers believe that the remote location of the island kept the great whites from being found for so long—and also had the added advantage of protecting them from being exterminated. Caged shark diving has now begun in this area, too, with as many as six sightings a day.

For those who crave the ultimate encounter with the great white, however, the best bet is one of two "hot spots" in South Africa: Gansbaii, 100 miles north of Cape Town, and Simons Town in False Bay. In both cases you will have a 99 percent chance of a close-up cage encounter. But there's a downside, too: you'll also experience the highly variable weather of the "cape of storms" known as the Cape of Good Hope. The visibility is a poor 6 to 40 feet with 15 feet the average. The water is also cold—with temperatures averaging less than 60 degrees Fahrenheit, you must really want to see the Great ones. It's a long way to go, you'll meet up with challenging conditions, but you might have the opportunity to see three great whites swim by your cage in a single day.

The Dive Feeding Controversy

Shark feeding has been stirring up controversy that seems to wax and wane depending on the number of shark attacks. The major argument against the practice is that the regular feeding of sharks changes their natural behavior and causes sharks to stay closer to the shore where they become a danger for swimmers, surfers, and anglers. In effect, these critics say, sharks grow too accustomed to people feeding them and associate people with food. Advocates of shark feeding, many divers among them, point to examples like French Polynesia where shark feeding has been going on for twenty years without any apparent adverse effects on humans or sharks. Nonetheless, the spate of attacks by sharks on waders and swimmers in Florida in 2001— 39 altogether—prompted critics of shark feeding to call for its ban. The state's Fish and Wildlife Conservation commission then proposed to prohibit dive operators from feeding sharks.

The commissioner had no doubts as to the need for the move. "There is no question it alters their behavior and is detrimental to Florida marine life," she declared. Scuba diving operators were quick to react, suing to stop the ban from taking effect. Representatives of the Diving Equipment and Marketing Association (DEMA) contended that there was no evidence that shark feeding posed any danger to humans, emphasizing that if the practice was risky then divers would have been attacked—and that hadn't happened.

In addition, these dives brought in millions of tourist dollars to the state. Ban advocates denounced the diving organizations. Thundered *In-Depth Magazine* in an editorial: "It has become apparent that pro-feeding forces have decided to pursue with renewed vigor a strategy that entails portraying their campaign as a valiant effort to protect 'divers' rights' from what they characterize as an unprecedented and unjustified assault by government." The writer contended that, while DEMA purported to protect "divers' rights," its true agenda was to make money while at the same time threatening a delicate marine ecosystem.

The commission subsequently backtracked and didn't impose the ban. Hawaii, on the other hand, has prohibited shark-feeding dives entirely. The measure, passed by the state legislature in 2002 with virtually no opposition, bans feeding sharks in state waters and forbids businesses from advertising or soliciting shark feeding. It is clear that passions over the issue have not abated and that banning advocates will take their fight to new battlegrounds in the future.

Shark Facts and Stats
Cages are used only in dive feeds with the blue, mako, and great white sharks.

Why the controversy? Critics contend that tossing out chum (fish and oil mixed with seawater for bait) encourages sharks to associate people with food. That, these critics say, is likely to increase the number of shark attacks along the coastline near these dive sites. Some dive operators have also come under fire for baiting sharks to bring them near the cages or boats to provide better photo opportunities for their customers.

Shark diving advocates refute the critics, pointing out that there is no proof that shark attacks have increased in waters around dive feeding sites. And they say that the practice of discarding huge quantities of fish parts overboard by fishing boats has been going on for years without any observable increase in the number of shark attacks. Moreover, shark diving enthusiasts say that shark diving, when it is done safely under qualified auspices, can provide divers with an unparalleled education about sharks. Through these encounters with sharks in their native habitats, divers are being recruited to serve the cause of shark conservation. But the debate about shark feeding dives is far from settled and may very well get more heated in the future.

The Addiction of Shark Diving

Shark diving is by no means something for all scuba divers. Some divers never get over their fear of sharks, but for those who do, the desire to see more is almost insatiable. Sharks are sleek, graceful swimmers, and they can be observed without intruding on them. Only a few sharks ever appear to be curious about the diver. Combine a potentially dangerous, beautiful shark and the adrenaline rush that comes with the encounter and you have the makings of a great adventure.

Swimmers who are comfortable with ocean swimming sooner or later find themselves snorkeling. The colorful fish and coral they observe in shallow waters usually stir their fascination and curiosity. But when they see others who wear tanks and dive to far greater depths and hear about the divers' close encounters with fish, many snorkelers get the urge to become a certified diver. Yet swimmers and snorkelers seldom get to see divers in action because divers don't want to be in shallow water, which is anything less than 60 feet. Divers far prefer the peace and tranquility that comes from being down so far that the only sound they hear is the gurgle of bubbles escaping from their regulators.

Diving with sharks is a natural progression and gradual addiction for people who develop a passion for scuba diving. The adrenaline rush of shark diving and the need to see sharks up close again and again are no doubt the reasons for the phenomenal growth in shark diving over the past 10 years. Certainly divers are attracted to the danger, although, as we've said repeatedly, most sharks are not dangerous and even those that are seldom bother divers. On the other hand, sharks are not to be taken for granted, either. And when one is speeding in your direction with his teeth bared, you would have to be a fool not to be alarmed.

Many people wonder if I am a "complete idiot" because I dive with sharks. I can remember feeling the same way when I first heard about other divers' encounters. Terrified of sharks when I started diving back in the late 1970s, I kept my eyes glued to one section of the reef rather than scanning the reef wall where sharks were likely to be found. Most of my early diving took place in the Sea of Cortez, and I never once saw a shark even though plenty of them live in those waters. On my hundredth dive I had my first encounter with a shark. I was diving in the Caribbean, and the reef shark's sleekness and beauty captivated me as it cruised along the reef wall, totally uninterested in me. I was hooked!

The adventure begins when the boat leaves the dock and the anticipation of the possibility of seeing sharks sets in. The adrenaline rush of diving with sharks is not much different than those I have felt jumping out of an airplane or bungee jumping off a 10-story tower in Cairns, Australia, or pushing the throttle of my Cessna T210 as I prepare for takeoff. Some of us are just adrenaline junkies; others simply enjoy diving with sharks even if their hearts aren't pounding in their chests each time they do so.

> **Shark Facts and Stats**
>
> Each year about 250,000 people in the world dive with sharks, making shark diving into a mini tourism industry on its own.

The Early Days of Shark Diving

Until recently there were only two sources of information about sharks—commercial fisheries and recreational divers. The fisheries, of course, weren't especially interested in research for scientific purposes; so it fell to divers to report back to the world what sharks were actually like in their watery habitats. In the 1970s, shark diving was still in its infancy and only the most intrepid divers were willing to swim with sharks. One of them was Carl Rosseler. The following is his account of those pioneering days underwater:

> In the late 1960s not much was understood about sharks. If you watched old movies of the early 1950s Hans Hass films or *Blue Water, White Death* in the 1960s you could see shark-diving techniques evolving during each shark-filming expedition. We simply did not know much about shark behavior, nor how they would respond to stimuli. So, we had to experiment with various ideas and see how different types of sharks would respond.

At the same time, there was an enormous body of myth and legend about sharks that made us wonder how much risk we were inviting when we went into the water with them.

In October of 1972, my great friend and partner, Dewey Bergman, used his contacts to charter a vessel for a diving adventure in tropical Australia. Our destination was Marion Reef, 320 miles out to sea off the Queensland Coast. We selected the northern tip of the eastern coral parapet, a site called "Action Point."

On this first "commercial" shark-feeding dive, six of us descended to the bottom at 60 feet with several good-sized fish carcasses wired together as bait. We tied that wire to a solid coral head, speared a passing fish to emit a sound signal to the sharks, and waited for them to respond. Half of the group, even after traveling so far, were so spooked by the fear of sharks ingrained in them that they stayed on the boat, kneeling on the rear platform and looking down at us through the clear water.

The sharks arrived in a swarm, and we quickly had 25 to 30 of them whizzing around us. We began learning lessons right away. For example, we realized very early that the sharks easily distinguished between the bait and us. They would zip over us, between us and around us, but never touched any of us. I have often said since that very first all-out feeding that sharks may not be smart about other things, but about eating they are geniuses.

Another immediate insight, which I have confirmed many times since, is that attacking sharks can swim so fast that your eye cannot even follow them—meaning, of course, that you cannot defend against them.

Since that first "public" shark feeding in 1972 I have conducted hundreds of feedings all over the world. An important note: when I have put on shark feedings I haven't just jumped into the water anywhere and found sharks. Instead, I always work with local experts and boat captains who know the area. We will then look for certain types of underwater terrain, which have yielded sharks in the past. Sharks tend to return to certain places regularly. Sometimes they are not only present, but they are sufficiently curious that we can get our photos without even feeding them.

I confess, though, that the most dramatic shark pictures occur in feeding situations. Given our preparation and experience, the sharks have almost never failed to perform. I never had a client nipped in more than a quarter-century of feeding sharks, and I now have confidence that well-run shark-feedings not only thrill divers who participate, but enlist those observers as friends who want to help protect sharks after sharing the excitement. Since sharks are endangered all over the world, they can use all the friends we can recruit.

Recently, on the occasion of his twenty-fifth diving expedition, Rosseler decided to celebrate by diving with great whites.

Recent research has suggested that in both South Africa and South Australia, more white sharks come to the coastal sites during the less hospitable months of southern winter—May through September. So, for my 25th expedition I chose a late April/early May cruise with my long-time friends, Rodney Fox and his son Andrew. I was armed with a new, thick wet suit I was anxious about being incapacitated with cold when I spent several hours at a time in the cages.

As they have so often done before, the great white sharks stalked the baits we offered patiently but relentlessly. They circled our cages looking for openings. They came in from the vast ocean from directions that were impossible to anticipate. They surprised us again and again. Sometimes they would hit a cage full of divers before anyone even saw them. Time and again, we saw behavior that convinced us one would never survive being stalked by these giants. It was my annual epiphany, and I laughed as I realized how these adrenaline-drenched moments brought me back year after year.

This great white shark experience organized by the Fox family is a transforming experience; I have had the testimony of dozens of dazzled clients on this. Some are so overwhelmed by the encounter that they return for one or even two more cruises in later years. All say that their friends see them differently after they have been with these predators. Great White Shark attacks out of the sun glare! For me, my photos of these massive carnivores are always among my most satisfying. Having a fifteen foot white shark a few ferocious inches from your lens is a test at several levels your self-control and ability to think in rapidly-changing circumstances determine whether you come home with pictures or not. I love that challenge above all others.

My Shark Tales

Eight years have passed since my first shark-diving expedition. Since then, I've had the thrill of diving in open water with hammerheads, Galapagos sharks, silkies, a wide variety of reef sharks, and even several whale sharks. To share a sense of just how exhilarating diving with sharks can be, I recount some of my favorite stories about shark encounters in the following sections.

Cage Diving for the First Time

I came up with the inane rationalization after seeing a few reef sharks here and there (after those first 100 dives were under my belt) that if I felt comfortable cage diving with sharks, I would head off to some of the world-class destinations (Cocos, Galapagos, Palau) that offered schools of "big stuff" such as scalloped hammerheads and mantas and also offered the possibility of realizing my dream (probably shared by all divers) of seeing a whale shark.

The closest destination to my hometown of Tucson, Arizona, for shark cage diving is San Diego. I was able to join a group from a Laguna Beach dive club on Bob Cranston's boat *Bottom Scratcher*. (Bob subsequently went on to become a famous underwater videographer.) Bob's destination was about 12 miles off the coast of San Diego, a spawning locale for blues and makos. There were a dozen guys on board, a woman chef, and me.

Technically speaking, the shark cage dive is very simple. The cage is tethered to the dive vessel about 25 feet from the boat and is sunk approximately 15 feet below the surface. Divers swim to and from the cage on a one-on-one basis with the shark master.

It is the responsibility of the shark master to be on alert for any shark activity that might pose a problem for divers under his watch. His primary role is to ensure the safety of divers, which means taking defensive measures when they're warranted. In some instances, the sharkmaster leads divers to and from the cage. In feeding dives they will attract and feed sharks so that divers can get closer and better photographs.

> **Taste of the Bizarre**
>
> On Fiji in the 1920s, a missionary reported a custom called shark kissing in which the natives captured sharks in a large net, and then waded out in the water to kiss them on their bellies before throwing them on shore. This custom was meant to keep the shores safe from shark infestation.

We had practiced entering and exiting the cage on the trip out to the shark habitat. We removed all unnecessary dive gear to avoid getting hung up on the cage, we all proved our ability to enter and exit the cage, and we all stood properly weighted on the floor of the cage. Many divers can manage the cage, but they are still phobic about plunging into the bottomless depth. Without a reef or bottom to orient themselves, some divers get vertigo. This was not the case on this trip; we all passed the checkout dive with flying colors.

To attract sharks, shark dive operators release bait or chum in the water. Back then, Bob stored tuna in his freezer. Today, chum buckets can be purchased at bait stores. It only took 12 minutes for the chum to attract enough sharks to tip the cages, tethered to a float, into the ocean. Two shark masters, garbed in heavy (25 pounds) stainless-steel suits from head to toe (including their hands), entered the water. They scanned the ocean between the stern dive deck and the cage to make sure there were no sharks between the descending divers and the cage.

The shark master hung on the top of the cage feeding the sharks mackerel to attract them closer to our group's cameras. Once in a while the shark's teeth would catch on the hand of the shark master, and he would have to push back the shark's snout to retrieve his arm. Although bits and pieces of chum were floating in the water, we were spared the sight of the grisly mess of dead horses that were once used to attract great whites. The technique of chumming may be more sophisticated and divers more shark savvy today, but even so you still sometimes come up empty handed. Carl Roessler (one of the first dive trip operators) once told me of a 10-day trip to Perth, Australia, when he and his crew had chummed 24 hours a day without attracting a single shark.

> **Shark Lore**
>
> Dive travel began in the 1960s when there were only a few dives in the Florida Keys and in the Bahamas.

When the moment of truth arrived, I could hear myself breathing on the dive deck. I signaled okay with a circle of my fingers, and the dive master told me to jump. With a giant stride, I hit the frigid 65-degree water and quickly descended to the cage. The cage was swaying like a ride at an amusement park, not so easy on the stomach. And there I was with two strangers. What if one of them freaked out?

A moment later, I forgot my apprehensions and became fascinated by the sharks. I wedged my fins under the bottom bar to steady myself and turned on my camera. Now I was focused on sharks gulping chunks of bait, totally distracted from the chill of the cold water and my concern about seasickness.

Time passed quickly as I snapped 36 frames. Our time allocation for two dives in the cage was 40 minutes. After 20 or so minutes had gone by, I found it no longer possible to ignore the chill in my bones. (Being a warm water diver, I was not adequately prepared with the proper wetsuit.) As I was contemplating the return topside to the boat, it suddenly occurred to me that I wouldn't be able to see the sharks behind me in open water.

> **Shark Lore**
>
> In the 1960s in the Bahamas, production staff working on James Bond films would release groggy tiger sharks in front of divers who would kick them in the face to make them behave aggressively for the cameras.

Exiting the cage was the most frightening part of the experience. By the time my turn came, the sharks had been in a feeding frenzy for more than two hours. Not wanting to scare us, the shark masters didn't tell us they carried "bang sticks" to ward off any aggressive sharks. But I ascended quickly with no problems and sprawled, emotionally exhausted, on the deck of the boat. Even then, I was already planning my next encounter with sharks.

Although I loved seeing the sharks, sharing a swaying cage in cold water with two strangers just wasn't for me. Although I did go cage diving again a few years ago, I much prefer being in the open water without a cage or being in a baited situation.

Scuba Diving with Hammerhead Sharks

"You'll want to be my dive buddy this week. Trust me on this." Scarcely were the words out of my mouth than the young man named Benji looked at me quizzically, wondering why a smiley, silver-haired lady would make such a definitive comment. Benji was young enough to be my son and was unaware that during the routine checkout dive, I was busy evaluating the air consumption of other divers.

> **Shark Lore**
>
> Credit for the Cocos Islands' discovery is given to a British whaler named Captain Belcher. When his ship departed the island in 1838, Belcher left behind a few pigs. Today the 5,000 descendants of those pigs are considered an environmentally destructive nuisance.

> **Shark Lore**
>
> The Cocos Islands teem with a variety of natural life. Scientists have identified 97 species of birds, two endemic species of reptiles, 57 crustaceans, 500 mollusks, 800 species of insects, several species of turtles, and 5 species of freshwater fish.

I was keeping an eye out for someone who had experience. The last thing you want to do when you go shark diving is to baby-sit an anxious buddy. For one thing, it reduces the time you can spend at depth with sharks (in this case scalloped hammerheads), and for another, it denies you the opportunity for an up-close experience with the sharks. I was looking for a buddy who could backroll from a Zodiac raft and descend quickly to depth. Benji was my man; he just didn't know why.

Twelve of us were willing to tolerate the excruciating 42-hour boat ride to the Cocos Islands, 300 miles south of Costa Rica, just to dive with schooling hammerheads, white tips, oceanic, and reef sharks, and—if we were lucky—whale sharks. Contrary to their negative reputation, hammerheads (the Cocos' primary attraction) are shy, elusive sharks who swim off at the sight or sound of a diver's bubbles. My 20 years of experience reinforced my hunch that only the first divers down to depth (and on this trip depth could be 150 feet) would be lucky enough to see the hammerheads.

The crew of our mother ship, the *Okeanos Aggressor*, divided the group into two Zodiac rafts. Benji must have trusted me because he switched his gear into my assigned raft. Benji and I entered the water and descended. This was open-water diving, so we had no shark cages for protection. We had to navigate through strong, shifting currents, always aware of riptidelike surges that could smash us against boulders covered with long-spined sea urchins. We could spend only minutes at depth looking for sharks before ascending for decompression. Benji's decision to be my buddy was rewarded on the first dive of the weeklong trip—we were the only divers to see hammerheads.

A Close Call

My heart began to pound as the six-foot blue shark swam toward me, nearing the diving cage that was all that protected me and my camera from the silvery, sleek-torsoed projectile. When the shark came close enough to look me in the eye, I came to a chilling realization: The cage's camera window was wide enough to admit the razor-sharp teeth! There wasn't time to think. With all my might, I took my small point-and-shoot underwater camera and punched the shark in the snout, my instinctive fear fueling the single blow. The shark quickly turned around and vanished. While the experience certainly didn't deter me from diving again as soon as the opportunity offered itself, I was always alert for any shark poking its snout into my business.

Cage Diving off San Diego

Not long ago, I revisited the up-close, adrenaline-filled experience of cage diving in the San Diego spawning grounds of blue and mako sharks. I signed up with San Diego Shark Diving Expeditions. Unlike my first experience in San Diego, when all the divers were having their first blue shark encounters, I learned that on this trip seven of the eight divers had dived with sharks before.

The biggest change was a new boat: the 30-foot *D&D II* (hope the initials don't stand for "Death and Disaster") had replaced the company's 63-foot *Bottom Scratcher* with its comfy lounge and meals on order. Tanks lined the sides of the D&D II, and the divers sat on backless aluminum benches. Box lunches were provided with cold drinks, and hot soup was served on the return trip. Additionally, the boat now carried only one shark cage (the *Bottom Scratcher* had two), which meant longer intervals between dives.

Although men continued to dominate the passenger list, one of the two shark masters on this trip was a woman named Jessie Harper. Jessie is in love with a job that would make most folks shudder. Even her parents don't want to hear about her adventures, but she's committed. She says she "feels invincible" when she dons her 22-pound chain-mail suit and jumps in the ocean to feed blue sharks. "I just can't get hurt too bad" with the suit on, she explains. "It's a real ego trip."

The petite 22-year-old college student has been diving since she was 17, taking less than five years to come up through the certification ranks and become a dive master. She was drawn to sharks since she began diving, but admits that her heart still skips a beat when an aggressive mako appears. Makos "really keep me on my toes; they're not as docile as the blue sharks." For that matter, makos even frighten away the blues, which they sometimes feed on.

Occasionally sea lions appear and also scare off the blues. The common view of sea lions as "shark food" isn't always true, says Jessie; the big animals often feed on the small blue sharks. "One day a sea lion gobbled a blue right in front of the divers who were filming inside the cage. That's seeing the food chain in action."

Clad in chain-mail suits and headphones that let them communicate with the boat crew, Jessie and owner Paul Anes swam around the cages releasing bait. Back on the boat, Captain Scott Sindby, a knowledgeable and friendly soul, used a GPS (global positioning system) unit to navigate the 9.5 miles to offshore spawning grounds in the La Jolla Abyss. The trip took about an hour and a half, during which time Scott offered divers the latest seasickness preventative. A Sea Pen (available only in Mexico) stamps a red dab of ink on the palm. A Dramaminelike substance then penetrates the skin on a time-released basis. "Don't use too much," Scott cautioned. "One diver painted her hand and slept the entire trip."

> **Shark Lore**
>
> In addition to bait, shark masters now use a "mako magnet" to attract makos. This electronic device emits a pitch that sounds like the cries of a wounded fish.

The boat operates with a crew of six, one of whose sole responsibility is to chop the bait (known as chum) used to attract sharks. In addition to the buckets of masticated mackerel, tuna, and sardines spread by the shark masters, larger chunks of bait are tossed overboard to attract sharks swimming near the surface. Tuna blood is mixed in for good measure.

One crewmember had a setup that, in the diving world, is the ultimate convenience for a man (and the envy of a woman): a dry suit fitted out with a condom catheter, which was attached to a P-valve that exited through the leg of his suit. (In diving, it's said that there are divers who pee in their wetsuits and those who admit to peeing in their wetsuits.)

Then it was time for the dive. We first did a checkout dive, familiarizing ourselves with entering and exiting the cage and checking if we were wearing enough weight to make us negatively buoyant (which makes it easier to stand in the cage). Experienced divers with extended strobes on their cameras were allowed to dive outside the cage, with the proviso that they would assume all liability for their own safety. They were instructed to stay next to the cage and not below, where ascending air bubbles might obstruct the view of divers in the cage. If an aggressive mako appeared, they were to put their backs to the cage and keep their eyes glued to the shark. If two makos appeared, they were to scurry into the cage.

The mako warnings proved useful. Twenty-three minutes after we began chumming, a six-foot mako came after the bait. Fortunately, the mako swam off, and we had only a smaller one darting around the cage while we were diving.

Fishing for Makos

A caged dive with makos was one thing. But what would it be like to go fly-fishing for them? I returned to San Diego to find out.

The thrill of casting a fly to a mako shark is hard to match. In addition to the skill and timing required in casting to catch large saltwater species such as sailfish, marlin, and tarpon, the angler must contend with the mako's brute strength, all the while admiring the beauty of its sleek, compact body.

Fly-fishing for mako shark is at once terrifyingly active and deeply philosophical and is one of the most challenging (and some say frustrating) examples of conservation fly-fishing. Even when hooked, the shark always wins: The sandpaper coarseness of its skin and tail either breaks the fly line (usually during a jumping episode), or the fish is reeled in and released at the side of the boat. Once a mako is hooked, the boat follows the direction of the shark; otherwise, the shark would strip the reel. If the angler is successful in bringing the mako to the boat, a custom-made gaff clipped to the line gently pulls the barbless, mackerel-patterned fly from the shark's mouth.

I was aboard guide Conway Bowman's boat in the Pacific Ocean near the La Jolla Bight. Here, deep-water canyons have become prime habitat for mako spawning; after a gestation period of two to three years, the mako gives live birth to as many as 15 pups. If the pups survive without being eaten by their mother or other makos, they are ready to hunt. Schools of sardine, herring, and mackerel feed the sharks until they weigh between 400 and

> **Shark Lore**
>
> The area of the Pacific between San Clemente, California, and Tijuana, Mexico, is called the "Mako Triangle" though it's popularly known as the "California Bight."

500 pounds. At maturity, the sharks leave the area; amazingly, nearly nothing is known about their adult whereabouts.

<table>
<tr><td>

Shark Facts and Stats

According to the book *Sharks: Silent Hunters of the Deep* (Reader's Digest, 1987), only 39 of nearly 400 species can grow more than 9 feet, and fewer than half can even reach a maximum of 3 feet.

</td></tr>
</table>

The 50-minute boat trip off San Diego aboard Bowman's 18-foot Parker outboard was a bone-jarring roller coaster of a ride. Despite the jarring trip, Bowman and I arrived at the fishing grounds in good spirits; Bowman proclaimed, "This looks like a great mako day." The dark gray Pacific Ocean was shrouded by fog, and three-foot southerly swells collided with a cross chop. I swallowed hard and nodded in a way that I hoped seemed enthusiastic.

A third-generation San Diegoan, the 34-year-old Bowman is a beach boy at heart. When he isn't fishing or working at his other day job (managing the Murray Reservoir in nearby La Mesa), he takes the surfboard off his car and heads for the waves. But fishing is his passion; he grew up fishing for bluegills, and then graduated to calico bass. Always fascinated by makos, Bowman developed his technique over time, experimenting with a variety of flies and bait. Now he's a huge mako fan, with serious interest in conservation of the species and a lot to say on those anglers who catch and kill the fish for food.

Bowman is a true angler, doing it for the joy of fishing. That doesn't mean he's not serious, though: He's recorded the exact location of each mako release achieved from his boat. Bowman begins each trip with some information gathering. On our trip, he used his GPS device to check the depth (less than 100 fathoms), water temperature (70 degrees), and current drift (southerly). This information is not just statistical; Bowman knows exactly where he wants to fish and, more important, the direction he wants the boat to drift.

Slowing the boat, Bowman next lowered a chum bucket filled with mashed bonito tuna. Particles of fish began to drift out of the bucket, clouding the water with fish particles and oil. We continued this "power chumming" until the chum line stretched about half a mile. The location of the line was highlighted by a flock of terns and a few shearwater and Hermann gulls, all looking for a feast along the chum line. While we waited for the mako to arrive, Bowman talked about his love for sharks and their strength and beauty while tying steel leaders using his homemade flies. The first mako approached the boat in less than an hour.

Fishing for mako is visual fly-fishing; although the angler uses the same baiting and casting routine for each shark, no two sharks ever react the same. Bowman began with a spinning rod, baiting it with a mackerel head to entice the shark closer. Once the mako took notice and began to follow, he tossed chunks of mackerel, trying to lure the shark within casting distance. (If a shark is about 3 feet long, Bowman recommends the 12-weight rod; larger sharks require a heavier 16-weight rod.)

The mako came closer while continuing to eat the mackerel chunk. Bowman warned me to keep the fly off the water during this process: He didn't want the mako tempted too soon or coming too close to the boat. If the shark leapt into the boat, explained Bowman, "it would be disastrous. The mako would tear this boat apart."

The mako receded a bit, and at Bowman's signal, I tossed the fly—but to no avail. Usually, if an angler is successful at this point, the battle begins. However, makos don't usually give an angler a second chance. But to our surprise, this one was different. Indifferent to conventional wisdom, the mako returned, majestic as ever. This time, after another taste of mackerel, it grabbed the fly—and I hooked it with all my might.

I'm a seasoned fly fisherman and an accomplished diver, but neither experience helped me here—maybe they even served up a false sense of security. All sense of self-confidence went out the window the moment I hooked the shark. It reared up, heading full-steam toward the boat, which offered the negligible protection of suddenly skimpy two-foot gunwales. I was all reaction and adrenaline, wrestling for control for maybe 10 seconds. Exploding like a firecracker from the ocean's surface, the wide-shouldered mako made a triple acrobatic leap before stripping 250 yards of fly line, sounding rapidly into the depths of the Pacific. It took me a few minutes to recover and quite a bit longer to digest the fact that my opponent was a shark half my size, a three-footer.

During two half-day trips, Bowman, and I had the opportunity to catch and release six makos, each of whom reacted differently to our presence. Some did aerobatics; others circled the boat as if we were the prey, and a couple "bull-dogged" (a term used by tuna fisherman for sounding or heading down). That's one of the reasons Bowman loves to fish for mako. Not only is it a visual sport that doesn't require trolling, but each fish also has its own personality, though all are aggressive and unpredictable.

Shark Facts and Stats
A cousin to the great white and salmon sharks, the short-fin mako, colored from olive to cobalt, is considered a top-of-the-pyramid ocean predator. This species, members of which have been clocked at speeds up to 40 miles per hour, covers a wider range that the great white.

When the next mako, a six-footer, came lurking, Bowman had the rod in hand to prove his angling prowess. After that I released several other three-footers, each time feeling more confident and each time reveling in the rush of the release. Four hours later, the chum bucket was empty, and our day of mako fishing was over. I endured another rough ride back to the marina, this time with every muscle aching from the fight. Bowman was quiet, but I did catch something about "California dreaming"—a dream in which the thrill and majesty almost overwhelm and in which the shark always wins.

The Least You Need to Know

◆ Shark diving is an adrenaline sport. Once you begin you always want to see more sharks "up close and personal."

◆ More than 200 shark diving sites around the world serve a quarter of a million divers, with more sites and divers being added all the time.

◆ When dive operators use chum, the shark diving takes place in cages to protect divers from feeding-frenzied sharks.

◆ Fishing for makos is a sport and a test of wills: yours and the shark's.

Chapter 18

Shark Attacks: Separating Truth from Myth

In This Chapter

◆ Whether shark attacks are on the rise

◆ Who is most in danger of being attacked by sharks

◆ Which species of sharks pose the most danger to humans

◆ What types of attacks sharks mount against humans

◆ What you can do to avoid shark attacks

Each summer seems to bring a new wave of shark attacks along the shores of the United States. Shark attacks were a media rage during the summer of 2001 (based on a few sensational incidents) until a more deadly human attack eclipsed them. But the facts do not support the alarmist school. Although sharks do present a danger to humans in some cases, they are hardly the deadly menace that the media often makes them out to be. This chapter explains the facts behind the scary stories and why so many misconceptions have arisen. You'll also find some useful tips to prevent attacks the next time you go swimming, surfing, or diving.

Taste of the Bizarre

After a spate of shark attacks in the summer of 2001, the sensationalist tabloid *News of the World* ran a banner headline proclaiming, "Castro Trained Killer Sharks to Attack U.S." The story was complete fiction.

The Shark Attack Scare

The shark attack that drew the most attention in 2001 occurred in July when a bull shark ambushed nine-year-old Jessie Arbogast in Florida, ripping off his arm. The boy's uncle subdued the shark and dragged the shark up to shore and then salvaged the boy's severed limb. Bull sharks were subsequently blamed for the deaths over Labor Day weekend in 2001 of David Peltier, 10, in Virginia Beach and Sergei Zaloukaev, 28, in North Carolina's Outer Banks. The two weekend attacks took place 135 miles apart, perhaps an indication that the same shark was involved.

Jessie's Uncertain Recovery

A year after the shark attack on Jessie Arbogast on a Florida beach, the boy's recovery from his injuries is still difficult. He continues physical, speech, and occupational therapy in his hometown of Ocean Springs, Mississippi. According to doctors, the prospects for a complete recovery are still uncertain, owing to the gravity of the wound he sustained: he lost both his right arm and a third of his thigh when he was attacked by a 7-foot-long, 200-pound bull shark. His uncle reacted quickly, pulling the shark to the shore where another rescuer shot it. The boy's severed arm was extracted from the shark's gullet and was reattached by doctors at Pensacola's Baptist Hospital. The severe blood loss and oxygen deprivation he suffered because of the attack left the boy unable to speak and possibly with permanent brain damage. Even with intensive therapy, he still remains partially crippled and is capable of producing only incoherent sounds.

Distinguishing Between Attacks

There are basically two types of shark attacks—provoked and unprovoked.

A *provoked* shark attack occurs when a human deliberately does something that causes a shark to attack. People have been known to pull on a shark's tail or poke a shark with a spear gun or other object. There are instances where people have cornered or cut off a shark's escaping into open water and there are those individuals who have been foolish enough to try to feed a shark by hand. Others have taunted sharks or otherwise behaved aggressively towards them. Obviously, most provoked attacks can be avoided if you exercise a little bit of common sense.

An *unprovoked* shark attack occurs when the shark assaults a person without that person having done anything to arouse his anger. (The shark, of course, may have a very good reason to attack, only it's just not clear to the poor human, who might unwittingly have made some provocative gesture that precipitated the attack.) Sometimes an unprovoked shark attack occurs when humans come into contact with sharks without meaning to or have used equipment—surfboards, for example—that attract the shark's attention.

The succession of fatal attacks that summer heightened fears that we were in for a real-life reenactment of *Jaws*. The truth is that there was no rise in shark attacks in 2001 over previous years. By September 2001, 52 shark attacks had been recorded in contrast to 84 for 2000, 58 for 1999, and 54 for 1998. The yearly average of shark attacks for the 1990s amounted to only 54.

The fact that shark attacks are relatively rare and that the overwhelming majority of shark species are harmless to humans doesn't appear to have made much of an impression. Why should that be? Perhaps the eminent Harvard biologist Edmond O. Wilson has a clue: "We're not just afraid of predators, we're transfixed by them ... because fascination creates preparedness, and preparedness, survival. In a deeply tribal sense we love our monsters."

> **Shark Facts and Stats**
>
> For every 1,000 people who drown in the United States one shark attack is estimated to occur. In South Africa one person is attacked by a shark for every 600 people who drown; in Australia there is one shark attack for every 50 people who drown.

How Many Shark Attacks Are There?

According to the best estimates, about 70 to 100 shark attacks occur each year, resulting in about 5 to 15 deaths. The estimates must be qualified because information about shark attacks and related deaths is hard to come by in certain corners of the world, especially in developing countries that may be loathe to admit to any problem that might cause tourists to stay away. One thing is clear: The death rate from shark attacks has shrunk over the years because of improved emergency services and medical treatment.

Even though more people are participating in recreational water activities, which should heighten the risk of intruding on turf the sharks consider their own, the fact is that in 2001, shark attacks dropped to 76 from 85 the year before in the United States. To put these numbers in another context, consider that, on average, African bees kill more people in the United States each year than sharks kill throughout the world. And every year, pigs and falling coconuts kill more people than sharks do.

Predictably, given the media attention to shark attacks, people aren't taking much reassurance from these statistics. (African bee attacks or fatal injuries resulting from falling coconuts don't sell papers the way that shark attacks do.)

To track the number of shark attacks around the world, a database called the International Shark Attack Files has been set up. These files include any type of injury caused by sharks and even record instances where the only injuries the sharks have inflicted are on surfboards or surf skis. Some of these injuries are only skin grazes where people come into contact with the sharks' rough skin. Some attacks are the result of needless provocations by humans that cause small, usually nonaggressive sharks such as wobbegongs, angels, and nurses to lash out. (People have been known to be so macho as to try to grab sharks by the tail!) Attacks by the smaller sharks such as the white-tipped and black-tipped reef sharks often appear to be unprovoked and often occur on reefs or in shallow water. In the majority of these cases, very little damage is done; the injury is even less than a bite from a small dog.

> **Shark Facts and Stats**
>
> In Florida, lightning killed 78 times more people during the past three decades than were killed by sharks.

Why Do People Think Shark Attacks Are on the Rise?

If you asked the average person on the street, that person would most likely say that shark attacks have exploded in recent years. Various theories are then invoked to account for this supposed phenomenon. Declines in the amount of fish (because of overfishing, particularly on the eastern seaboard of the United States) are said to have made sharks so desperate for food that they are now turning to human meat for sustenance. There is absolutely no proof to back up this assertion. Nor is there any evidence to support the idea that government restrictions against catching sharks has caused a rise in shark population. On the contrary, shark populations are dwindling because many sharks are being caught before they mature.

A third theory, with no more evidence to bolster it than the other two, is that commercial fishermen have shunned bull sharks, who are among the most predatory of all sharks. As a result, more bulls are now swimming in the seas, posing heightened risk to unwary humans. Indeed, this theory has an element of truth. Heavy-bodied, aggressive bulls certainly have no compunction about going after humans (or any other creature for that matter). Yet fishermen have not necessarily avoided bulls so much as bulls have avoided the fishermen. By swimming in shallow waters and even in

> **Shark Facts and Stats**
>
> Since 1994, the number of shark attacks in Florida has exceeded 20 in every year except 1996. The number peaked in 2000 at 38, including one death.

rivers and lakes, bulls are able to avoid the nets and lines that fishermen cast into the sea and thus present less of a target.

As I pointed out in Chapter 17, some people contend that shark feeding demonstrations have acclimated sharks to humans, making humans more vulnerable to attacks. Again, little in the way of evidence proves this case one way or another.

Where Do Shark Attacks Occur?

Most shark attacks take place near shore, inshore from a sandbar or between sandbars where sharks feed and can sometimes become trapped during low tide. Another potentially hazardous location is the steep drop-off of a reef where sharks congregate because that is also where their prey usually gathers. Spearfishing and surfing in areas inhabited by seals and other shark prey also attracts sharks to humans who find themselves cast into the role of prey instead of predator.

Who Gets Attacked?

Sharks certainly have attacked scuba divers, but they don't do so very often. In Australia, where diving is popular and sharks are plentiful, there have been only three recorded fatal attacks on divers during the last 20 years.

According to the book *Shark Attacks* by Mac McDiarmid, 9 out of 10 shark attacks happen within about 4 feet of the surface, where swimmers and anglers are more likely to be found. One third of those attacks are fatal. Great whites, you may recall, typically attack on or very close to the surface, ambushing their prey from below.

In certain parts of the world (off the coast of Australia and California in particular), *abalone* divers are at heightened risk because they work in cool waters frequented by seals, which are ideal conditions for attracting great whites. These divers also spend a great deal of time in the water. In California, observers began to notice a curious trend: Abalone divers were being attacked only north of Point Conception but not south. It turned out that local regulations banned the use of scuba diving equipment in the northern waters; that meant that the divers had to stay closer to the surface where they were at greater risk of shark attacks.

> **What Does It Mean?**
>
> **Abalone** is the name given to certain marine snails found on rocks near the shores of warm seas (except the western Atlantic). They feed on seaweed.

Spearfishing carries special risks as well. Spear fishermen are required by law to stay on the surface because they are not allowed to use scuba equipment. Moreover, spearfishing involves dying fish and loss of blood, which attracts sharks of all species, even those who are ordinarily nonaggressive.

The Three Kinds of Shark Attacks

There are three major kinds of unprovoked shark attacks, according to experts. The most common are hit-and-run attacks that typically occur in the breaking wave surf zone favored by swimmers and surfers. In hit-and-run attacks victims rarely get a glimpse of their attacker, and the shark usually inflicts a single bite or slash wound and then slips away, never to return.

The most likely explanation is that these attacks are cases of mistaken identity because of poor water visibility, breaking surf, strong currents, and other difficult environmental conditions. Sharks may be initially attracted by splashing, shiny jewelry, colored swimsuits, or contrasting tan and white skin (especially involving the soles of the feet) and become confused, mistaking a human for their normal prey. Once the sharks realize that they have made a mistake, they have no reason to add insult to injury by taking a second bite of such an unpalatable dish. Some of these attacks might also be related to dominance behaviors that have nothing to do with feeding and might be a way of establishing territorial possession or turf and then chasing off an intruder.

In most of these incidents, hit-and-run victims usually sustain relatively small lacerations, often below the knee, that are rarely life threatening. When they are life threatening, the lacerations have severed an artery, creating severe blood loss. Which sharks are responsible for these hit-and-run attacks is unclear because of the nature of the attack—the culprits slip away before they can be identified. In northern California, the culprit is most likely the great white preying on sea lions. In Florida, where 20 to 30 hit-and-run attacks take place each year, evidence implicates the bull (*Carcharhinus leucas*), black tip (*Carcharhinus limbatus*), and black-nose (*Carcharhinus acronotus*).

Shark Facts and Stats

About 9 out of every 10 shark attack victims are men, reflecting the fact that a greater proportion of men participate in recreational water sports than women.

The two other types of shark attack, which are less common and cause greater injuries and most of the fatalities, are bump-and-bite attacks and sneak attacks. Victims of these attacks are usually divers or swimmers in somewhat deeper waters. But in some parts of the world these attacks can occur closer to shore in shallow waters.

In bump-and-bite attacks sharks initially circle their intended victim, often bumping him or her just before they strike. Sneak attacks, as their name suggests, occur without any warning. In both types, the shark returns for second or third helpings, inflicting repeated bites and slashing wounds. As a result, the injuries are more serious and can often prove fatal. Whereas hit-and-run attacks are probably a result of mistaken identity, the other two types of attack appear to be intentional either because of feeding or antagonistic behaviors.

The Most Dangerous Sharks

Almost any large shark (meaning six feet or longer) can represent a potential threat to humans (though the biggest sharks, the basking and whale sharks, eat only plankton and small fish and are harmless to humans). Most species do not deliberately attack humans unless provoked. Of nearly 400 species, only 11 are known to have attacked humans, and of those only 3 have been implicated in the vast majority of recorded attacks: the great white (*Carcharodon carcharias*), the tiger (*Galeocerdo cuvier*), and the bull (*Carcharhinus leucas*). All of these sharks, which I discussed in Chapter 7, reach large sizes, consume large prey (marine mammals, sea turtles, and fishes), and range over vast distances, meaning that they can be found in waters all over the world. One male great white was tracked thousands of miles from the California coast to the warm waters off Hawaii, a distance of 2,300 miles. The attacks perpetrated by these three species are mostly of the bump-and-bite and sneak variety. Other species involved in attacks include the great hammerhead (*Sphyrna mokarran*), shortfin mako (*Isurus oxyrhynchus*), the Galapagos (*Carcharhinus galapagensis*), and the oceanic white tip (*Carcharhinus longimanus*).

Oceanic white tip sharks sometimes travel in schools and can be extremely savage. As their name implies, they prefer deeper waters, so they seldom attack swimmers close to shore. On the other hand, they have been held responsible for a large number of fatal attacks on shipwreck and air crash victims.

> **Shark Lore**
>
> Amanzimtoti, a popular swimming beach in Mozambique in Africa, has been given the nickname of "the worst shark attack beach on earth." Although the neighboring city of the same name is featured as a tourist destination, the beach has had more than 12 shark attacks. All have occurred in murky water.

The Fiercest Predator of All: The Great White

The great white is the largest shark and has a high percentage of fatal attacks. Great whites don't just confine their attacks to humans; they go after boats, too—a potentially dangerous situation because they have the bulk and ability to crush a large hull.

"[I]t is clear that a shark heading, even at a slow speed, for the hull of a boat can shatter it like a walnut," writes shark researcher Xavier Maniqut. "No wooden or plastic hull can withstand such a snoutbutt."

In Australia, sharks have long been known to bite gaping holes in hulls, rip off pieces of a boat, and leave large teeth embedded in hulls. In his book *Close to Shore*, Michael Capuzzo recalls a famous incident that took place in Australia in April, 1946. A man and his son were fishing from a boat off the coast of New South Wales when a 20-foot shark took the line and charged the boat, ripping off the rudder, flinging it high into the air, and savaging it "like a mad dog." Then the shark made off with the rudder between his teeth.

The next story, according to the correspondent, a retired professor of ocean engineering at Florida Atlantic University in Boca Raton, Florida, who posted it on a website devoted to sharks, may be exaggerated, but he attests to its credibility. In any case, it is too good to leave out. In March 1973, two orthopedic surgeons and an anesthesiologist, all ardent fishermen, were sailing in waters about 30 miles west of Isla Coiba in Panama. During this time, these waters were filled with blue crabs who were surfacing in large numbers to feed or mate, attracting a large number of predators including large silk snappers. In turn, these predators attracted larger predators who fed on them, the largest of whom were sharks. Many of these sharks measured 15 to 18 feet in length. One, however, appeared to the three physicians and their guide to be well over 20 feet, which they guessed had to be a great white.

After the first sighting, the suspected great white disappeared. As the four were eating lunch, two makos showed up about 100 to 150 feet apart. One of them reared up under the boat and started shaking it. It was all the men could do to keep from toppling overboard. When they were able to get their bearings, they looked up to find themselves staring at the head of a great white, who had the entire rear of the mako and the two 55 Johnson motors in his mouth. To keep himself from sliding aft the guide had his hand on the shark's nose. As the astounded doctors watched, the guide pushed off from the nose and grabbed the console. Then, with a mixture of acrobatic skill and sangfroid, the guide turned on both engines, still stuck in the shark's mouth, and threw them in gear, producing "great clouds of meat, cartilage, teeth, and blood [which] shot all over the men, the boat, and the water." The boat surged forward, but it didn't get very far. One engine was so

Shark Lore

A report from Steve Benevides, a sports fisherman, on witnessing a great white devouring a large elephant seal: "I could not believe anything could bleed that much. Blood, birds, water, guts, and fat flew in all directions at once, a truly grisly scene. There was nothing exciting about it. It was raw, primordial, and I felt like I was seeing something not intended for my eyes."

badly mangled that it stopped running, the other was partly operable. The great white (if indeed that was what the shark was) no longer posed any threat, however. He was sinking slowly into the water in a great pool of blood.

A Dissenting Opinion on Great Whites

In earlier chapters, I cited research carried out in the 1990s that suggested that great whites did not care for human flesh. They didn't consider it sufficiently tasty or fatty, and if they did attack humans it was because they mistook them for other prey such as elephant seals or sea lions. George Burgess, a shark biologist and director of the International Shark Attack File, conducted a worldwide study of great white attacks that shows that in the majority of the 170 recorded attacks on humans (56.9 percent of the cases) humans received only a single bite and were "spit out." The great white attacks on pinnipeds also can involve only a single bite. The shark is content to wait until the prey bleeds out, often dragging it as far as three quarters of a mile away from the point of attack.

According to Burgess, great whites do not necessarily have an aversion to humans. In a third of the attacks in his study, he notes that occasionally great whites bite their human victims repeatedly, clearly intending to feed. In such cases, "multiple bites occurred, including many instances in which victims were wholly consumed." "Humans are not uniformly unpalatable," he writes. It is difficult to take this as a compliment.

Great White Attacks on Inanimate Objects

Great whites don't always go after live prey. Great whites have attacked boats, buoys, and crab traps. The assortment of objects that they have bit into raises questions about their ability to distinguish between what might make a tasty and nutritious meal and what they would be better off foregoing altogether. These attacks have been reported in waters all over the world—Australia, Japan, South Africa, Canada, South America, and the United States—with reports of these attacks extending back to the middle of the nineteenth century.

In one July 1953 incident on the southeastern coast of Cape Breton Island, Nova Scotia, Canada, a great white stalked a dory for several days running, much to the astonishment of fishermen on the vessel. One witness said that the behavior of the shark reminded him of the way in which an African lion might stalk a Thomson's Gazelle on the savannah. As soon as the dory set out to sea the great white would reveal itself by sticking its dorsal fin out of the water astern of the boat. This pattern went on for several days until the great white suddenly attacked, smashing a 20-centimeter hole through the bottom of the boat. The two fishermen on board were flung into the sea—one drowned, the other was rescued after clinging to the hull of the dory for several hours. Interestingly—and to the relief of the survivor—the shark did not return after its initial assault. From the tooth left embedded in the hull scientists were able to deduce that the great white was about 12 feet in length and weighed about 1,200 pounds. The fact that the great white lost all interest in the vessel—and indeed in its human passengers—may lend some weight to the argument that they often make mistakes about the identity of the prey they choose to attack.

Shark Attacks and Air and Sea Disasters

Most shark attacks involving sea disasters when a plane or ship goes down in shark-infested water probably involve bump-and-bite and sneak attacks. In 1957, for instance, a Pan-Am plane crashed into the ocean about 1,200 miles from Hawaii. Of the 65 people on board, 19 were killed by sharks before rescuers could reach them. The following two stories show what can happen when survivors of shipwrecks are left in the water with sharks.

The USS *Indianapolis*

Possibly the most spectacular example dates back to World War II. The USS *Indianapolis* occupies a portentous place in the history of the Second World War. In July 1945, the ship with 1,200 men on board was entrusted with the fateful mission of delivering the components of the second and third atomic bombs, which would be dropped on Hiroshima and Nagasaki and force Japan's surrender. Once the boat had completed its mission, it set sail from Guam, bound for Leyte in the Philippines. On July 30, 1945, at about midnight, the USS *Indianapolis* was struck by a Japanese submarine and sank in 12 minutes.

With no time to put lifeboats into the water, the sailors donned their lifejackets and jumped into the sea. It wasn't long before sharks appeared, but they did not attack. Rather, they seemed to be checking out the sailors. About 900 men were alive at this point. "So we thought, well this is not too bad, we'll be picked up before the day is over," recalls Woody James, one of the survivors. "They know we are out there. They know we're due in the Philippines at 11:30 today, so if we don't show up they'll be out this afternoon looking for us. We're okay."

But they weren't okay. Because of the clandestine nature of the ship's mission, no one had alerted naval authorities that the ship had gone down. The next day passed, and the men remained afloat, desperately awaiting rescue, while sharks swam about them, still without attacking. During the days the heat was unremitting, but at night it was freezing cold. "Oh, you start praying for the sun to come up, and it finally did," James said. "Then a couple hours after that, we started praying for it to go down so we can cool off again. Then the sharks showed up again. They were all around and close, and we screamed and made all the commotion we could in the water and tried to scare them away, and it kind of quieted down." Another day went by. "In the afternoon the sharks got bad again. It was really terrible." That night the sailors heard anguished screams as men fell victim to the sharks. By morning's light, 100 men had been killed by sharks. It wasn't until August 8 that the surviving crewmembers of the *Indianapolis* were finally rescued—316 out of a total of 1,199 sailors.

A Deadly Attack in Australia

There are many harrowing accounts of shark attacks, but this one from Australia captures the horror in particularly vivid detail. The story centers on three people who were aboard a fishing trawler east of Queensland: Ray Boundy, the skipper; Dennis, the deckhand; and Linda, Dennis's girlfriend. On the night of July 25, 1983, their boat capsized, and they were thrown into the water. Using a surfboard, some foam, and a lifesaver, they managed to stay afloat. Although they spotted sharks in the water, they felt sure they would be rescued before the animals posed any threat.

But rescue didn't come. After circling them for a while, the sharks moved in for the attack. One bit Ray lightly on the knee. A few minutes later, a wave knocked the three off their surfboard. By the time they'd resurfaced, a shark had torn off Dennis's leg. Realizing that the blood would only draw other sharks and put his girlfriend and Ray in danger, Dennis began swimming away. Sharks attacked him a second time. "He was just screaming, and I couldn't believe that anyone could have that much guts to get his mates out," Ray recounted later. He described the attack "like watching a human being fed through a mincer."

At four in the morning, a shark began to circle the surfboard to which Linda and Ray were clinging. Suddenly, the shark attacked Linda, pulling her underwater. "It flung itself into the air and got the top half of her and turned her upside down," Ray recalled. "It was just so

Shark Facts and Stats
Is the threat of shark attacks overblown? Take San Francisco where there were 596 reported cases of dogs biting humans in 1998. By contrast, there were only 108 unprovoked shark attacks recorded along the Pacific Coast of North America during the *entire* twentieth century and only 8 of those attacks were fatal!

quick, and she squealed, and it shook her like a rag doll … She didn't say anything but was mumbling …." Fortunately, Ray caught a wave over a reef into shallow water and eluded a third attack. When he was finally rescued, he said he believed all the attacks were the work of one shark, but experts disagreed.

Sharks vs. Dolphins

While sharks and dolphins are not known to be natural enemies and usually keep a cautious distance, they do confront one another from time to time—even in captivity. Surprisingly, the dolphins occasionally emerge the winner in these contests. In the 1950s, for example, at the Miami Seaquarium, a sandbar shark began to show excessive interest in a newborn bottlenose dolphin calf, which impelled three adult male dolphins to attack it, butting the shark repeatedly in its stomach and gills until it died. In another reported case, a dolphin off the coast of California killed a two-foot leopard shark.

The adversarial relationship between the two species caught the interest of the U.S. Navy, and in the 1960s Naval specialists trained bottlenose dolphins to attack large sharks by butting their gill pouches, one of their most vulnerable spots. The dolphins turned out to be quick studies, learning how to attack sandbar, lemon, and nurse sharks.

But dolphins drew the line at bull sharks. It didn't matter that they had successfully mastered other sharks of similar shape or build—they would shun the bulls entirely. Researchers have concluded that dolphins are able to distinguish species of sharks that are dangerous to them and others that they can beat up without any difficulty. That some 75 percent of dolphins in the wild bear scars from shark bites suggests that they are not always able to escape those sharks that can dominate them, and presumably many of the dolphins didn't live to swim another day. The controversial Naval dolphin-training program, by the way (which inspired the movie *Day of the Dolphins*) has since been abandoned.

Antishark Devices

To keep sharks from preying on swimmers, authorities in charge of coastlines have experimented with different types of barriers and devices with varying degrees of success. In Natal, South Africa, for instance, nets have been employed to catch sharks before they can come too close to the shore. These nets, which are about 656 feet long and about 19 feet wide, are attached to buoys anchored to the seabed in water about 40 feet deep. These nets have reduced shark attacks by 90 percent, catching an average of 1,245 sharks per year—mainly Zambezi (bull sharks), great whites, and tigers who are responsible for most attacks. Australians have also tried protecting their beaches with nets. In Queensland these nets have killed more than 38,000 sharks. In 2000, 800 sharks were caught of which 65 percent were great whites or tigers, the species frequently implicated in shark attacks. The downside to using these nets is that the nets also snare dolphins, stingrays, and turtles. By attaching battery-operated pingers to the shark nets that scare off dolphins, researchers hope that they can reduce dolphin catches.

Shark Lore

For scuba divers, cameras make effective weapons to ward off sharks; otherwise a sawed-off pole or a shark billy club—yes, there are such things—can serve just as well.

Another antishark device called a Protective Oceanic Device POD (or SharkPOD for short) is useful to individual divers. It relies on electricity for its effect, and the technology was developed by an Australian company. Remember that sharks are very sensitive to electricity. What the SharkPOD does is to create an electric field around the user. As sharks approach the field, they begin to experience discomfort that intensifies as they come closer; they then begin to suffer unbearable muscle spasms that cause them to veer off.

Because SharkPOD is so expensive, however, it is used mainly by commercial divers. However, some companies are now developing similar but less costly devices for recreational diving and boating. Some researchers also contemplate a time when an entire beach area can be protected from sharks by an electrical barrier.

These devices are controversial, though. Some evidence suggests that the user has to be in the water for it to work because several attacks have occurred when the device failed to function effectively when the diver was getting out of the water. A related problem is that some divers, unaware that sharks were in the area, simply never bothered to turn on the devices.

The Big Bite

Just how much power does the bite of a shark actually have—and is it all that it's cracked up to be? And is a shark bite more dangerous than the bite of lions, say, or other predatory animals? The answer is that no one really knows because there is little hard data to draw on to settle these questions.

To measure the power of a bite experts refer to four basic measurements: strength, pressure, force, and power. The "strength" of a bite is defined as resistance to

continues

continued

being deformed. That is to say, you have to be careful of biting off more than you can chew or else you might do damage to your teeth or jaw. If you chip a tooth or lose a filling by biting down on a hard bagel, for example, you will immediately understand what is meant by the strength of a bite.

Then there is the "force" of a bite to consider. Force may be defined as a "push" or "pull" in a particular direction. "Pressure" may be defined as force as measured by a particular area of the jaws and teeth. Similarly, "power" may be defined as force as measured by a particular period of time.

On the basis of these measurements, it appears that shark jaws are actually *less* strong than those of either humans or crocodiles. That's because it takes considerably less force to warp or distort the jaws of sharks than those of either humans or crocodiles. (On the other hand, it's probably easier to shatter the jaws of humans and crocodiles than those of sharks with a forceful blow.)

Measuring the pressure of a shark bite is much harder given the complex ways in which muscles, connective tissue, and cartilage move together. Assessing the force and power of a bite is also problematic; how do you measure the duration of maximum force during a bite? Moreover, sharks do not necessarily exercise maximum force each time they take a bite. On the contrary, sharks often test unfamiliar objects, taking a nip rather than clamping down with all the force or power it can muster.

Perhaps the best known experiments on shark bite pressure were carried out by James Snodgrass and Perry Gilbert in 1965. The researchers employed a special device called a shark "gnathodynamometer" or bite-meter. The device is basically a steel cylinder with a soft aluminum core, with 12 steel ball-bearings fitted into grooves on its surface. This contraption was then cocooned in four plates of polyvinyl chloride and wrapped in mackerel so that the sharks would go near it. Three species of sharks were given the opportunity to try the treat—a tiger, a lemon, and a dusky. The researchers then examined the depth of indentations the ball bearings pressed into the aluminum core after the shark had bitten into the fish. The maximum pressure for the tip of a single tooth, was the equivalent of three metric tons per square centimeter.

This measurement has been interpreted as the equivalent of about 18 tons per square inch, which would mean that a shark with a 10-inch mouth could exert a total force of 180 tons. But that would be incorrect since the device only measured the pressure *at the tooth tips*. It would be a mistake to multiply this over the total area of the mouth. In other words, the pressure is maximized by being con-centrated in a very small amount of space. Analogously, a knife is effective, not because of the total area of the blade but because when you apply pressure all the force is concentrated on the edge of the blade.

The Snodgrass-Gilbert experiment proved to have some limitations. For one thing, they were unable to determine to what extent the pressure of the sharks' bites was absorbed or distributed by either the fish or PVC wrapping. Nor could they be certain whether the sharks were biting in the same way they would ordi-narily. The novelty of the device might have caused them to bite more carefully than they would if the prey had been familiar. Even the proximity of the researchers might have affected the results of the study.

Until more sophisticated methods of measuring the strength and power of shark bites are devised, we will have to rely mainly on anecdotal evidence. Most victims of shark bites report that shark bites are typically not very forceful—excluding, of course, those of great whites or other aggressive predators—and appear to be either intended to be threatening or exploratory rather than to inflict damage. So the question remains open as to whether sharks are capable of exerting even greater bite pressures than what researchers have recorded to date.

Preventing Shark Attacks

You can take some sensible precautions to minimize the chance of being attacked by sharks:

- Stay out of water at night, at dusk, or before sunrise, when sharks are most active.

- Because sharks like to attack solitary targets, you are better off swimming in groups. The same advice holds true for divers.

- Don't wander too far from shore where it's more difficult to get help.

- Don't swim if you are bleeding from an open wound. (Shark experts disagree as to whether it is safe if you are menstru-ating.)

 **Shark Lore**

Scuba divers are advised not to dive with dolphins because sharks may attack dolphins—and the human divers in their midst.

- Shiny jewelry is known to attract sharks and should not be worn in the water.

- Steer clear of waters where seabirds are diving, where there is bait fishing, or where seals or sea lions congregate.

- Avoid excess splashing because it can lure sharks.

- Exercise caution between sandbars or steep drop-offs, which sharks often favor because their prey are often found in these areas in large numbers.

- Remember that shark attacks occur rarely, but they may present a danger if they are provoked, intentionally or inadvertently. By taking proper precautions and behaving sensibly in the water you can minimize the chances of an attack. Most sharks want nothing to do with you—don't give them an excuse to decide that you are a subject of interest, after all.

The Least You Need to Know

- Most shark attacks on humans take place in shallow waters, affecting mainly swimmers, surfers, and fishermen.

- Many shark attacks inflict only minor injury, such as grazes and flesh wounds.

- Three shark species pose the greatest danger to humans: great whites, bulls, and tigers.

- Great whites are the largest and deadliest predator of all and have been known to crush boat hulls.

- By taking sensible precautions while swimming and diving, you can do a good deal to avoid shark attacks.

Chapter 19

More Dangerous Creatures and Deadly Beauties

In This Chapter

- ◆ Sharks versus other dangerous water creatures
- ◆ The threat to humans from venomous marine life
- ◆ The most lethal marine creatures
- ◆ How to avoid dangerous sea creatures

Sharks garner all the fame for water attacks because of the media frenzy that follows any shark attack. In most cases, the shark is not the aggressor. Most hit-and-run attacks occur in the surf where a shark has been attracted by splashing or tempted by a hooked fish trying to escape from an angler. Shark attacks are usually a case of the shark mistaking a human for its normal prey. For example, evidence points to the shark confusing the surfer on his board with the shark's favorite meal of sea lions. Sometimes an attack occurs because people have invaded the sharks' territory, especially when the sharks gather for breeding.

Open water attacks are different. In this case, an accident at sea (a boat capsizing or a plane crash) usually results in injured passengers bleeding in the water, making them susceptible to becoming shark prey. (Actually, the sound of a crash or ship collision is very effective in drawing sharks from quite a distance, even before blood gets into the water.) Victims of unwarranted shark attacks have gruesome injuries and oftentimes bleed to death. These attacks make headlines.

Although sharks garner all the attention, they are by no means the only deadly creatures in the sea. The bite or sting of other deadly sea creatures is not a hit-and-run affair. Attacks by these creatures are usually defensive in nature, a reaction to the swimmer or diver who, unwittingly or not, invades their territory.

Dangerous or Deadly?

Pioneer shark diver Carl Roessler feels that …

> [E]veryone knows that sharks are dangerous because sharks have countless, effective press agents. Thousands of magazine articles, TV documentaries, and Hollywood spectaculars have told their story brilliantly. When you have Steven Spielberg telling the world how dangerous you are, your reputation is assured. There are many other marine creatures, though, whose armament is also lethal, but almost always defensive. For that reason, as well as the sharks hogging the limelight, most of the other dangerous marine animals are barely known.

Any creatures who emit toxin can potentially be deadly. Whether a creature is dangerous or turns deadly is a subject of conjecture. In one situation, the creature may not kill its victim because the individual has an immunity to the venom or receives a nonlethal dose; another person might succumb to a stronger, more lethal dose from the same kind of animal. The size of the victim, the circumstances in which he or she is attacked, and the dosage of the toxin all play a key role in the outcome of the encounter. Although we have tried to make a distinction between dangerous and deadly creatures in this chapter, bear in mind the possibility that categorization is not always a matter of black or white.

Taste of the Bizarre

Jellyfish have no bones, cartilage, heart, blood, or brain. Their bells are 95 percent water. They are the real "no-brainer."

The Box Jellyfish

The box jellyfish (also known as the marine stinger or sea wasp) can kill a human in four minutes. And box jellyfish are fast—they can swim in bursts of up to 5 feet per second.

The bell, or body, of a fully grown box jellyfish can be as large as a basketball, with trailing tentacles reaching as far as 10 feet in the water. Although the bell is difficult to see, the far-reaching tentacles are almost invisible. A mere brush with one of as many as 60 transparent tentacles is usually deadly. Each tentacle carries millions of poison capsules called *nematocysts*, which is enough poison to kill 60 adults! In some cases, the poison from a box jellyfish's tentacles causes the victim's heart to slow down or stop almost immediately. The box jellyfish also attacks the respiratory and lymphatic systems.

Each tiny half-millimeter nematocyst, when released in $^3/_{1,000}$ of a second, acts like a hypodermic needle injecting its poison directly into the skin. Unlike venomous sea snakes, who usually bite in only one place, box jellyfish can inject their poison over a large portion of the body, making treatment much more difficult. Antivenin is available, but it has to be administered quickly in order to be successful.

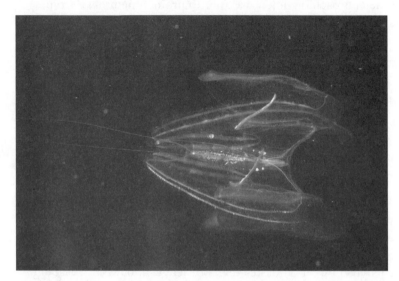

Each tentacle of the box jelly-fish carries enough poison to kill as many as 60 people.

Shark Facts and Stats

You should know these key facts about the box jellyfish:

- ◆ Box jellyfish tend to be seasonal and swim in shallow water.
- ◆ Covering your body (many swimmers in Australia use pantyhose) is an easy way to prevent stinging.
- ◆ Vinegar or antivenin needs to be applied immediately in the event of an attack; if neither is available, urine is recommended.
- ◆ Never wipe the injury. Wiping only spreads the nematocysts, increasing the size of the injury.
- ◆ Shortness of breath is a symptom of a potential fatality.

The Lion's Mane Jellyfish

The most genuinely lethal nonshark marine creature that Roessler ever encountered was the lion's mane jellyfish. While he was diving near Busuanga in the southwestern Philippines, a hurricane in the area whipped up the seas. The captain of the boat he was on sought refuge in a sheltered bay. That night, although the ocean was still troubled, the sky was clear. After dinner, the divers made their way to the upper deck as a full moon blazed overhead. To their astonishment, the entire surface of the water around the boat was writhing with thousands and thousands of pail-sized pink jellyfish! The divemaster explained that millions of jellyfish infest the interior shallow lagoons if they sense the approach of violent weather to protect themselves from waves that could toss them around and possibly damage them.

The following morning Roessler woke to leaden skies, filled with anticipation of being able to photograph as many jellyfish as possible before the weather again deteriorated. During his first dive, juvenile pink jellyfish were everywhere, and he snapped pictures with abandon. About midway through the dive, he spotted a monstrous white jellyfish with iridescent blue trim. This big daddy had a diameter the size of a 55-gallon drum. At the time Roessler didn't have any idea what kind of jellyfish he was observing, but he instinctively felt the menace of its majesty and size.

A year later, he sent a picture of the jellyfish to the Monterey Bay Aquarium to be used for an exhibit. The photo editor called a couple of days later and said, "By the way, did you know you were diving with lion's mane?" "No," Roessler replied, "But it looked pretty dangerous." "Dangerous? It could have killed you in 90 seconds!" Roessler may be one of the very few to have had such an encounter with the lion's mane jellyfish. These jellyfish might kill faster than box jellyfish, but they don't plague beaches the way box jellyfish do.

Shark Facts and Stats

Here are some facts about the deadly lion's mane you should keep in mind:

- Lion's manes are a lethal form of jellyfish found in temperate waters of Australia but are known to flourish as far north as the Arctic.
- Lion's manes have stinging tentacles that can extend more than 20 feet that are used to ensnare prey.
- The sting of a lion's mane can bring on death, possibly faster than even box jellies.

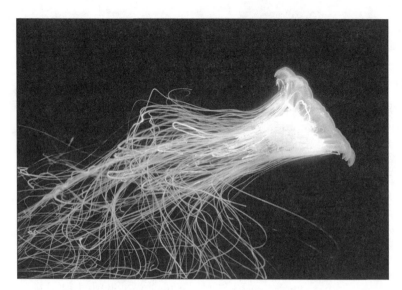

The lion's mane jellyfish is one of the most lethal forms of marine life.

(Photo courtesy of Monterey Bay Aquarium Foundation)

Lion's mane jellyfish have bells as large as 8 feet in diameter, and their tentacles can reach more than 20 feet. Juveniles are pink, turning red as they mature and becoming brownish-purple as adults. They are found in the temperate waters of Australia and extend as far north as the Arctic.

Lion's mane tentacles extend outwards in a fan-like pattern, trapping all but the smallest fish. Adults frequently travel in the company of small fish that live near the bell while avoiding the stinging tentacles. This proximity gives the fish protection from other predators because few will approach a large lion's mane jellyfish. This kind of symbiotic relationship is known as *commensalism* because one organism benefits from another and neither suffers any harm from the association.

The Blue-Ringed Octopus

One of the deadliest creatures in the ocean is the blue-ringed octopus. The two known species of blue-ringed octopus are the larger eight-inch *Hapalochlaena lunulata* and the smaller, more common one-ounce *Hapalochlaena maculosa*. Scientists have studied blue-ringed octopuses and have discovered that they are quick learners with a keen memory and the ability to solve problems.

Taste of the Bizarre

In Thailand, a tourist was found dead on the beach. He had not drowned, and there were no signs of major trauma. A small incision was found on his shoulder. It is suspected that he found a blue-ringed octopus in a tidal pool, which he picked up to carry on his shoulder. It bit him, and he most likely died in a few minutes.

Usually found in shallow coral reefs and tidal pools in Australia, blue-ring octopuses look deceptively cute and come in shades of brown or yellow. They are the size of a golf ball with a tiny parrotlike beak strong enough to bite through a wetsuit. But don't pick one up—by the time you see the electric blue rings, it's too late!

The bite of the small blue-ringed octopus renders you paralyzed and unable to breathe in three minutes. Initial symptoms of poisoning include nausea, hazy vision, and blindness, loss of the sense of touch, and the inability to swallow or speak. Sometimes the victim has fixed, dilated pupils. Even if the victim is still conscious, he or she may be incapable of responding. That's quite a trip in a few minutes.

What's Their Poison?

The blue-ringed octopus bite causes a small laceration with no more than a tiny drop of blood and little or no discoloration. Bites are usually reported as being painless. Sometimes the victim doesn't even know that he has been bitten. Nonetheless, the absence of pain doesn't begin to reflect the severity of the injury. The blue-ringed octopus has neuromuscular paralyzing tetrodotoxin venom that blocks sodium channels in the victim, causing motor paralysis. Scientists have determined that a single adult blue-ringed octopus can fatally paralyze 10 humans. The last memory the victim experiences is the sight of blue rings—they become visible only when the octopus is about to attack.

Blue-ringed octopuses have the unique quality of having two types of venom. The one they use most effectively for killing crabs is considered relatively harmless to humans. The second one is similar to the toxin found in puffer fish and is sometimes used as a defense against predatory fish. Both types of venom are found in one of two glands, each the size of the octopus's brain.

> **Shark Facts and Stats**
>
> Invisible tentacles drifting yards away from the bell of the jellyfish or the painless bite of the blue-ringed octopus can kill and can do so less violently and more quickly than any shark attack. Both jellyfish and octopuses are found in shallow water and tidal pools, an area frequented by swimmers or beach-goers.

The poison, contained in the octopus's saliva, is frequently not injected. Blue-ringed octopuses either secrete the poison in the vicinity of their prey, wait until it is immobile, and then devour it or else they envelop the prey with their eight tentacles and then deliver the fatal bite. Each of tentacles has a suction cup that the octopus controls by creating a vacuum to either maintain or relax its grip.

No antidote exists. The only possible treatment is heart massage and artificial respiration until the poison has worked its way out of the body, which can take hours. Envenomizations may require supportive treatment including mechanical ventilation.

Most divers are aware of the nasty reputation of the blue-ringed octopus, but they seldom see them because the octopuses prefer deeper depths. However, they can appear unexpectedly. In one instance, Dr. Roy Caldwell of the University of California at Berkeley was studying mantis shrimp at Lizard Island off the North Queensland coast of Australia. While collecting promising looking rubble on the bottom, he would signal his teenage daughter with a few yanks on the line to pull up the collection bag, transfer the rubble to plastic bins, and send the bag back down to be refilled. One morning she mentioned that one rock oyster shell "had something soft and squishy inside." At first he assumed it was a small sea cucumber and dismissed the comment. Suddenly encountering a blue-ringed octopus, he quickly ascended, and using his dive mask to scoop up the octopus, he gingerly transferred the creature to a bucket.

Don't Be Fooled by Size

Deadly marine creatures aren't always big. Roessler was photographing tiny reef creatures in the Philippines when his presence flushed a blue-ringed octopus out of a coral crevice:

> Blue-rings are anything but aggressive and would hardly fill your hand if fully splayed. The stories of their killing people have always come from the victims handling the octopus; they will bite to defend themselves, then infuse the wound with a deadly neurotoxin. It's a bad way to go.

Shark Facts and Stats

The following list summarizes what you should know about blue-ringed octopuses:

- They inhabit easily accessible tidal pools.
- Their colorful appearance can attract the curious beach-goer.
- They can use one of two types of venom, one that they spit to immobilize their prey and another that produces a deadlier but painless bite.
- The blue rings for which they are named are visible only when they attack.
- Their poison has no antidote.
- Victims can die in three minutes unless artificial respiration is applied for the lengthy period it takes for the venom to pass through the system.

Blue-ringed octopuses can be found ranging from the seas of Japan to Australia. They are most frequently sighted while hunting for their favorite meals: crabs found in tidal pools. The octopuses camouflage themselves in the lighter colored rock and sand, waiting to spit their venomous saliva if a crab scurries into a tight space. If they're picked out of the pool, stepped on, or otherwise provoked, the disturbed creatures turn yellow and display those bright blue rings in the blink of an eye.

The blue-ringed octopus has two types of venom: one for killing crabs and the other to defend against predatory fish (and occasionally intrusive humans).

The Saltwater Crocodiles

Known to Australians as "salty," the world's largest reptile has a broad, stubby snout and ferocious-looking, cone-shaped teeth. Although a saltwater crocodile's average length is approximately 12 feet, larger males have been reported. Grayish brown with brownish yellow sides, saltwater crocs have rows of bony scales on their neck, with webbed back feet to aid in swimming. Transparent eyelids enable them to clearly see their prey underwater. Scientists think they can survive to the ripe old age of 100. The habitat of the Australian saltwater crocodile is primarily the coastal areas and rivers in the northern part of Australia and throughout Asia. These crocodiles are capable of swimming thousands of miles.

> **Shark Facts and Stats**
>
> Temperature determines the sex of the baby crocodile. If the egg is nested in a mount-shaped nest made of mud and plants at 31.6 degrees Celsius, it will become a male. If the temperature is hotter or colder, the egg will be a female.

Saltwater crocodiles are most frequently spotted on a log or muddy riverbank with their mouths wide open. Although they hardly make for glamorous models for toothpaste, this posture enables crocodiles to regulate their body temperature.

The saltwater crocodile's feeding strategy is to lie still near water's edge and then pounce upon a victim in the blink of an eye. The usual prey of younger crocs is fish and crustaceans such as crabs. Adult saltwater crocodiles attack and eat anything that passes by first overpowering and then drowning them with teeth designed for holding. Although their typical prey is fish, reptiles, and mammals such as the Australian dingo or wallaby, they have been known to kill domestic cattle and, yes, people. (Their cousins, the alligators found in southeastern United States, are known to prey on small pets wandering by a pond or water hole on a golf course.) Not until the prey has drowned will the crocodile break the animal into smaller pieces with a violent flicking of his head to snap or break bones. Although very few people are devoured by crocs, about 12 unwitting people have wandered into a crocodile's path to meet their demise in the past 20 years.

A Personal Encounter with a Dangerous Croc

A dangerous saltwater crocodile had been sighted previously in the underwater cave called "Mirror Pond" on Mane, one of many mangrove islands in the Russell chain in the Solomon Islands. "We do not know the behavior of this man-eating crocodile," admitted our divemaster Scott Waring. The crocodile usually could be seen lying on one of the cave's ledges. Waring advised us that the crocodile had previously attacked a snorkeler, but it had never bothered a scuba diver. But he added a cautionary note: "As you follow me through the 250-foot underwater passageway to reach the cave, please leave me plenty of room to escape!"

Then Waring's wife, Diane, put in, "It's only a small croc and it isn't always there." Confidence bolstered, some of us foolishly decided there was "safety in numbers." Those steel tanks on our backs made us feel invincible. There were five of us altogether including the divemaster and myself. I brought up the rear, figuring in case of an evacuation it was "last in, first out."

Following in single file, we threaded the twisting passage at a depth of 30 feet, carefully avoiding the stinging fire coral growing on the wall. As we approached the entrance to the underwater cave, the passage wall narrowed while still leaving an open slot extending to the surface of the ocean. The opening provided sunlight and clear visibility as we navigated the passageway.

At the end of the passage the cave widened to about 30 feet in diameter. The ceiling of the cave extended above the surface of the water. Mangrove roots gripped the coral around the edges of the pond. Branches of felled trees cluttered the water, providing lots of hiding places for the crocodile.

continues

continued

Waring immediately sighted the crocodile resting on a ledge and signaled for our attention. I looked up to see a six-foot, man-eating crocodile lunge into the water, swim across the surface of the cave, and then climb onto another ledge. When I surfaced for a better view, the crocodile lunged back into the pond. Adrenaline pumping and hearts pounding, the five of us spontaneously backpedaled out of the cave, retracing our path through the passage.

From Diane's use of the word "small" to describe the creature, I had imagined a 12-inch aquarium-size croc. What had I been thinking? It is rare that a diver would ever venture into circumstances where an underwater passage would lead into the interior of an atoll and surface at a pond inhabited by a crocodile. In any event, we should have rethought our bravado and not entered the passage at all.

Shark Facts and Stats

Here's what you need to know about "salty":

- Saltwater crocs lying on the shore with their mouths wide open are not sleeping. They are thermoregulating (not unlike birds) their body temperature while they wait for prey.
- Salty has an appetite for anything; the bigger the croc, the bigger the prey.
- Crocs drown their prey before they break them apart to devour them.
- Odds of surviving a crocodile attack are rare. Give the saltwater croc a wide berth.

The Textile Cone

The textile cone is an attractive-looking snail, but its beauty is deceiving. A nocturnal, carnivorous feeder, this species of snail lives in warm, tropical waters such as Hawaii. Textile cones feed on worms, mollusks, and small fish.

Cones detect prey by using a siphon that contains chemoreceptors. When prey is within reach, textile cones use their proboscis to inject venom. Within the snail, a tubular duct that is several times longer than the snail itself is attached to a muscular bulb, which is thought to be capable of providing the necessary force to inject the venom.

Taste of the Bizarre _____

Before the days when it became politically incorrect to touch or take shells or anything else from the sea bottom, a naive man on one of Carl Roessler tours picked up a textile cone and stuck his "treasure" inside his glove. Back on the boat, Roessler and crew were horrified to see what might have been a deadly encounter. Fortunately, it was daylight, and the cone was sleeping or didn't feel threatened.

The proboscis impales the prey with its harpoon-like tooth and tethers itself to the victim; then the proboscis pierces the tissue that's been exposed. The venom paralyzes within a second or two, leaving little opportunity for the prey to escape. Once the prey is paralyzed, the textile cone retracts the cord by which the prey is attached and engulfs the prey through the radular opening of the proboscis. The cone's stomach can distend to make digestion easier. The textile cone shell can quickly reload for multiple envenomations.

Shark Facts and Stats

Here are some facts about the textile cone snail:

◆ Textile cones rank high on collectors' lists because of their beauty.

◆ Encounters with textile cones are rare because they are usually found in deeper water and feed at night.

◆ Cones do not extend their proboscis until they attack, so divers might consider the shell to be empty when the snail is retracted into his shell.

◆ Cones and any other shells should never be touched.

Fatal Sea Snakes

Sea snakes are found in the tropical and warm temperatures of the Indian and Pacific oceans, the Persian Gulf, throughout Asia, and extending from Africa to America, and from Siberia to Tasmania. But they are not found in the Atlantic Ocean. Sea snakes used to be common in Australia and tropical Pacific waters; however, the demand for snakeskin goods has put them in danger, not unlike what has happened with sharks. The trade in snakeskin persists even today. Because the animals reproduce very slowly, the population will need years to recover even if it is left alone.

Most sea snakes are three to four feet long and have round scaly bodies with flat tails and valve-like nostril flaps. They are not considered aggressive unless provoked. There are two main kinds of sea snakes. The sea kraits are brightly marked serpents with black, blue, yellow, or white bars. They return to land to lay eggs above the tidewaters and to bask. Quite mobile on land, sea kraits are efficient climbers of mangroves.

The other kind is known as a true sea snake. These snakes bear their young live and avoid ever coming ashore. When these snakes are accidentally washed ashore, they are totally helpless and unable to move. These live-bearing species give birth to only 2 to 10 young at a time. There are approximately 50 species of true sea snakes, and all are venomous, although only a few species have been implicated in serious human envenomations or fatalities. One species, the yellow-bellied sea snake, occasionally forms massive floating islands consisting of thousands of intertwined individuals. Fish that mistake the island for a shelter provide easy prey for these snakes.

Several features enable sea snakes to adapt and survive in aquatic environments. Their tails, when flattened into a paddle-shaped oar, propel them through the water. Their nostrils are equipped with a valve to keep them closed while the snakes are submerged. Fangs, found in poisonous land snakes, are absent in sea snakes. Sea snakes can commonly hold their breath for half an hour, but they have been known to stay underwater for more than an hour. Some people confuse sea snakes with eels and other fish. Eels can be quite similar in shape to snakes, but they have gills and smaller scales. Like the turtle, sea snakes are air-breathing reptiles and need to resurface for air.

By nature, sea snakes are shy and not aggressive in the water. Most reported cases of fatal bites from sea snakes involve fishermen who catch them inadvertently in trawl nets. These snakes have also been known to lose their sense of humor during their mating season in winter and become quite aggressive. They may be very persistent in following a diver, and they require many kicks to discourage their approach.

The Danger of Sea Snakes

A popular misconception suggests that sea snakes are harmless because their mouths are too small to bite. The truth is that they can easily swallow fish more than twice the diameter of their necks and can easily bite a diver's hand. Their venom is a heat-stable, nonenzymatic protein that blocks neuromuscular transmissions. Symptoms may occur in minutes or be delayed as long as eight hours after a bite. The victim may experience nausea, difficulty speaking and swallowing, blurred vision, weakness, numbness, or stiffness. More severe reactions involve paralysis, drooping eyelids, dark brown urine, lockjaw, and difficulty breathing. The venom is 2 to 10 times as toxic as that of a cobra, but less is delivered at a time: Only about one-fourth of persons bitten develop symptoms.

Sea snakes have a delivery apparatus developed for small prey and so they are not very hazardous to humans. Nonetheless, one type of sea snake, the olive sea snake, has been reported to be curious about divers and has been known to entangle itself around a diver's legs. Most likely, these animals follow divers to pick up an easy meal from stirred-up bottom sediments—another good reason to control your buoyancy.

The puncture wound from a sea snake bite usually shows one to four marks, although as many as 20 are possible. The snakes' short fangs, easily dislodged from their sockets, may be embedded in the wound or wetsuit. Victims typically experience a symptom-free interval of 10 minutes to several hours. If generalized symptoms do not appear in six to eight hours, significant poisoning has likely not occurred. The initial symptoms may be euphoria and anxiety with restlessness, thirst, nausea, and vomiting. More severe symptoms may develop and extend centrally from the bite. These include painful muscle spasms and ascending paralysis that may lead to respiratory failure and death.

Sea snakes are known to be shy, except during mating season, and human deaths from their bites are relatively rare.

Photographer Robert Yin encountered a banded sea snake in Fiji. He admits to being somewhat nervous when he thought about these snakes being considered one of the most poisonous in the world. "Ten years ago, if someone had asked me to go diving in a place infested with sea snakes," he said, "I would have wondered what I had done to offend this person so that he wanted me dead. Now that I have learned much about the behavior and good nature of these curious reptiles, I would not pass up a chance to dive into a snake pit." So he cautiously followed the snake as he tried to photograph it, even knowing its venom could be 2 to 10 times more toxic than that of a cobra—and a cobra can kill an elephant.

Very few people are ever bitten by sea snakes, however, and if bitten, some victims never show any symptoms. How can this be? Sea snakes have the ability to control the amount of venom they inject when they bite. This ability allows them to hold onto their venom and use it for acquiring a meal rather than for defense. Their small teeth are designed for biting and holding fish and usually cannot penetrate a wetsuit. As a result, the dosage is usually too low to do harm. No specific antivenin exists for sea snake bites but most general antivenins are effective.

How much of a threat sea snakes pose to humans can vary considerably, as the following account by Carl Rosseler illustrates:

> We had a divemaster bitten in the Coral Sea. He had placed an Astrotia Stokesii sea snake (very potent) into a pail with an onion sack over it to keep the snake in. The snake started to escape; when the divemaster tried to push it back under cover, it bit him. He stood there, waiting to die. After a few minutes went by, and then hours, we realized that the snake had not envenomated the bite. Later, a scientist told me that if sea snakes killed everyone they bit, who would be alive to carry the tale that they were dangerous? So they venom-bite to eat and digest food, but unless they are in fear of death, they bite only to warn that they are dangerous and running out of patience.

Shark Facts and Stats

Hunter Rock in the Philippines, a seamount buried 60-feet beneath the sea, is inhabited only by sea snakes. The snakes live in holes and feed at night on the water's surface. Although they are not aggressive, they need to return to the surface to breathe. Divers are advised to view them in their holes and avoid running into them while they are coming up for air.

The Adaptive Secrets of the Sea Snake

Sea snakes possess a neurologic toxin. The question has been raised as to whether this is an aquatic adaptation. Remember, the snakes' nostrils are sealed while underwater. If fish escape their bites, sea snakes, unlike their land cousins, cannot follow a scent trail to recover their lost prey. That is why they need to be effective at killing or paralyzing their prey quickly on their very first bite.

Other scientists debate the aquatic adaptation of the sea snake and believe they originally developed their neurotoxic venom as a terrestrial species. According to one researcher, Dr. Martin S. Farber, "the ability of sea snakes to seal their nostrils, a trait common to other vertebrates which have made the transition from a terrestrial to an aquatic existence, is an adaptation to an undersea existence." He also expresses some doubt as to whether the snake's "ability to bear live young is truly an aquatic adaptation, as other sea snakes which can be terrestrial also have that ability."

What Does It Mean?

Snake blenny fish, with their long, thin snakelike bodies, have developed a venom of their own that is similar to that of sea snakes. Biologists call this **convergence,** a phenomenon that occurs when two animals from different branches of the evolutionary tree adopt similar characteristics because they have similar lifestyles.

Shark Facts and Stats

Here is what you need to know about sea snakes:

♦ Sea snakes are rarely aggressive unless provoked.

♦ Sea snakes can deliver a potent venom but usually do so in low doses, and many humans attacked experience no symptoms because the dosage is so low.

♦ At higher dosages of sea snake venom, victims may experience symptoms ranging from nausea and numbness to paralysis and lockjaw and rarely death.

♦ Most antivenins are effective against the sea snake toxin.

The Deadly Stonefish

The deadly stonefish, *Synancea horrida*, is a member of a family of warty ambushers who remain utterly motionless and indistinguishable from the background clutter of a busy reef. They are found on reefs from Australia and the Solomon Islands to the Indian Ocean. They can be dull brown, purple, or florid pink and grow to an average size of 16 inches in length, but some have been recorded nearly twice this size.

Approximately 20 species of stonefish belong to the scorpionfishes (*Scorpaeniformes*) family. All have similar needlelike dorsal fin spines. This undisputedly ugly species has a rough, scaleless body, lumps and fleshy growths, a large, upward-turning head, and protuberant eyes deeply set in the bony hollows of the head. The stonefish's large upturned mouth is partially disguised by a notched fringe of skin. Stonefish use their large front fins to scoop out a depression in the sand or mud and lie motionless awaiting their prey. As their name suggests, the coloring and shape of stonefish camouflage them perfectly as they lie half-buried among stones or in rock crevices.

Carl Roessler recalls his most memorable sighting of a stonefish. It happened one day as he was swimming along a remote beach on the north coast of Papua New Guinea with nine other divers. Halfway through the dive, one of his clients settled down onto the reef to take a picture. As his leg came closer, a huge lump of reef moved! Grabbing the diver's leg, Roessler pulled it away just as the diver was about to put it down on the flaring, poison-tipped spines of a huge pink stonefish. And the stonefish wasn't alone—another stonefish was nearby. The divers proceeded to photograph the two camouflaged fish until they ran out of film. After swimming back to the beach to reload their cameras, they returned to the reef to take more stonefish pictures, but not one of the 10 divers could locate those two big camouflaged stonefish on a reef that wasn't more than 50 yards long!

Stonefish are easily mistaken for coral reefs where they lie in wait for prey; severe injury can result from coming into contact with their venomous spines.

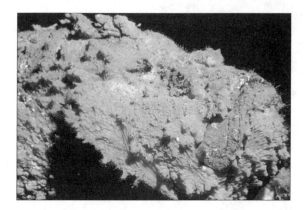

The stonefish is acknowledged to be one of the most venomous fish in the waters of the Indo-Pacific and northern Australian waters, from Brisbane to 400 miles north of Perth. Stonefish may be resting disguised in the exposed sand and mud of tidal inlets or at depths of around 40 feet. While lying on the seabed, they become totally camouflaged appearing as part of an encrusted rock.

Stonefish feed on small fish and shrimp. When prey swim by, the camouflaged stonefish gulps them down with lightning speed, in less than a second.

To protect themselves from attacks by bottom-feeding sharks and rays, stonefish have 13 venomous spines lined as a row along their back. For this reason the stonefish is dangerous if stepped on or caught. When pressure is applied to the spines, the stonefish's 22 venomous glands automatically expel their contents. It takes a few weeks for these glands to regenerate and recharge.

The venom creates excruciating pain, and the accompanying swelling can cause irreparable tissue damage. The severity of the symptoms depends on the depth of penetration and the number of spines involved. If the encounter is severe, there is also muscle weakness, temporary paralysis, and shock, which may result in death if not treated. Fatalities are known to have occurred in the Indo-Pacific region but not in Australian waters.

You can protect yourself from stonefish injury by wearing thick-soled shoes and treading very lightly—spines can pierce through a shoe! Treatment can be as simple as immersing the stung area into hot water, but antivenin is required if the injury is severe.

Shark Facts and Stats

Here is what you need to know about the stonefish:

- Stonefish can be dangerous if they are stepped on accidentally and their sharp spines penetrate the skin and release their venom.
- The severity of the symptoms depends on the depth of penetration and the number of spines involved. Severe injuries can cause muscle weakness, temporary paralysis, and shock, which may result in death if not treated.
- Thick-soled shoes are necessary to protect against penetration by the spines; the spines are capable of piercing lighter-soled shoes.
- Treatment of less severe injuries can be as simple as moistening the injured area with hot water. In more severe injuries, antivenin is required.

The Prickly Lionfish

Compared to other stonefish, the lionfish, which is also a member of the Scorpionfish family, is a raving beauty. This extraordinary fish uses long, fanlike pectoral fins and branched dorsal fin to hover near coral or swim lazily in the current. The brightly striped body may be eye-catching, but those grooved spines, like the stonefish, are equipped with potent venom, which can have serious and even fatal effects in humans.

Lionfish are usually found in depths of at least 80 feet and in waters warmer than 78 degrees Fahrenheit. They can grow up to 17 inches long and have maroon bodies with vertical white stripes. Their most distinctive feature is a fan of prickly spines that secrete a poison that can cause severe pain, numbness, paralysis, and even death. The sting of the lionfish is similar but usually less severe than that of the stonefish. The severity of sting depends on several factors including the number of stings and the age and health of the victim.

In the spring of 2002, the lionfish was reported prowling the waters off the East Coast of the United States, where it hadn't been sighted before. Divers along the East Coast had sighted the lionfish since the early 1990s. But it was only when commercial fisherman off St. Augustine, Florida, hauled a specimen in that its presence was confirmed. Subsequently, divers have sighted lionfish from south Florida up to North Carolina and Long Island, New York.

What is still a mystery was how the lionfish migrated 10,000 miles to the Atlantic from Southeast Asia and Australia where it ordinarily lives. Scientists believe it impossible for a tropical fish to survive the journey through cold waters and so speculate that they might be the progeny of discarded aquarium pets. Other marine biologists theorize that ships traveling from the South Pacific to the East Coast inadvertently transported larvae of juvenile lionfish; then they were released on the East Coast when the ballast water was pumped out. It is feared that the lionfish, if it is present in large enough numbers, can do great damage to the ecosystem, often driving out native species.

Shark Facts and Stats

Here is what you need to know about the lionfish:

♦ Like the stonefish, lionfish have venomous spines.

♦ The sting of a lionfish is generally less severe than that of the stonefish.

♦ The extent of the injury depends on several factors including the number of spines causing the injury and the health and age of the victim.

♦ Treatment with antivenin may be necessary in severe cases.

Sea Urchins

Sea urchins are the porcupines of the sea. Found in tidal pools and in rocks along the sea bottom, sea urchins have poisonous sharp spines that can penetrate human skin and break off. And when they penetrate the skin, they stay and stay, creating a protracted infection.

Sea urchins are members of the phylum *Echinodermata*, the same group that includes sea stars, sand dollars, sea lilies, and sea cucumbers. Like all echinoderms, sea urchins do not have a brain. Worldwide inhabitants, the 700 different species of sea urchin have spiny, hard shells. These invertebrates move very slowly along the seabed, and many of them have venomous spines. The biggest species is the red sea urchin (*Strongylocentratus franciscanus*).

Their hard outer body is similar to that of sea stars and sand dollars. The outer skeleton, known as a *test*, is comprised of 10 fused plates. The spines can rotate extensively around the plates. Alternate sections have holes for the sea urchin's tube feet, which are controlled by a water vascular system. By changing the amount of water inside the test, sea urchins can extend or contract the feet, allowing them to move.

The sea urchin's beaklike mouth, which is used to scrape rock clean of algae, is located on the underside of the urchin's body. Sea urchins, like some sharks, eat just about anything that floats by. Their sharp teeth can grind plankton, kelp, periwinkles, and hard shell barnacles and mussels. Sea urchins are also able to regrow teeth to replace worn-down ones. Tiny stinging structures called *pedicellarines* are used for defense and for obtaining food. Waste is eliminated through the anus, located next to the genital pores on the top of the test.

Mating and fertilization are external. Females release several million tiny, jelly-coated eggs through five gonopores. As they develop, the tiny larvae (called *pluteus*) swim in the open sea and are a component of zooplankton. It takes several months for juvenile sea urchins to form. The time lapse for juveniles to become reproductive adults varies between two to five years.

Sea urchins are a delicacy for birds, sea stars, cod, lobsters, foxes, and sea otters, and you'll find them in any sushi restaurant. When sea urchins die, the tests covered with tiny bumps where the spines were attached are sometimes found along beaches.

Long-spined sea urchins can prove treacherous if someone accidentally touches their venomous spines.

Shark Facts and Stats

Here is what you need to know about sea urchins:

- ◆ Sea urchins live on the sea floor where divers may accidentally step on them.
- ◆ Many sea urchins have venomous spines that can penetrate the skin. Once the spines have become embedded, they can cause long and painful infections unless treated.

Fire Corals

Fire corals, which are not true corals, probably get credit for delivering the most stings. Divers often mistake the bright yellow-green and brown skeletal covering of fire coral for seaweed, and accidental contact is very common. Fire corals are widely distributed in tropical and subtropical waters. They have very small nematocysts or stinging cells located on their tentacles, which protrude from numerous surface pores. In addition, their sharp, calcified external skeleton can do further injury by scraping the skin.

Once contact is made, the victim knows it immediately because the burning or stinging pain increases during the next half-hour. The signs of a sting are obvious: a red rash with raised welts appears followed by itching. Some encounters result in swollen lymph glands, nausea, and vomiting.

The recommended treatment is to rinse the area with seawater. Fresh water only intensifies the pain. Vinegar or isopropyl alcohol will ease the pain. Tentacles should be removed with tweezers. The extremities of the tentacles should be immobilized because movement can spread the venom. Hydrocortisone cream is helpful for itching but should not be used if any signs of infection are present. If the victim develops an allergic reaction, indicated by shortness of breath or swelling in the tongue, face, or throat, he or she should be treated for an allergic reaction. Otherwise acetaminophen or ibuprofen should stop the pain.

Shark Facts and Stats

Here is what you need to know about fire corals:

- ◆ Fire coral is not a true coral and is often mistaken for seaweed.
- ◆ Fire coral has tentacles laden with special stinging cells that can produce a rash, itching, swollen lymph glands, nausea, and vomiting.
- ◆ Saltwater (not fresh), vinegar, and isopropyl alcohol should be applied to the injured area, and the tentacles should be removed with tweezers.

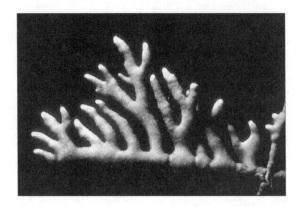

Fire coral, often mistaken for seaweed, can cause severe rashes in people who come into contact with its stinging tentacles.

Crown of Thorns

The crown of thorns is a sea star with long, sharp arms and red-tipped spines. Each one of its 6 to 23 arms, which are often reddish brown in color, is filled with venomous glands. Found in large quantities along the Great Barrier Reef in Australia, these sea stars eat and destroy coral. They prefer to live in sheltered areas such as lagoons and in deeper water along reef fronts where there is less disturbance by currents, tides, weather, or other environmental conditions.

The crown of thorns feeds on coral polyps by expelling its stomach out through its mouth to cover a chunk of living coral. As it secretes digestive juices, it kills the coral and then sucks in the resulting "soup." After feeding it moves on, leaving a patch of white or a coral skeleton. The crown of thorns usually feeds twice a day for several hours. Although it will eat most types of coral, it prefers the branching tubular and staghorn type of corals.

The poisonous spines of this sea star contain toxic compounds called *saponins*. These spines are intensely painful to humans who step on or touch on a crown of thorns, and the injury can cause occasional nausea and vomiting. The skin may turn a dark blue, and tissues may become swollen.

Like the sea urchin, juvenile and adult crown of thorns use tiny tube feet to move. They are prolific breeders, too, releasing millions of eggs during their breeding season. Females shed eggs into the water, which are fertilized by sperm simultaneously released from nearby males into the water.

During the plankton stage, the larva develops a large saclike structure until it settles on a reef where the larva metamorphoses (changes) into a juvenile starfish. Juveniles have five rudimentary arms, but additional arms develop rapidly as it begins feeding on algae. At six months the starfish changes its diet and begins feeding nocturnally on corals while hiding from predators during daylight hours. Predators include the giant triton, the helmet shell, harlequin shrimp, Maori wrasse, puffer fish, and several species of triggerfish.

> **Shark Facts and Stats**
>
> Here's what you need to know about crown of thorns:
>
> ◆ The crown of thorns is a sea star with several arms, each of which contains venomous glands.
>
> ◆ It inhabits lagoons and is found in large numbers in the Great Barrier Reef of Australia.
>
> ◆ The spines cause painful injury to humans who step on or touch it.
>
> ◆ Symptoms from contact include occasional nausea and vomiting as well as swollen tissue.

The Least You Need to Know

- Sharks are less deadly than many creatures that have not received the same publicity and media frenzy.

- Many of these creatures, such as the jellyfish, are easily encountered in shallow water.

- Protection can be as simple as covering the body with pantyhose or a more attractive Lycra suit.

- Most people would go out of their way to avoid a saltwater crocodile, yet they would not hesitate to pick up the beautifully patterned textile cone shell.

- There are two species of sea snakes, but only one is terrestrial.

- Stonefish and lionfish belong to the same family; both are capable of releasing venom from their spines.

- The sea urchin is equipped with envenomed spines that can cause injury and infections.

- Fire corals, which are not true corals, are known for causing the most stings to victims because they are easily mistaken for harmless seaweed.

- The crown of thorns is a starfish with envenomed spines that is known for devouring coral.

Chapter 20

The Growing Threat to Sharks

In This Chapter

- ◆ Why are sharks are so crucial to the environment
- ◆ How many species of sharks are in danger of extinction
- ◆ What makes finning so repellent
- ◆ How sharks are caught in large numbers
- ◆ Why basking sharks are at particular risk

Let's face it—sharks aren't lovable. People swoon over whales and dolphins, but they're scared of sharks. Sharks are portrayed in movies like *Jaws* as menacing creatures from the deep, always craving human flesh. Sharks are fished because they are objects of fear and disdain, but their cartilage and skin are valuable as well—the former for its potential therapeutic properties and the latter for its use in handbags and shoes. Their fins are especially coveted because they are used to make a soup considered a delicacy in Asia. Many experts believe that many sharks are in danger of extinction. But why does it matter whether sharks disappear from the seas? This chapter answers this question.

The Reasons Sharks Matter

Sharks matter for environmental, scientific, and economic reasons. They are the apex predators in the sea, meaning that they occupy the top rung of the marine food chain. As apex predators, sharks keep fish and shellfish populations from getting out of control. Eliminating apex predators from any area results in environmental imbalance in that area. When you consider the fact that the ocean environment constitutes four-fifths of the planet's surface, it stands to reason that an imbalance in four-fifths of the planet is likely to cause a lot of problems for the inhabitants of the other fifth, including us. Reduced numbers of sharks can put commercial fisheries at risk as well.

Sharks continue to represent a great mystery. We don't know very much about their natural history, and we are completely in the dark about certain species. Many species may still remain to be discovered. Although we know that shark cartilage cannot cure cancer (see Chapter 16), that is not the same as saying that sharks have no therapeutic research value for humans—quite the contrary. They seem nearly impervious to infections and circulatory diseases. Cancer in sharks appears to be relatively rare. But if researchers are to continue to investigate the shark immune system in hopes of one day applying its secrets to fight human illness, they will need to have sharks to examine. Some species may offer therapeutic benefits that others do not, but we'll never know if, as we are already doing, we eliminate them from the oceans.

Last, but hardly least, there's also an economic incentive for saving sharks. According to one estimate, every shark that is killed is valued between $5 and $50. On the other hand, every shark that is left alive could possibly generate $50,000 in income. We've all read about sharks that drive tourists away from beaches and resorts, but sharks turn out to be a great lure for tourists as well. Almost a quarter of million divers choose to dive with sharks every year, and the number of shark tours that are being offered every year is also increasing. (Go online to www.google.com and do a search for shark dive and find out for yourself.) Consider the equipment that enthusiasts buy to go on the dives and you can begin to get a sense as to how much money a live shark is worth. Whale sharks, for example, have such great value to the tourism industry that thousands of divers travel each year to Ningaloo Reef in Australia just for a chance of diving with the whale sharks and happily pay more than $3,000 for the privilege. According to DEMA (Dive Equipment Manufacturers Association), American recreational divers spend $1.4 billion annually on shark dive tours.

Shark Lore

The impact of dwindling numbers of sharks is already being felt. In Australia, at least one lobster fishery is threatened because lobster-eating octopi have proliferated because sharks that preyed upon them have begun to disappear.

The Threat of Overfishing

Overfishing threatens stocks of all kinds of fish in the world. Stocks of commercial fish in coastal waters off New England, for instance, have become so depleted that legislation now imposes severe restrictions on fishermen. But bony fish have an advantage over cartilaginous fish: They reproduce more readily, enabling them to better sustain their population. Fishing of sharks, by contrast, has put many shark populations in danger of extinction. Sharks are falling victim to an ever more efficient global fishing industry, which sometimes operates with little regulation.

Counting the Endangered Species

Of the world's 350 plus species of shark, the World Conservation Union Red List 2000 lists 79 species as imperiled, ranging from "critically endangered" through to "lower risk near threatened." Estimates of the numbers of sharks who are killed each year range from 100 million to a high of 200 million sharks.

The picture becomes more disturbing when you get to specific cases. In just one decade (between the mid-1980s and mid-1990s), populations of dusky sharks and sandbar sharks along the eastern coast of the United States declined by more than 80 percent! Worldwide, the sand tiger shark and the great white shark are similarly threatened. The mortality rates of sharks in U.S. waters from commercial fishing have averaged 20,000 metric tons per year. According to computer models and statistical analysis, catches more than 10,000 to 12,000 metric tons impede the ability of these targeted species to reproduce at sustainable rates.

> **Shark Facts and Stats**
>
> According to experts, shark harvesting is unsustainable at a level of more than 100 million sharks annually and yet that level has been maintained or exceeded in recent years.

Commercial fishermen so prized porbeagle sharks (swift, pelagic sharks) that by 1960 they were virtually fished out. Commercial fishermen stopped fishing for them because it cost them more in gas money searching for them than they could get back from sales of their catches. Thirty years later, even though porbeagles have not been hunted, their populations still have not recovered.

This situation is hardly an aberration; many shark fisheries around the world have gone through boom and bust cycles, resulting in alarming declines in the shark population. Shark fishery crashes have occurred among the California soupfin shark in the 1940s, the Australia schoolfin shark from the 1940s through the 1970s, the basking shark in the 1950s and 1960s, and the porbeagle shark in the 1960s. The same pattern is now repeating itself on the eastern seaboard of the United States.

The depletion of shark species is inextricably linked to the decline of other fish populations. That's because as certain types of commercial fish are being wiped out in response to increasing worldwide demand, fishermen have moved farther afield, fishing in places that they previously had ignored. As a result, sharks in these newly targeted areas who had been left alone before are now at heightened risk of being killed.

The Long History of Overfishing

Overfishing isn't a new phenomenon by any means. According to researchers, overfishing seems to have been going on for hundreds, perhaps thousands, of years; the effects of overfishing are being felt today in the collapse of coastal marine ecosystems.

For a long time scientists attributed the collapse of these coastal ecosystems to pollution, increased nutrient runoff, and climate change, which are all fairly recent trends. But suspecting that they were missing the big picture, researchers at the Australian National University in Canberra took another approach. Why not look at conditions in ancient oceans as a basis of comparison? Researchers pieced together a portrait of the seas from marine sediment evidence dating back about 125,000 years as well as from archaeological information about early human coastal settlements some 10,000 years ago and records of trade from the fifteenth century to the present. Coral reefs, the researchers found, did not begin to die only a few decades ago. Populations of marine mammals, fish, and shellfish have been decreasing for centuries and invasions of alien species (blooms of algae, for instance) have been going on for a long time as well. That isn't to say that these noxious trends haven't accelerated in recent years due to human activity, only that they can be traced back to what our ancestors were doing eons ago.

Long-Term Domino Effect

The depletion in coastal waters of large marine vertebrates such as whales, sharks, rays, seals, crocodiles, turtles, cod, and swordfish has set off a domino effect that can have a significant impact even centuries later. In every case the researchers looked at, overfishing preceded—and probably precipitated—the collapse of the ecosystem. The evidence suggests that when marine vertebrates are taken out of the food chain, the marine environment suffers significant, possibly irreversible damage.

Sea turtles offer an instructive example. Amerindians in the Caribbean hunted these turtles for food long before Columbus set sail from Spain in 1492. But from an examination of ancient trash dumps, researchers concluded that over the centuries sea turtles must have been hunted to extinction. Even though these animals were harvested in only one region, the impact was felt over a wide area. That's because these turtles traveled long distances to forage for food and then returned to their homes. By over-harvesting these turtles at one location, the Amerindians were inadvertently contributing to their extinction in coastal waters far away.

You might think that the disappearance of sea turtles from Caribbean waters hundreds of years ago, while regrettable, shouldn't make much of a difference to the overall health of the marine ecology today, but it does. Sea turtles are among the many species that curbed the growth of algae. One by one, these plant-grazing species were wiped out, leaving only sea urchins to curb the algae spread. Then in the 1980s, the urchins were decimated by disease. Now there was no species left to keep the algae in check. The algae were free to overrun and kill the corals and keep new coral from growing. So the extinction of sea turtles, far from being a historical footnote, has had lasting and calamitous repercussions 500 years or so after the fact.

A similar pattern is seen in the elimination of sea otters from Northern Pacific waters. Aboriginal Aleuts hunted sea otters as far back as 2,500 years ago. Because sea otters are the major predators of sea urchins, the overfishing of the otters allowed the sea urchin populations to increase unimpeded. Overgrazing by the sea urchins in turn led to the devastation of kelp beds, and that change resulted in changes in wave action, water quality, and the rate of silting. So the actions of people thousands of years ago has had unforeseen and largely negative effects on today's marine ecosystem. It's impossible to predict what impact the depletion of sharks will have on the marine ecosystem, but from evidence drawn from the destruction of other marine vertebrates we can safely say that the long-term consequences are likely to be significant. After all, given their standing as the apex of marine food chain, sharks have more influence on the health of the environment than sea turtles or sea otters.

The Reasons Sharks Are Hunted

Shark fishing has a history going back thousands of years. Sharks were originally caught with wooden or bone hooks for their meat and their teeth, which were employed for tools and weapons. In the United States, commercial fishing of sharks began in earnest in the 1930s and 1940s. By that time, sharks were coveted for their skin, which could be turned into leather for high-priced shoes, belts, and handbags. Shark liver oil was also prized for its rich Vitamin A content. When Vitamin A was synthesized in the late 1940s, interest in this byproduct of the shark dwindled, but the belief that the shark has life-saving properties has scarcely faded. As discussed in Chapter 16, shark cartilage is now (mistakenly) seen as an anti-cancer agent. And although shark meat was once shunned in the United States, it has recently begun to win acceptance as part of the American diet. In many parts of the world shark meat is considered a staple, especially in developing nations where it is one of the major sources of protein.

Of course, sharks are also killed because of fear. Many people kill sharks because they regard them as a menace or simply as "trash fish," disposable creatures who have nothing to recommend them.

The Despicable Practice of Finning

One shark byproduct commands higher prices than either shark cartilage or sharkskin. And that product involves the act of maiming known as *finning*. Finning is the practice of cutting the fins off living sharks and then tossing the mutilated creatures back into the sea to die. Shark fins are harvested so they can be used as an ingredient in shark fin soup, which is a delicacy in Asia. And they are lucrative: Shark fins can sell for $25 or more per pound off right off the boat, making them one of the more valuable seafood products. To some fishermen fins have the same trophy value as the horns of rhinos. So lucrative are shark fins that even when sharks are caught unintentionally with other fish, fishermen take their fins, reasoning that otherwise they would be throwing money away.

The Cost of Shark Fin Soup

In Asia or western Canada, a bowl of shark fin soup served in a restaurant can be priced between $100 to $300. Among the sharks preferred for the soup are sandbars, blues, hammerheads, porbeagles, makos, threshers, bulls, and black tips.

Tens of thousands of sharks were killed for their fins alone in Pacific waters off the United States. In 1998, the number of sharks finned in the waters surrounding Hawaii topped 60,000. What makes the practice even more wasteful—not to mention appalling—is the fact that fins make up only a tiny percentage of a shark's total body weight. In effect, finning sacrifices 95 to 99 percent of the shark to get at the other 1 to 5 percent. Yet until 2000 when the U.S. Congress imposed a ban, finning was allowed to proceed without legal interference. But any hope that congressional action would diminish the practice has to be weighed against the decision by the People's Republic of China to permit finning, which has increased demand in mainland China and Hong

Kong, where residents consume almost six million pounds of shark a year, mostly in the form of soup.

Bycatch: The Threat of Long Line Fishing and Gill Nets

Bycatch is the term commonly used to refer to marine life that inadvertently ends up trapped by long lines or nets. One way or another, the result, of course, is the same: the majority of the animals die. Although sharks are targeted specifically—for their fins, cartilage, or other attributes—or for recreational sport, the majority of sharks that are killed are casualties of bycatch. That is to say, most sharks are collateral damage, trapped by nets or lines that were intended for commercial fish such as salmon, swordfish, or mackerel.

Taste of the Bizarre

In a strange and still unexplained incident in November 1993, 188 people were admitted to hospital after eating the meat from a single shark in a town on the southeast coast of Madagascar. Almost everyone who ate the shark was afflicted with a variety of neurological symptoms—notably lack of muscle coordination (ataxia)—but almost no nausea or vomiting. Nearly 30 percent of the victims died. Nothing like this had happened in this area before—fishermen had eaten the same kind of shark for years without suffering any ill effects. Scientists were able to rule out bacteriological and chemical agents as a cause of the poisoning but were able to isolate two toxins from the shark's liver. How those toxins came to be there are unknown.

An estimated 80 percent of fish killed are caught by long lines. Long line fishing is a popular method of fishing in which a line bristling with baited hooks is thrown into the water behind a boat. Long line commercial fishermen catch huge numbers of sharks because the sharks have the bad luck to end up on the other end of the line, not because they were the intended targets. As a result, they end up being left to rot in the sea.

Drift net fishing, by contrast, targets a far greater number of fish at a time. In this process large nets are deployed in the water, and held up by buoys. These floating nets (also known as gill nets) sometimes stretch 30 miles in length and indiscriminately trap every large creature in their path, sweeping up whales and sea turtles as well. When sharks (or any marine animal for that matter) blunder into the nets, their gills get stuck; the more they struggle and try to extricate themselves, the more entangled they become. Eventually they either drown or starve to death. Smaller sharks or marine animals considered of no commercial value are tossed back into the water dead. Gill nets account for about 14 percent of the commercial catch.

The Threat of Recreational Fishing

Commercial fisheries are not the only threat to sharks. Sharks are drawn to fishing boats and no wonder: Anglers are after the same prey sharks are. With a few notable exceptions, such as makos and blues, sharks are relatively easy to catch using a hook and line, so they fall victim in great numbers to sports fishermen. Many anglers take advantage of these circumstances to catch a shark as a trophy and display the tail fin on the boat. Although no one knows for certain, it is estimated that as many as 40,000 of these trophy fins are on boats throughout the world.

> **Shark Facts and Stats**
>
> Recreational anglers catch approximately 1,000 mako sharks a year in North Atlantic waters.

The Case of the Mako Shark

Many mako sharks are caught in long-line fishing primarily as a result of bycatch in commercial fisheries in the Atlantic Ocean. Mako sharks were not the intended target; they just happened to be at the wrong place at the wrong time. No one knows for sure how many mako sharks are killed in this manner because these catches often go unreported and the sharks are usually discarded.

In an effort to document the toll being taken on these sharks by long line fishing, the Food and Agriculture Organization of the United Nations (FAO) began listing mako shark catches (the technical term is *landings*) in 1987. In the first couple of years of the study, the relative number taken by U.S. commercial fishermen as part of bycatch was relatively low, but the small numbers did not reflect the bycatch in the long line fisheries of several other nations, including Cuba, Denmark, Venezuela, Korea, Taiwan, Japan, Spain, and Canada.

> **Shark Facts and Stats**
>
> In 1989, 100 million sharks perished in commercial fisheries, according to the Shark Specialist Group of the International Union for the Conservation of Nature and Natural Resources (IUCN) Species Survival Commission.

Makos appear to be more at risk because their patterns of migration parallel those of commercially desirable swordfish. Since the 1970s, U.S. swordfish fishing has continued to expand so that it currently extends over much of the western North Atlantic from the Grand Banks to the equatorial zones off South America, including the Gulf of Mexico and the Caribbean Sea. Japanese and Spanish fisheries have similarly expanded into North Atlantic waters in search of swordfish, placing makos at heightened risk, even though they are not specifically being targeted—a classic case of guilt by association.

Safety Nets

Nets are also being used around beaches in countries such as Australia and South Africa to protect swimmers and surfers. As discussed in the previous chapter, these nets, put up to protect swimmers and surfers from shark attacks, catch thousands of sharks each year, the majority of whom are not the least bit aggressive toward humans. (What's more, these nets trap dolphins and sea turtles and other fish.) New technologies such as chemical substances similar to fish toxins are in development in the hope that sharks can be kept away from beaches without killing them. (Chapter 21 discusses how some countries are reexamining their use of protective nets in hope of reducing shark mortality.)

Shark Lore

A large set of jaws from a great white shark may be worth up to $10,000 to collectors.

The Threat to the Basking Shark: A Study in Overfishing

Basking sharks owe their name to their apparent habit of basking in the sun. Commonly found in the Irish Sea and off the south and west coasts of Ireland and Scotland, basking sharks were originally known as sunfish (or sailfish, because of their tall dorsal fins) and were once thought to be a species of whale. Basking sharks have been hunted for hundreds of years, forming the basis of a cottage industry of fisheries in Ireland, England, Norway, and Scotland. In the past, fisheries had to rely on handheld harpoons thrown from small rowing boats in order to catch basking sharks.

Until this century, basking sharks were coveted for oil that could be extracted from their livers. One liver could yield between 80 and 200 gallons of oil. This oil was used for lighting and tanning. In addition, their meat was sometimes used for food, and their skin was turned into leather. However, by the beginning of the twentieth century, with mineral oil being so abundant and cheap, the production of shark liver oil no longer made economic sense. Nonetheless, as oil prices rose after World War II, oil from the basking shark was seen as an alternative, and for several years it was used as a lubricant in high-altitude aircraft as well as for cosmetics and as a vitamin substitute.

Basking shark fisheries sprung up off the California coast as well between 1924 and 1937 when the shark meat was used for fishmeal and shark liver oil enjoyed brief popularity as a "cure-all" tonic. After World War II, a larger fishery took root using surplus U.S. Army vessels in tandem with a small plane to search for sharks close to shore, netting about 200 basking sharks a year between 1947 and 1949. At one point racketeers sought basking sharks for squalene that they used to adulterate olive oil. The fishery was abandoned when the commercial value of basking sharks declined.

Techniques for hunting the sharks became more sophisticated as well in the postwar era, ensuring that greater numbers of baskings would be harvested. Fisheries used nets or nonexploding harpoons instead of hand-held harpoons. (Exploding harpoons proved damaging to the tissue and the soft cartilaginous skeletons of sharks.)

Oil from basking sharks is no longer a profitable commodity, but that hasn't let baskings off the hook. They are still being fished in waters off Norway, Portugal, California, and Scotland mainly for their fins, which are used for soup. For many years the Norwegians have had the dubious distinction of being the major hunters of the basking shark. Ranging from the North Sea as far as the southeast coast of Ireland and as far as Iceland, Norwegian fishermen travel in small wooden vessels fitted with specially made shark harpoons fired from a whale gun. The shark fishing begins in spring and only comes to a halt when the stocks decline in August or September. To conserve the basking shark, the European Union now imposes restrictions on the total numbers of basking sharks that can be caught.

Trying to pin down how many basking sharks are being killed and what impact these killings are having on the shark population as a whole is difficult. That's because very little is known about the basking shark's natural history, although this shark is the second largest fish in the sea. For instance, basking sharks show up in British coastal waters each April, but where do they come from? Researchers are unsure. Nor can they say why the baskings migrate to Britain in spring and or what happens to them after they depart in the fall.

Researchers who study marine life have begun to notice an alarming phenomenon. Animals that feed close to and on the water surface are most at risk of being caught. A disproportionate number of these at-risk animals—in the case of the basking shark about 95 percent—are female. The elimination of so many females belonging to a single species (whose numbers are unknown in the first place) has a devastating effect on the sustainability of the population as a whole.

Extinctions of species occur in nature all the time—think of what happened to the dinosaurs. What is changing, though, is the rate at which species are becoming extinct, and that number has been increasing dramatically. Most of the extinctions since prehistoric times have occurred over the last 300 years, according to estimates. Most of the animals who have disappeared over the last 50 years have become extinct during the last decade. Given the vulnerability of the basking sharks and the lack of knowledge as to how many of them exist, conservationists fear that the sharks, too, may vanish before long unless governments, fisheries, and environmentalists act decisively to protect them.

The Least You Need to Know

- Many species of sharks are in danger of extinction because of overfishing by commercial fisheries and sports fishermen.

- The dwindling of sharks, who are the apex predators of the oceans, can lead to a critical ecological imbalance.

- Finning is the controversial practice of taking fins to make shark fin soup and killing sharks in the process.

- Although not always specifically targeted, hundreds of millions of sharks are killed every year because they are trapped by long lines or in large gill nets—a casualty of bycatch.

Chapter 21

Preserving the Sharks

In This Chapter

- ◆ What makes sharks so vulnerable to overfishing
- ◆ How the lack of knowledge about sharks hampers conservation efforts
- ◆ What people do to protect sharks worldwide
- ◆ What you can do to aid conservation efforts

Chapter 20 discussed the increasing threat to sharks, pointing out that experts now believe that nearly 80 species may be in danger of extinction. But the paucity of data about shark behavior, habitat, and the populations of various species hamstrings conservationists and scientists. Some species, such as the basking and great white, appear to be more in danger of extinction than others, but far more research is needed to know just how grave the risk is. In the meantime, as this chapter explains, governments, prodded by environmental organizations and others, are gradually responding to the threat.

However, in spite of new legislation and international accords, the crisis has hardly abated. In many instances, governments pay only lip service to shark conservation; in other cases, they look the other way while millions of sharks are exterminated as a result of finning and bycatch. But conserving sharks is too important to be left to governmental agencies alone. Each one of us can contribute to this critical effort. At the end of the chapter, we'll tell you how.

Understanding What Makes Sharks Vulnerable

Chapter 20 discussed the various methods that humans have employed for hundreds and even thousands of years to hunt sharks. Certainly the development of large gill nets and the expansion of fisheries have contributed to the alarming increase in shark catches that are putting so many species of sharks (and other marine life) at risk. However, sharks also have particular characteristics that make them especially vulnerable.

Knowledge about sharks is essential in helping to conserve them. If scientists can accurately determine the migratory patterns of a certain species, we as a society will be in a better position to protect that species from overfishing. On the other hand, the data scientists have already collected about migration and habitats have also helped commercial fishing interests find sharks with more ease.

Rate of Maturity

Getting a handle on the age of sharks is often difficult because so many species haven't been adequately studied. Sharks typically live to 15 to 30 years, but some species seem to live well beyond 50. Longer lived sharks grow slowly. Dusky and sandbar sharks, for example, grow less than five inches a year while they're young and only a couple of inches or so as adults. Tiger sharks, on the other hand, grow quickly at first (about 10 inches a year) and then slow down as they reach maturity. Commonly, sharks reach sexual maturity relatively late in life. The dusky shark matures at 17 years, for instance, and the sandbar matures at 15 to 16 years old.

> **Shark Facts and Stats**
>
> Black tip and Atlantic sharpnose sharks reach sexual maturity at four to seven and three to four years of age, respectively—much more quickly than most other shark species.

Slow Reproductive Rate

Most female sharks don't develop new eggs until after giving birth. On average, sharks who are commercially targeted give birth about every two years (this includes the gestation period). The gestation period of spiny dogfish, which are commercially sought-after sharks, is 18 to 24 months, which is the longest of any vertebrate.

However, because their gestation and egg development occur concurrently, they are able to produce litters every two years.

The typical litter sizes of sharks often make sharks more vulnerable. Unlike fish, who can lay hundreds or thousands of eggs at a time, sharks usually have small litters. The spiny dogfish has 10 or less; the black tip produces only 4 to 8 pups, and the sandbar shark has about 10.

Typically then, a shark needs anywhere from 8 to 20 years just to reach sexual maturity; another year or more may then be consumed in pregnancy and gestation. Even then, a female then may produce a litter of only 4 to 10 pups, and they have to grow for another 9 to 21 years before they can reproduce. Should the cycle be interrupted the population can dwindle to the point where it is unable to sustain its numbers. If the population reaches critically low levels, it may take decades to recover—and that's only if further fishing is halted or severely curtailed.

> **Shark Facts and Stats**
>
> In terms of litter size, tiger sharks are exceptional in that they can produce about 30 to 40 pups per litter and occasionally produce more than 50.

Because bony fish usually reach sexual maturity at an early age (often at two to three years of age) and reproduce by laying eggs (rather than giving birth to live young as many species of sharks do), their population has a much greater chance of being maintained. Fish lay thousands or even millions of eggs and sperm that produce thousands of larvae, young, and adult fishes. Even allowing for the fact that predators devour many of these eggs, enough survive to ultimately develop into fish and replenish the population.

Fishing in Mating Areas and Nurseries

In many respects the shark might be notoriously unpredictable, but when it comes to breeding and giving birth, many species of sharks are very predictable—much to their detriment. Because these sharks return seasonally or annually to specific mating areas, commercial fishers know exactly when and where to find them. And they often don't have far to look because the sharks' nursery areas are often located in inshore shallows or estuaries. Nurseries, you might recall, are waters that offer abundant sources of food for young sharks

> **Shark Facts and Stats**
>
> Some shark species, such as hammerheads and sharpnose, gestate and develop eggs at the same time (rather than go through a separate period of gestation and egg development). They can therefore mate immediately after giving birth, producing yearly litters.

and also are sheltered from predators, usually larger sharks. Fishing isn't the only threat to sharks in these shallow waters; commercial and residential development and pollution pose grave hazards as well.

Shark nurseries are popular for commercial and sports fishing for many of the same reasons that sharks inhabit them: the presence of so many other fish to feed on. The result is that sharks are often the unintended victims of shrimp trawlers and sports fishers hoping to catch other types of fish. In this sense, sharks become bycatch, the marine equivalent of collateral damage.

In addition, federal environmental protections that extend to open seas do not extend to inshore nurseries, meaning that they must be regulated state by state. The record so far is spotty: Florida and Texas have strictly protected inshore nursery areas while other states are more lax. Florida, for instance, limits catches to one shark per person per day or two sharks per boat.

Predictable Migratory Patterns

The most commercially desirable species of sharks are predictable in another way that makes them so susceptible to overfishing. Most species of sharks in the western North Atlantic follow specific routes on their seasonal migrations, typically moving northward along the east coast of the United States as water temperatures increase in the spring and summer and shifting south in the fall as temperatures drop. Migrations between deep and shallow waters also follow predictable patterns, based on water temperature and breeding periods. Fishermen tracking these patterns just "follow the pack" in order to harvest their catches.

> **Shark Facts and Stats**
>
> The mako is a restless shark, as tagging demonstrates. Of the 231 makos recaptured (an estimated 4 to 9 percent of the total tagged), some were reported to have traveled almost 2,500 miles from where they were originally captured.

Identifying Shark Vulnerabilities

To summarize, the following facts are important to keep in mind when assessing the vulnerability of sharks:

♦ Sharks who are most sought after by commercial and sports fisheries don't reach sexual maturity until 8 to 20 years of age.

♦ Most harvested species of sharks have small litters every one or two years.

♦ Because sharks are drawn to specific nurseries and breeding areas, they can be easily tracked and fished.

♦ Predictable migratory routes of large, ocean-going sharks allow fisheries to follow the pack and hunt them.

Preserving the Sharks

The grave threat to sharks has galvanized people around the world into action. Grassroots movements have gathered enough support to push governments and international bodies to impose restrictions on overfishing and finning. But officials in many parts of the world, including the United States, are still lagging behind in conservation efforts.

To combat overfishing, state and federal management have already put plans in place to restrict the number of sharks that can be legally killed. But for a long time one of the most controversial practices—finning—remained legal.

Shark advocates received one of their most significant victories in December 2000 with the passage of legislation to protect sharks. It took a two-year battle before Congress finally acted to prohibit shark finning. "By addressing this egregious waste, Congress has established a strong and consistent national shark policy and reasserted U.S. leadership in addressing global threats to these exceptionally vulnerable fish," said Sonja Fordham, shark fisheries specialist for the Center for Marine Conservation. Up until Congress acted, finning in the Pacific had continued unimpeded in spite of several international fishery agreements deploring the practice.

Shark Facts and Stats
Between 1989 and 1991, high-seas fisheries caught 11.6 to 12.7 million sharks a year as bycatch. Most of these sharks were caught by Korean and Taiwanese fisheries that were searching for tuna.

The United Nations Gets in the Act

Conservationists have also been active internationally. The growing threat to the great white, for example, has impelled several countries (the United States, South Africa, and Australia among them) to enact legislation to protect them. But great whites are not the only endangered species even though they are arguably the best-known sharks.

A plan adopted in 2000 by member countries of the Food and Agriculture Organization of the United Nations calls for "concrete and specific steps to improve the conservation of sharks and sharklike species (skates and rays) at the national, regional, and global levels." But to take these steps, the UN agency needs to work out two major issues: how to fund the effort in a cost-effective manner and how to identify which species of sharks are most at risk.

Lack of knowledge hampers the proper environmental management of many shark populations even in an advanced country such as the United States. The task is both biologically complex and politically sensitive. An additional complication is that in contrast to other managed U.S. fisheries that focus on a single species such as king mackerel or striped bass, almost 40 species of sharks are involved in harvesting in the North Atlantic alone. Each species has distinctive behavior, habitats, and ways of reproduction. That requires different strategies specifically tailored for each species rather than trying to manage sharks as a whole. But how can each species be managed individually if so little is known about its characteristics, behavior, habitats, and population size?

But the situation is too urgent to wait while the needed data is assembled. Already governmental agencies, often at the urging of environmental groups, have begun to put measures into place to protect sharks. In some instances, they have revisited earlier decisions: If in the past they placed emphasis on protecting humans from sharks, today officials are more inclined to think about protecting sharks from humans. Take, for example, the changing attitude of authorities in charge of one of South Africa's most popular beaches.

Rethinking Protective Nets

Bycatch isn't only a phenomenon limited to long line fishing. As noted in Chapter 18 on shark attacks, several countries, including the United States, Australia, and South Africa, have established protective nets near beach areas to protect swimmers against shark attacks. In South Africa these nets have been in place in swimming areas for about 40 years.

Durban, South Africa's most popular holiday city, was the first to install nets in 1952 after a series of shark attacks, several of which resulted in fatalities. The nets were about 656 feet long and about 19 feet wide and were attached to buoys anchored to the seabed in water about 40 feet deep.

Although the Durban experiment was a success, it was overshadowed by attacks at resorts not far down the coastline from Durban that failed to put up the nets. During a 107-day period extending from Christmas 1957 to Easter 1958 that became known as "Black December," sharks claimed the lives of five people. Local authorities scrambled to find a solution to restore the confidence of panicked beach-goers. Instead of duplicating Durban's example, they tried other alternatives. They erected enclosures built of wooden poles, wire, and netting, but they were swept away by the rough surf. A naval frigate dropped depth charges to kill marauding sharks. This strategy was little more successful: a few sharks were killed to be sure, but many more fish were wiped out—and that attracted yet more sharks. Not until 1964 did the provincial officials settle on the protective nets that resisted sharks and surf alike.

The netting served its intended purpose: Tourists didn't have to fear being bitten by sharks. The nets reduced shark attacks by 90 percent, catching an average of 1,245 sharks per year. But the nets had an unintended effect as well, which was to trap a disturbing number of harmless sharks as well as stingrays, turtles, and dolphins.

Now South African provincial officials are beginning to have second thoughts about these nets, wrestling with two different and sometimes conflicting goals: How do they continue to protect swimmers and protect sharks and other marine life at the same time? Nonetheless, scientists are convinced that this dilemma can be resolved without imperiling swimmers, surfers, or sharks.

Catching Sharks with Nets

To find out exactly what effect the protective nets were having, provincial authorities tended the nets 20 days each month and released any live animals they found, including sharks. Dead sharks underwent laboratory analysis so researchers could collect data about shark behavior. In spite of these efforts, officials believed that the nets were killing too many sharks unnecessarily. By reducing the number of nets and avoiding overlap between nets, the researchers managed to cut down on the bycatch without increasing the risk to swimmers. In Australia, concerned authorities also decided to reduce the number of nets, which diminished the number of sharks being killed by 25 percent without posing any additional risk to swimmers. These results are still preliminary, and more studies are necessary to assess the effect of net reduction.

Researching Shark Net Alternatives

Other protective strategies are being pursued as an alternative to nets. They have to meet two objectives: protect swimmers and surfers and avoid environmental damage. One alternative is the use of "drumlines," which are floats made out of recycled oil drums anchored to the seabed with baited hooks attached. These baited hooks attract sharks, usually only species specifically targeted because they are dangerous. It's hoped that some combination of drumlines and nets will prove most effective. SharkPODs, which I mentioned in Chapter 18, are another alternative; these devices produce electric fields to prevent sharks from getting close to the beaches.

Moving to Protect Sharks in U.S. Waters

Sharks have had to wait a long time to get respect. It wasn't until the early 1990s that the U.S. government officially acknowledged that sharks were imperiled by overfishing and moved to do something about it. The responsibility for the conservation effort fell mainly on the U.S. National Marine Fisheries Service (NMFS). Initially, the agency developed a management plan to address the problem. Unsurprisingly, the first recovery plan it devised was imperfect in conception and, in terms of its goals, was wildly optimistic. All the same, it has still proven useful to researchers, fisheries, and conservationists alike. As new biological and fishery data becomes available, the plan is adjusted accordingly.

> **Shark Facts and Stats**
>
> Out of the 21,000 shortfin makos tagged and released to date, only 84 have been reported recaptures, most within 30 days from the original date of capture and within 50 miles of the initial site. This small sampling is insufficient to make good management decisions.

What Does the NMFS Plan Say?

The NMFS shark management plan covers the area from 200 miles offshore inward to state waters, an area that is called the Exclusive Economic Zone (EEZ). The plan is based on management of 39 species classified in three species groups:

♦ Large coastal species, made up of the major sport and commercial target species including the sandbar, black tip, bull, Galapagos, reef, tiger, lemon, nurse, scalloped hammerhead, great white, basking, and whale

♦ Small coastal species, made up largely of small species close to shore and caught primarily by sports fishers or as bycatch including Atlantic and Caribbean sharpnose, smalltail, and angel sharks

♦ Pelagic species, comprised of offshore and deepwater species that are harvested primarily as bycatch of tuna and swordfish long line fisheries, but are also targeted by sport fishers, including longfin and shortfin makos, porbeagles, oceanic white tips, and blues

In 1990, the NMFS determined that the threat to each of these groups ranged significantly. Small coastal sharks, according to the NMFS, were not overfished, and although pelagic sharks were well fished, they were not overfished. The situation was more critical when it came to large coastal sharks, which were substantially overfished. As a result, the NMFS established annual poundage quotas, called total allowable catches (TACs), for each of the heavily fished groups. No restrictions were placed on small coastal sharks. The numbers of large coastal sharks who could be harvested would be adjusted upward each year as their stocks recovered. Sport fishers were restricted to two sharks per boat per trip for combined large coastal sharks and pelagic sharks and five sharks per person per day for small coastal sharks. In addition, the sale of recreationally caught sharks was forbidden. The plan went into effect in 1993.

Although the plan was conceived with the best of intentions, it did not envision just how long it would take shark stocks to recover. As scientists and conservationists weighed in with data that they had collected, the plan was modified to reduce fishing limits to 4,000 pounds per trip. This limitation was imposed because of the advent of "sweepstakes" style fishing during the first regulated year (1993), resulting in exhausting quotas in certain waters early in each fishing season as well as disproportionate catches in areas influenced by seasonal migratory patterns of major shark species. Officials of the Fisheries Service realized that the evidence argued for further reductions instead of increases in quotas.

> **Shark Facts and Stats**
>
> According to National Oceanic Atmospheric Administration (NOAA), many shark species found along the southeast coast of the United States declined in number as much as 80 percent between the 1970s and 1980s.

> **Shark Facts and Stats**
>
> Recent fishery studies conducted by the National Marine Fisheries Services (NMFS) off the western Atlantic and the Gulf of Mexico have concluded that the depletion of up to 85 percent of regional shark resources is attributed to overfishing.

Are Governments Dropping the Ball on Shark Conservation?

According to sampling carried out by the U.S. Fish and Wildlife Service, several species of sharks are in danger of extinction: makos, elephant fish, lemon sharks, hammerheads, and great whites. In the last several years governments and international organizations have hammered out a range of multilateral agreements intended to draw attention to the perilous state of many shark species and institute regulations to protect the most vulnerable among them. The most important international conservation effort came in 1999 when member states of the UN Food and Agriculture Organization (FAO) adopted The International Plan of Action for the Conservation and Management of Sharks.

Although the FAO plan calls for its 87 member governments to assess the condition of sharks in their fisheries, which is the first crucial step to conservation, the response has been less than overwhelming. Three years after the adoption of the plan, few of the member nations with shark fisheries had carried out the assessments. Worse, 47 member countries didn't show any indication that they were going to prepare a national shark plan at all. Even the U.S. Fish and Wildlife Service has been dilatory in coming up with badly needed information on endangered sharks. The Humane Society International and Defenders of Wildlife, a Washington-based conservation group, have recommended that at the very least, both the basking and great white shark should be added to the UN list of endangered U.S. species, but the government has so far not done so. It is one thing, of course, to recognize that there is a problem and draw up a plan to deal with it, but it is quite another to put the plan into action.

Recommendations for Saving Sharks

The conservation of endangered sharks doesn't depend only on governments. Concerned environmentalists and even anglers can all lend a hand. Conservation efforts, as mentioned earlier, depend on getting adequate information. If you don't know how many sharks there are to protect, or you have no idea where they are likely to feed or breed, how can you take measures to protect them?

Tagging is seen as one efficient way of gathering valuable data. Through tagging researchers have been able to track the movements of sharks through the oceans and learn, for instance, that a pelagic shark who was swimming in New York waters in one year is the same shark who was cavorting off Brazil five years later. But efforts to recruit taggers (who are usually amateur anglers) are still lagging. The National Marine Fisheries Service has enlisted over 6,500 taggers on the east coast, but fewer than 100 on the west coast.

Tagging also has its drawbacks. Sharks that are caught, tagged and released may suffer increased mortality from trauma if the tagging has not been done properly. Misapplied tags can impede growth and sometimes kill the shark. Nonetheless, the

> **Shark Facts and Stats**
>
> The National Marine Fishery Service and the California Department of Fish and Game have successfully adapted a spear gun to tag sharks. This device allows the tagger to accurately place the tag at the base of the dorsal fin with minimum risk to the shark.

benefits of tagging by amateur anglers, who can cover a far wider geographical range than researchers, almost certainly outweigh the potential for harm.

Once adequate data can be collected several steps can be taken to protect species most at risk:

- ◆ Impose shark size limits for commercial and sport anglers.

- ◆ Improve monitoring of recreational and commercial catches.

- ◆ Prohibit finning of all cartilaginous fish in regions where the practice is not already banned.

- ◆ Close state waters to shark fishing during the season when sharks are giving birth or hatching eggs.

- ◆ Close some or all shark nursery areas to fisheries that take large numbers of juvenile and adult sharks in their bycatch.

- ◆ Prohibit the use of gear (such as gill nets) that result in high levels of bycatch and/or the use of devices that cause unnecessarily high mortality in sharks.

- ◆ Require commercial fisherman to tag bycatch and undersized fish.

- ◆ Develop tag-and-release training programs.

How You Can Help

Even if you don't fish and are not in a position to catch and tag sharks, you can support the objective of shark conservation in several ways. One is by supporting conservation organizations that work to protect all marine life. You can also help by refusing to buy products made from a shark including vitamins, liver oil, and sharkskin boots. Don't patronize restaurants that serve any kind of shark or shark fin soup. If you see shark on the menu, express your displeasure. Write to companies that manufacture shark fin soup to express your disapproval. Keep yourself and your friends and family informed by reading books about sharks and regularly checking with relevant websites. You'll find a valuable list of websites dedicated to shark conservation in Appendix A. In Appendix C, you can obtain information about a website operated by the Monterey Bay Aquarium called Seafood Watch. Seafood Watch offers a valuable guide to choosing what kind of seafood you can consume in good conscience and what kind to shun.

The Least You Need to Know

◆ Because sharks grow slowly, have small litters, and reach sexual maturity late in life, shark populations are more at risk of overfishing than bony fish.

◆ South Africa, Australia, and other countries are adopting alternatives to protective nets that cause less harm to sharks.

◆ Regulations are being implemented in the United States and abroad to curtail overfishing of sharks, but far more needs to be done.

◆ Individuals can make important contributions to the cause of shark conservation.

Resources in Print and Online

If you need any evidence that the subject of sharks is a source of continuing fascination, you needn't look farther than your favorite online bookstore. Several popular books on sharks, written from a variety of perspectives, have been published just in recent years. In the following listing, you'll find a sampling of some of the more notable books with a brief description of their contents. But to learn the latest about shark research and sightings your best bet is to look on the web. There are a multitude of websites devoted to sharks, some run by aquariums and natural history museums, others hosted by divers and other enthusiasts. In this appendix, you'll find a list of those I've found to offer credible and timely information presented in a lively and generally nontechnical manner.

Websites

Thousands of websites are devoted in whole or in part to sharks. Some are instructional, others full of entertaining stories, and still others, hosted by universities and research centers, may be more academic and scientific in nature. The following list is not meant to be comprehensive but rather is intended as a guide for readers interested in learning more about sharks and related topics. With the web in constant flux, we cannot guarantee that all sites will still be up and running when you try to access them.

General Information About Sharks

Enchanted Learning
www.enchantedlearning.com/Home.html

Enchanted Learning is a valuable educational site with a glossary and information on individual sharks, shark anatomy, and the evolution of sharks. Although intended for schoolchildren, it can be a good resource for adults as well. (It also contains information about dinosaurs, astronomy, oceans, and many other subjects about the natural world.)

The Pelagic Shark Research Foundation
www.pelagic.org/conservation/

The Pelagic Shark Research Foundation runs this site, which emphasizes conversation of pelagic sharks. The mission of the foundation is to develop and assist projects that contribute to a better understanding of elasmobranchs, with an emphasis on those that contribute to their conservation and management.

New Brunswick.net
new-brunswick.net/new-brunswick/sharks/behavior.html

Run by the province of New Brunswick, this site contains a section devoted to sharks, including information on behavior, myths, dangers, tales, species, and links.

Biosis
www.biosis.org/zrdocs/zoolinfo/fish_col.htm

This page is full of links to sites on sharks and other fish.

The Rodney Fox Shark Museum
www.rodneyfox.com.au/

Rodney Fox, an Australian filmmaker and shark expedition leader, is regarded as a miracle survivor after being attacked in 1983 by a great white shark. His abdomen was fully exposed with all ribs broken on his left side. His diaphragm was punctured, his lung ripped open, his scapula was pierced, and his spleen exposed as was the main artery from his heart. To this day he has part of a great white tooth embedded in his wrist. But far from bearing any grudges, he has made the conservation of great whites part of his life's work and the focus of his personal website.

Australian Museum Online
www.austmus.gov.au/fishes/search.cfm

The Australian Museum Fish site has sections profiling a variety of sharks, is well illustrated, and provides recommended reading lists.

Awesome Sharks
www.everwonder.com/david/sharks

This site focuses on various aspects of sharks: anatomy, scientific classification, shark attacks, updated news about sharks, and conservation efforts.

Sharks, Information and Conservation
www.brunel.ac.uk/admin/alumni/sharks/shbiol.html

This site provides basic information about sharks, such as their buoyancy, physiology, and family tree.

Ocean of Kno
wwww.oceanofk.org/sharks/sharks.html

This basic guide to sharks (which includes information on senses, diversity, and anatomy) is intended for schoolchildren.

How Stuff Works
www.howstuffworks.com/shark.htm

This site is a basic, well-illustrated survey of shark information.

Shark Research Program of the University of Florida
www.flmnh.ufl.edu/fish/Sharks/sharks.htm

Run by the University of Florida, this site is linked to the International Shark Attack File that documents incidence of shark attacks worldwide.

Shark Conservation

The United States National Marine Fisheries Service
www.nmfs.noaa.gov/

The official site of the National Marine Fisheries Service, which is devoted to protecting fish stocks, provides information about sustainability and research programs.

The Monterey Bay Aquarium
www.montereybayaquarium.org/cr/cr_seafoodwatch/sfw_howto.asp

This site hosted by the Monterey Bay Aquarium features "Seafood Watch," which makes recommendations on which seafood to eat and which to avoid on the basis of the sustainability of different species of fish and shellfish. (For a preview please see Appendix C.)

The International Union for Conservation of Nature and Natural Resources
www.flmnh.ufl.edu/fish/Organizations/SSG/SSGDefault.html

Managed by the International Union for Conservation of Nature and Natural Resources, an umbrella group of governments and NGOs, this site features articles on shark conservation and an online shark newsletter with back issues available. This site is also associated with the Florida Museum of Natural History.

Aquatic Network: Save the Sharks
www.aquanet.com/sharksav.htm

This site focuses on the conservation of great whites. Although the site itself doesn't have much, it does offer many links to sites on pelagic sharks, shark conservation, and research.

All About Sharks
www.ozemail.com.au/~bilsons/SHARKS.htm

This Australian site has lots of e-mail postings about shark encounters and other useful information.

Shark Evolution

Elasmo.com
www.elasmo.com/

This site offers information about the latest fossil finds.

About Prehistoric Sharks
www.sharkattacks.com/prehistoric.htm

This fairly comprehensive survey of prehistoric sharks has sections devoted to fossils, individual early sharks, and megalodon.

JT's Sharks Teeth
www.jtssharksteeth.com/

This site is devoted to modern and primitive shark teeth (including a section on megalodon); it offers links to other sites focusing on shark fossils.

Shark Research

The Center for Shark Research
www.marinelab.sarasota.fl.us/~rhueter/

This site bills itself as "the largest center devoted to the scientific study of sharks and rays." The Mote Laboratory is one of the pioneers in research on the shark immune system.

Reefquest.com
www.reefquest.com/expeditions/expeditions.htm

Reefquest Expeditions, hosted by a South African research and educational program, offers a varied site with information on shark diversity, biology, evolution, behavior, and so on with several sections devoted to the great white shark.

Suggested Reading

Ainley, David G., and A. Peter Kimley, eds. *Great White Sharks: The Biology of Carcharodon Carcharias.* San Diego: The Academic Press, 1998.

This collection of the latest information on the ecology and behavior of great white sharks covers anatomy, physiology, evolution, distribution, population dynamics, and interactions with humans. It's also illustrated with photos.

Allen, Thomas B. *Shadows in the Sea: The Sharks, Skates, and Rays.* New York: Lyons Press, 1996.

Allen describes what scientists have learned about sharks and their relatives, the skates and rays. He also covers the shark's role in folklore and cuisine and considers the commercial shark-fishing industry. The book contains a species-by-species profile of each type of shark.

———. *Shark Almanac.* New York: The Lyons Press, 1999.

This book begins with an overview of shark biology, anatomy, and behavior and then proceeds to describe about 100 species of sharks. This illustrated book also has chapters devoted to shark attacks and a discussion of the precipitous decline in shark populations and what conservationists are doing to save them.

———. *Shark Attacks: Their Causes and Avoidance.* New York: The Lyons Press, 2001.

This book offers a fairly comprehensive look at shark attacks from around the world and profiles sharks who show the most aggression toward humans.

Benchley, Peter. *Shark Trouble.* New York: Random House, 2002.

If Benchley inspired fear for sharks with his best-seller *Jaws,* he comes to their aid in this personal account of encounters he has had with sharks while diving all over the world. He points out the threat of extinction confronting many species of sharks and offers a cautionary tale about what would happen if all sharks were to vanish from the planet. He also includes a chapter on how, as an impoverished freelancer, he came to write *Jaws* in the first place.

Capuzzo, Michael. *Close to Shore: A True Story of Terror in an Age of Innocence.* New York: Broadway Books, 2001.

This harrowing narrative describes the 1916 shark attacks on the New Jersey shore that inspired Peter Benchley to write *Jaws.* Three adults and one child died in the spree, thought to have been perpetrated by one or more bull sharks.

Castro, José. *Sharks of North America.* College Station: Texas A&M University Press, 1996.

Castro, a scientist for the National Marine Fisheries Department, provides an overview of sharks indigenous to U.S. and Canadian waters and a profile of each species.

Ellis, Richard, and Edward Ellis. *The Book of Sharks.* New York: Knopf, 1989.

The book examines the biology, ecology, and evolution of sharks and includes biographies of important scientists and conservationists. It's also illustrated with paintings and photographs.

Gottlieb, Carl. *The Jaws Log: Twenty-Fifth Anniversary Edition.* New York: Newmarket Press, 2001.

Gottlieb, who wrote the screenplay of the blockbuster film *Jaws,* recounts the mishaps and disasters that occurred in the making of the movie. Of special interest to film buffs, the book includes an introduction by Peter Benchley.

Hamlett, William, ed. *Sharks, Skates, and Rays: The Biology of Elasmobranch Fishes.* Baltimore: Johns Hopkins University Press, 1999.

This introduction to elasmobranch morphology and biology is intended for graduate students.

Stanton, Doug. *In Harm's Way: The Sinking of the USS Indianapolis and the Extraordinary Story of Its Survivors.* New York: Henry Holt & Co., 2001.

After dropping off components for the atomic bombs that would be dropped on Japan, the USS *Indianapolis* set sail from the Philippines. On the night of July 29, 1945, it was hit by a Japanese torpedo and quickly sank. Hundreds of survivors of the initial attack waited for rescue for a week as sharks circled and eventually killed many of the group. The book makes for compelling reading; it is an attempt to give a full account of a little-known incident before the last survivors die. To his credit, the author never allows his passion for his subject to stand in the way of his factual presentation.

Taylor, Valerie, and Ron Taylor, eds. *Great Shark Writings.* New York: Overlook Press, 1997.

This compendium of writings about sharks ranges from the adventures and discoveries of scientists such as William Beebe and Eugenie Clark to accounts of survivors of shark attacks. The book also includes legends from Polynesia and the Indian Sea, shark-fishing stories, and tales of adventure from other parts of the world.

Shark Attacks

The Florida-based International Shark Attack File (ISAF) investigated 91 alleged incidents of shark attacks on humans throughout the world in 2001, the most recent year for which statistics are available at the time of writing. Of these, 76 incidents were determined to be unprovoked, which are defined "as incidents where an attack on a live human by a shark occurs in its natural habitat without human provocation of the shark." Unprovoked attacks include incidents involving sharks and divers in public aquariums or research holding pens.

"Provoked attacks" usually occur when a human initiates physical contact with a shark—for instance, when a diver is bit after grabbing a shark or is attacked while removing a shark from a net. In 2001, the ISAF determined that four cases were provoked. The remaining reports included cases where sharks inflicted injuries on people who had already died, often as a result of drowning, and two cases in which sharks attacked boats. Other incidents were either discounted or were dismissed because of insufficient information.

The 2001 total of 76 unprovoked attacks was lower than the 85 unprovoked attacks recorded in the previous year. Yet the number of unprovoked shark attacks has grown at a steady rate over the past century. Overall, the 1990s experienced the highest attack total (536) of any decade, and the 2000 and 2001 totals continue that upward trend.

Five fatalities occurred in 2001, which was down from 12 in 2000. The 6.6 percent fatality rate was significantly lower than the 1990s decade average of 12.7 percent. The five fatalities occurred in the Cape Verde Islands, Mozambique, and United States (one each in Florida, North Carolina, and Virginia).

Continuing the trend of recent years, the majority of attacks (82 percent or 62 attacks) occurred in North American waters, including 55 from the United States, 4 in the Bahamas, 2 from Mexico, and 1 in Cuba. The 55 attacks in the United States are only one less than the total in 2000. Elsewhere, attacks occurred in South Africa (4), Australia (3), Brazil (3), the Cape Verde Islands (1), the Marshall Islands (1), Mozambique (1), and New Zealand (1).

Florida had most of the unprovoked attacks in the United States with 37, only one less than the total for that state in 2000. Other attacks in the United States were recorded in South Carolina (6), Hawaii (4), California (2), North Carolina (2), Texas (2), Alabama (1), and Virginia (1). Within Florida, Volusia County had the most with 22 incidents. This number is attributable to high recreational use of its waters by residents and tourists, especially surfers. Other Florida counties that had attacks in 2001 were Broward (4), St. Lucie (2), Brevard (1), Manatee (1), Monroe (1), Nassau (2), Escambia (2), and Duval (2).

Of all the groups of recreational water users, surfers experienced the most unprovoked attacks in 2001: 35 incidents or 49 percent of confirmed cases. Other attacks involved swimmers/waders (21 or 29 percent), divers/snorkelers (11 or 15 percent), and kayakers (4 or 6 percent). One attack (1 percent) occurred when someone simply waded into the water.

Although the summer of 2001 was dubbed "The Summer of the Shark" by one newsmagazine because of a spate of sensational attacks (with two fatalities), the figures reveal another story. The number of shark attacks for both the United States and Florida were almost identical to those of the previous year (which did not draw particularly high media attention). Meanwhile, the international total was down 11 percent from that of 2000. More important, the incidence of serious attacks, as measured by the number of fatalities, was less than half the average yearly total for the past decade.

The ISAF also takes strong exception to the theory advanced by some observers that U.S. east coast fishery regulations enacted in 1993 have resulted in the expansion of shark populations, which in turn has led to an increase in attacks. For one thing, the number of shark attacks has been rising throughout the past century—many years before regulations were put in place. The rise in attacks can be accounted to human population growth and the increasing popularity of aquatic recreation. There's also reason to believe that the increase is a result of greater efficiency in documenting the incidence of cases. Given the slow rate of maturation among sharks, shark populations could not possibly have returned to pre-fishing levels of the early 1980s in eight years. At current harvest rates, the ISAF estimates that it will take decades to get to that point. Most sharks born in 1993 have not yet reached sexual maturity, let alone produced offspring capable of attacking humans!

The International Shark Attack File, which is internationally recognized as the definitive source of scientifically accurate information on shark attacks, is a compilation of all known shark attacks. In existence since 1958, it is administered by the American Elasmobranch Society, the world's foremost international organization of scientists studying sharks, skates, and rays, and the Florida Museum of Natural History at the University of Florida. You can find more information on shark attacks at the museum's website: www.flmnh.ufl.edu/fish/Sharks/sharks.htm.

Seafood Watch

Seafood Watch is a program instituted by the Monterey Bay Aquarium to promote consumer awareness of seafood. With demand for seafood increasing, stocks of fish around the world are being depleted with adverse impact on the marine ecosystem. The program emphasizes the importance of sustainable seafood, which is fish or shellfish caught or farmed in ways that allow for the replenishment of the stock so that its survival is ensured for the future. The Monterey Bay Aquarium drew up a fact sheet that classifies seafood by its suitability for consumption based on the fish's sustainability.

There are three lists. The first includes seafood that can be consumed in good conscience. A second list is made up of seafood that can be eaten without undue concern, but that, under certain circumstances, should be avoided. For instance, some clams caught in the wild may be contaminated by pollutants. A species of fish may be sustainable in one region and becoming depleted in another region, so it would behoove the customer to first find out where the fish originated before ordering it. The third list indicates what seafood should be avoided all the time because the food source is endangered. These lists can be downloaded from the Monterey Bay Aquarium website at www.mbayaq.org/cr/cr_seafoodwatch/ sfw_regional.asp, printed, and carried as a wallet-sized card for easy access. You can click on any fish or shellfish in each of the lists on the website to obtain additional information.

Best Choice

Abalone, farmed

Catfish, farmed (United States)

Caviar, farmed

Clams, farmed

Crab, Dungeness

Halibut

Hoki

Lobster, rock (California and Australia)

Mussels, farmed

Oysters, farmed

Sablefish (British Columbia and Alaska)

Salmon, canned

Salmon, wild-caught (California and Alaska)

Sanddabs

Sardines (sprats/brisling)

Shrimp/prawn, trap-caught

Squid (calamari)

Striped Bass, farmed

Sturgeon, farmed

Tilapia, farmed

Tuna, albacore

Tuna, canned white (albacore)

Tuna, yellowfin (troll/pole)

Caution

Clams, wild-caught

Cod, Pacific

Crab, imitation (surimi/krab)

Crab, king

Crab, snow

Lobster, American

Mahi-mahi

Mussels, wild-caught

Oysters, wild-caught

Pollock

Sablefish (California, Oregon, Washington)

Salmon, wild-caught (Oregon, Washington)

Scallops, bay

Shark, thresher

Shrimp, bay

Shrimp, U.S. wild-caught (all sources)

Sole (Pacific)

Swordfish, (U.S. West Coast)

Trout, rainbow (farmed)

Tuna, canned chunk light

Tuna, yellowfin

Avoid

Caviar (beluga/osetra)

Chilean seabass

Cod, Atlantic/Icelandic

Lingcod

Monkfish

Orange roughy

Rockfish (Pacific snapper/rock cod)

Salmon, farmed (Atlantic salmon/farmed Chinook)

Scallops, sea

Sharks, except thresher

Shrimp, wild or farmed (international)

Sturgeon, wild-caught

Swordfish (Atlantic)

Tuna, bluefin

I want thank the Monterey Bay Aquarium for giving me permission to use this important list in our book.

Diving Information and Resources

There are several ways to get a look at sharks. In recent years, aquariums have created tanks holding the more docile reef and bottom-dwelling sharks. Looking for a closer encounter without Plexiglas, sign up for a scuba certification class. This appendix provides some general information about diving. If you get bitten by the aquatic bug, check here for details to get you started on your underwater adventures.

Diving Instruction and Certification

Many exotic destinations offer "resort courses" which will get you under the water with an instructor. If you enjoy diving, you will be required to take a course to become certified. No responsible dive operator will permit you to dive without first seeing your certification (C-card).

Contact the following organizations for information about scuba diving classes in your area:

- National Association of Scuba Diving Schools (NASDS): www.nasds.com

- National Association of Underwater Instructors (NAUI): www.naui.org

◆ Professional Association of Diving Instructors (PADI): www.padi.com

◆ YMCA courses: www.ymcascuba.org/ymcascub/dive.html

General Information on Scuba Diving

If you would like more information on whether you want to enroll in a scuba course, the following sites provide enlightenment on health issues and expand on the information that is taught during certification courses

The Mt. Sinai Medical Center Memorial Library

www.mtsinai.org/pulmonary/books/scuba/sectionb.html

This site provides an overview of recreational scuba diving, including detailed descriptions of equipment, certification requirements, and information on issues relating to depth and decompression. This site is technically oriented with links about scuba diving history, quizzes, myths and misconceptions, the respiratory system, air pressure, and women and diving.

Zoologist Mark Carwardine

www.markcarwardine.com/wheretowatchsharks/index.html

This site lists shark watching and diving sites around the world.

Undercurrent Newsletter; The Private, Exclusive Guide for Serious Divers

www.undercurrent.org

This site has an online newsletter that reviews and evaluates numerous destinations as well as the latest developments in shark research. The June 2002 newsletter of *Undercurrent*, for instance, reported on a new $400 electronic shark repellent called SharkPOD.

NOVA Online produced for PBS

www.pbs.org/wgbh/nova/sharks

Sponsored by the PBS series *Nova*, this site is based on a documentary about shark diving in the Coco Islands in Costa Rica.

Diving Expeditions

If you check the web you can find countless sites hosted by tour organizations that sponsor shark diving tours for recreational and sports divers, whether you are just starting out or are an experienced diver interested in deep water diving. This section provides information about shark diving locations that are featured in this book. Keep in mind that this information is subject to change.

Cocos Islands, Costa Rica

Best time to travel: The ocean temperature is warmer (74 to 82 degrees) during the dry season of November to May, but the diving is reputed to be better in the wet and "misty" season of June, July, and August. During summer months, whale sharks migrate through the islands, and hammerheads school in shallower water.

Transportation: American Airlines provides nonstop service (an approximate three-hour flight) between Miami or Dallas to the capital city of San Jose, Costa Rica.

Visa: Issued at airport.

Language: Spanish, but English is widely spoken.

Money: Colon, but U.S. dollars are generally accepted and required in the Cocos.

Cocos Park Fee: $25 per diver per day plus a $10 daily dive tax payable only in U.S. dollars.

Accommodations: Because divers are required to arrive the day prior to departure for the islands, accommodations are necessary in San Jose. San Jose has many destination resorts, but the following are two smaller, more charming properties:

- Hotel Grano de Oro: Calle 30 between Avenidas 2 and 4; e-mail granoro@sol.racsa.co.cr or fax 011-506-221-2782.

- Barcelo Amon Plaza: Avenida 11 and Calle 3; e-mail amonpark@sol.racsa.co.cr or fax 011-506-257-00284.

Boat departure: The *Okeanos Aggressor* departs from the port of Puntarenas, a two-hour drive to the west coast. The Aggressor Fleet provides van transportation both ways. A C-card or proof of dive certification is required to board the ship. This trip is recommended only for experienced divers. For more information, contact Aggressor Fleet at 1-800-348-2628, go to www.aggressor.com, or e-mail info@aggressor.com.

Diving: The approximately 42-hour trip (300 miles) from Puntarenas to the Cocos can be grueling depending on ocean conditions. Diving conditions in the Cocos are limited to about five seamounts. There is a lot of surge and current near rocks covered with spiny sea urchins. This is a trip for experienced divers.

For more information: Galapagos Aggressor. 1-800-348-2628 or go to www. aggressor.com or e-mail info@agressor.com.

Park fee, dive tax, and departure tax: The Costa Rican government requires a $105 U.S cash only conservation fee to dive the Cocos Islands. There is also a $28 U.S. dive tax. Costa Rica has a $17 departure tax as well.

Galapagos, Ecuador

Best time to travel: The Galapagos Islands are also a destination for experienced divers. The water is a cool 72 to 78 degrees. Wetsuits and gloves a necessity. Divers wanting to better insure the opportunity to see whale sharks and hammerheads should sign up for itineraries that include the remote Darwin and Wolf islands, most of which are inaccessible for land excursions.

Visa: A U.S. passport is required; visas are issued on arrival.

Language: Spanish, but English is widely spoken

Currency: The sucre is no longer printed. U.S. dollars are used.

Galapagos Park Fee: $125 plus a $17 exit fee payable only in U.S. dollars

Transportation: American Airlines flies nonstop from Miami to Quito. Continental flies nonstop from Houston to Guayaquil. An overnight is required in both directions from either city. The gateway city to the Galapagos is Guayaquil flown by TAME airlines. A connection can be made from Quito or non-stop from Guayaquil, an hour and a half flight.

Accommodations:

- In Quito—Alameda Real: Fax 011-593-2-565759 or e-mail apartec@uio.satnet.net.
- In Guayaquil—Unipark Hotel: Fax 011-593-2-328352 or uni_gye@ oroverdehotels.com.

San Diego, California

San Diego Shark Diving Expeditions runs daylong Saturday trips twice a month. The cost is $260. The trip includes two 30- to 40-minute cage dives. All divers must be certified and experienced. A hooded wetsuit should be included with your dive gear. Hanging gear, with the exception of the air gauge, is detached for ease in entering and exiting the cage. Underwater cameras and video are available for rental. Contact Mr. Paul Anes at 6747 Friars Road, Suite 112, San Diego, CA 92108-1110. You also can call him at 619-299-8560 or toll-free at 1-888-SD-SHARK. The fax number is 619-299-1088, and the web and e-mail addresses are www.sdsharkdiving.com or info@sdsharkdiving.com.

Mako fly fishing season runs from May to November. Bowman prefers to fish five days before the phase of either the new or the full moon (when tidal movements attract bait, which attracts the sharks). A half-day fishing trip costs $250. For information, contact Conway Bowman by calling 619-286-4625, e-mailing info@bowmanbluewater.com, or going online to www.bowmanbluewater.com.

Glossary

Note: The only shark species cited in this glossary are those that are mentioned frequently in the book. Because there are nearly 400 shark species, space does not allow the inclusion of them all.

abalone   Name given to certain marine snails found on rocks near the shores of warm seas.

abyssopelagic zone   A frigid region of the ocean where light never penetrates and that is suited only to highly specialized types of marine life.

Acanthodians   Primitive fish identified as the first jawed vertebrates who lived about 400 million years ago.

allometry   The science of tracking changes in animal growth and behavior in order to obtain a comprehensive portrait of the animal being studied.

ampullae of Lorenzini   A special network of nerves in the shark's head that allows the shark to detect electrical and magnetic impulses in order to find prey and navigate.

anal fin   A fin found at the tail end of some species of shark (also present in pairs at the tail end of some fish).

angel shark   Flat-bodied, bottom-dwelling sharks with a blunt snout.

antibodies   Proteins in blood that are generated to fight invaders called antigens. They are also known as immunoglobulins.

antigens   *See* antibodies.

aplacental viviparity   A process of birth (formerly known as ovoviviparity) among certain species of sharks in which the babies hatch from eggs, but develop inside the mother's body; there is no placenta to nourish the babies, however.

barbel   Sensory whiskerlike projections near the nostrils and mouth of some sharks, such as the nurse shark, that are used for smell and touch.

barnacle   Small parasitic shellfish who attach themselves to whales, boat hulls, rocks, and other underwater objects.

basking shark   A large, sluggish, harmless filter feeder; it is the second largest shark after the whale shark.

basihyal   A shark's tongue; it is a small, thick, relatively immovable piece of cartilage found on the floor of the mouth of sharks and fishes. Most sharks don't seem to use it, except for cookie-cutter sharks who use it to rip "flesh cookies" out of their prey.

bathypelagic   Refers to living in the deep ocean near the bottom.

benthic feeders   Organisms (plants and animals) that live in or on the bottom of a body of water including angel sharks, frilled sharks, and wobbegongs.

black tip shark   Also known as the spinner shark, this common shark has black markings on the tips of the dorsal and pectoral fins and is found in shallow waters and in reefs in the western and eastern Atlantic.

blue shark   A large, sleek pelagic shark with long, pointed fins and a pointed snout who is popular with sports fishing enthusiasts.

bottom feeders   *See* benthic feeders.

Bradyodonti   A class of fish who have an upper jaw fused to the braincase and a flap of skin (the operculum) covering the gill slits. This class includes chimaeras.

bull shark   Also known as the cub shark, the Ganges shark, the Nicaragua shark, and the Zambezi shark, the bull shark is a large, fierce predator who eats fish, rays, other sharks, and just about anything else. Bull sharks can live in fresh as well as salt water and are known to be aggressive toward humans.

buoyancy   The ability to keep afloat. Sharks are buoyant because of their oil-rich, oversized livers.

buoyancy compensator   A device used by scuba divers to regulate their level of buoyancy.

bycatch   The capture of noncommercial fish as a result of the use of long lines or nets intended to trap commercial fish. Millions of sharks are victims of bycatch.

caged diving   The use of a protective cage in diving, ordinarily employed with mako, great white, tiger, and other dangerous sharks.

Carcharhiniformes   An order of sharks with five gill slits, two dorsal fins, an anal fin, no fin spines, the mouth behind the eyes, and nictitating eyelids. This group includes cat sharks, requiem sharks, and hammerhead sharks.

cartilage   Firm, flexible tissue that compose shark skeletons and is found in the ears, nose, and joints of humans.

cartilaginous fish   Known by the scientific name of Chondrichthyes, these fish have skeletons made of cartilage, not bone. They include sharks, rays, skates, and chimaeras (ratfish).

caudal fin   A fin found toward or at the tail of an animal.

cephalofoil   A structure particular to the head of scalloped hammerheads.

cetaceans   Members of an order of marine mammals that includes toothed and baleen whales, dolphins, and porpoises.

chimaera   Also known as a ratfish, the chimaera is one of 35 species of cartilaginous fish who are closely related to rays and skates. Chimaeras have compressed bodies, rodentlike teeth, smooth skin, and whiplike tails. They all live in cold water and are oviparous (they lay eggs).

Chondrichthyes   Cartilaginous fish, including the sharks, skates, and rays that have a structure of cartilage.

chum   Bait used to attract sharks, usually composed of fish and oil mixed with seawater.

cladoselache   The earliest complete fossil shark who lived about 400 million years ago. Fossils of this ancient shark have been found in the Cleveland shales with their stomach contents intact, revealing that they ate fish.

claspers   Modified male organs that sharks used to grasp hold of the female during mating.

cleaner wrasse   A small fish that feeds off the parasites of sharks and other larger fish.

cloaca   A cavity in the female shark that serves a double function: reproduction and digestion.

cneoselachkian   An early form of modern shark who existed between 65 and 2 million years ago.

cold-blooded   Refers to animals that rely upon the temperature of the surrounding environment to regulate their own temperature. Most sharks are cold-blooded, but a few, such as the mako and the great white shark, can raise their temperature above that of the water for short periods of time when they need energy.

commensalism   A form of symbiosis in which two species form an association that is harmless to one and benefits the other, such as the relationship between sharks and pilot fish.

copepods   Minuscule crustaceans (related to shrimp) who are a common food source for marine life but who in certain cases, such as with the Greenland shark, can also become parasites.

countershading   A scheme of body coloration seen in sharks and some other animals in which the top and bottom sides of the animal are colored differently for camouflage. In sharks, their tops are much darker than their bellies.

crustaceans   Mostly marine animals (invertebrates) who have an exoskeleton (outer skeleton) and jointed legs including copepods, barnacles, lobsters, crabs, shrimp, and crayfish.

ctenoid   A type of fish scale with small points on the surface that are rough to the touch.

cycloid   Smooth, rounded fish scales found in herring, salmon, bluefish, tuna, and many other fish.

dermal denticles   Also called placoid scales, these small, hard, toothlike structures have a layer of enamel, dentine, and a central pulp cavity. Sharks' teeth and skin are composed of this type of scale.

dive computer   A miniature computer used by divers that offers vital information about depth, nitrogen uptake and elimination, water temperature, when to ascend, and other data.

dorsal fin   A fin on an animal's back.

ears   Shark ears are very sensitive to low-frequency sounds. The endolymphatic pores on the top of the shark's head are the only outward indication of shark ears.

ecomorphotype   A classification of sharks based on their habitat, body structure, and behavior.

elasmobranchs   Cartilaginous fish including sharks, rays, and skates with an upper jaw that is not fused to the brain case, no swim bladder (which bony fish have), an advanced electroreceptive system to detect electrical impulses, a spiracle, skin with placoid scales, teeth that are modified placoid scales, and five to seven separate slitlike gill openings.

electroreceptors   Special organs particular to sharks that allow them to pick up electric impulses in order to locate prey and to navigate.

endolymphatic pores   Openings in a shark's head where the shark's ears are located. *See also* ears.

epipelagic zone   The uppermost zone of the ocean that is rich in plankton, a food source for filter-feeder sharks.

estuary   The place where a river meets the sea.

eyes   Shark's eyes vary in shape and size depending on the species; sharks can see very well even in dim light. *See also* tapetum lucidum.

feeding frenzy   A phenomenon in which several sharks are driven into a frenzy by the prospect of food to the point where they are oblivious of pain, even fatal wounds.

finning   A practice by commercial fishermen of cutting off the fins of a shark—in effect killing it—for fins that are used as an ingredient in shark fin soup, which is considered a delicacy in Asia.

free diving   Diving while holding one's breath, a practice followed by commercial divers in Japan and Korea.

filter feeders   Animals that consume food by taking in seawater and straining out food such as crustaceans, small fish, and plankton. The whale shark, basking shark, and megamouth shark are filter feeders who filter water through their gill slits.

fin   A part of aquatic animals that helps them swim, steer, and balance in the water. Sharks have four (and sometimes five) types of fins: pectoral, dorsal, caudal, pelvic, and anal. These fins often but do not always appear in pairs.

fossil sharks   Most fossil evidence of early sharks comes from the few hard parts of sharks (teeth and skin) that left impressions. The earliest primitive sharks had double-pointed teeth, were up to 3 feet long, ate fish, and lived about 400 million years ago. *See also* cladoselache.

ganoid   Interlocking, diamond-shaped scales that are rough to the touch and are found in some primitive fish.

gills   Respiratory organs of sharks, fish, and amphibians that help them breathe underwater. Sharks have five to seven gills depending on the species.

gill pumps   Muscles in the mouths in some species of sharks that force oxygenated water into and through the gills.

goblin shark   Rarely seen, slow-swimming, bottom-feeding shark who is about 11 feet long with very unusual features and is found at great depths in the western Pacific Ocean, the western Indian Ocean, and the western and eastern Atlantic Ocean.

great white shark   A large oceanic predator who can grow up to 23 feet long and weigh more than 7,000 pounds. Great whites have 3,000 teeth and eat pinnipeds (sea lions and seals), small toothed whales, otters, and sea turtles. These sharks have attacked humans, but it is unclear as to whether they have any craving for human flesh.

hammerhead shark   A species of sharks who have odd, wide, elongated heads. They eat fish, including rays, other sharks, squid, octopuses, and crustaceans.

heart   Sharks have a two-chambered heart with an atrium (also called the auricle) and a ventricle.

helicoprion   A primitive form of fish who lived about 250 million years ago and might be an ancestor of modern-day sharks.

heterodontoids   A shark family also known as horn or bullhead sharks whose name is derived from the Latin meaning "different teeth," which refers to the fact that their teeth are spiked in front for prying and holding and flat in back for crushing shellfish.

horn shark   A bottom-dwelling, sluggish shark who is about three to four feet long. This shark has rounded fins, a blunt snout, a dorsal fin spine, small, pointy teeth in the front of its mouth, and flat teeth in the back (for shellfish). Oviparous, this shark lays corkscrew-shaped eggs in rock crevices.

ichthyologist   A scientist who studies fish.

invertebrate   Animals without backbones including insects, crustaceans, worms, jellyfish, sponges, mollusks, bivalves (clams, scallops, and oysters), and protozoa.

jaws   In sharks, jaws are hinged and loosely connected to the skull (or brain case). They are capable of protruding when capturing or consuming prey.

juvenile   An animal weaned from its mother but not yet sexually mature.

Lamniformes   An order of sharks with an anal fin, five gill slits, two dorsal fins, no fin spines, the mouth extending behind the eyes, and no nictitating (blinking) eyelids that includes basking, goblin, megamouth, great white, sand tiger, and mako sharks.

lateral line   A network of fine, fluid-filled vessels that run along a shark's body under the skin along the length of a shark and help the shark navigate by detecting the intensity and direction of vibrations in the water.

lemon shark   A yellowish shark who is about 8 to 10 feet long and lives near the surface and at intermediate depths.

leopard shark   A bottom-dwelling shark who preys on worms, clams, crabs, shrimp, octopus, and small fish. These sharks grow up to 6 feet in length and reproduce in aplacental viviparity (eggs are hatched in the mother's body) with up to 30 pups in a litter.

liver   The large, oily livers of sharks provide buoyancy because the oil is lighter than water.

Iodonts   A group of extinct primitive fish with cartilaginous bodies who may be ancestors of modern sharks and rays.

longfin mako   A pelagic shark about 14 feet in length who is very similar to the shortfin mako, but with longer pectoral fins and a blunter snout. Less common than shortfin makos, longfin makos reproduce via aplacental viviparity, bearing their young live. Makos are found in tropical and temperate oceans.

marine mammals   Mammals who live in the sea and breathe air including whales, dolphins, seals, sea lions, and sea otters.

megalodon   An ancient shark who lived 25 to 1.6 million years ago and is now extinct. This shark may have reached a length of 40 feet or more.

mesopelagic zone   Also known as the twilight zone. A layer of water about 3,300 feet deep where most fish, invertebrates, and marine mammals feed.

nanotesla   A measure of magnetic force; sharks are believed to use magnetic fields for navigation.

neritic zone   The most productive area of the ocean close to the surface.

nictitating membrane   An eyelid that in certain species of sharks, such as the great white, protects the eye from being injured by thrashing prey while the shark is feeding.

macrophages   White blood cells that surround, ingest, and destroy bacteria and other foreign organisms in a process called phagocytosis (literally cell-eating) that produces an inflammatory response.

megamouth shark   A filter-feeding shark discovered in 1976 who grows to be over 16 feet long and feeds nocturnally on plankton, shrimp, and small fish. Only 14 examples have been found, mainly in the Pacific Ocean.

mermaid's purse A common name given to shark's eggs, which can have unusual and beautiful shapes.

mollusk Marine invertebrates with soft, unsegmented bodies including squids, octopuses, snails, clams, and oysters.

mutualism A form of symbiosis in which two dissimilar organisms enjoy a close association to the benefit of each.

nostrils In sharks and rays, nostrils are found in pairs on the underside of the snout. Water continually flows through the nostrils, giving the shark olfactory information. The nostrils are not used for breathing.

nurse shark A large, sluggish shark who is generally harmless unless provoked. Nurse sharks have strong jaws, a stout body, and a wide head. They are nocturnal hunters.

oceanic white tip shark A large, thick-bodied, slow-moving shark with very large, paddle-shaped pectoral fins and white tips on the pectoral and dorsal fins and tail. This shark can grow to about 13 feet long and is not closely related to the smaller white tip reef shark. Found in tropical and subtropical waters, oceanic white tip sharks are known to be aggressive toward humans.

omnivore An animal who eats both other animals and plants.

opportunistic feeder Animals who eat whatever food is available at the time.

oviparous A method of giving birth in which the young are hatched from eggs.

ovophagy Cannibalism in the womb of a female shark in which a stronger embryo eats a weaker one.

ovoviviparous *See* aplacental viviparity.

paleontology The study of ancient forms of life, principally by examining fossils in rock formations.

Paleozoic era A geological period 540 to 245 million years ago characterized by an explosion of new life forms. Sharks originated in this period. It culminated with the largest mass extinction in history and was followed by the Mesozoic era.

parasite An animal who lives off another animal (the host) without benefiting the host.

pectoral fin A wide, flat fin located in the chest area.

pelagic Ocean-going animals; pelagic sharks include the great white, blue, and mako sharks.

pilot fish   Small fish who have formed a symbiotic relationship with sharks in which they feed off scraps of food left over by the sharks. *See also* commensalism.

pineal gland   A gland that regulates the body's internal clock. In some species of sharks it is a thin translucent "window" in the skin and skull underneath that regulates the shark's response to light and darkness.

pinnipeds   Marine mammals such as sea lions and seals who are often the favorite prey of sharks.

placoderms   Bony-plated, jawed fishes who long ago became extinct.

placoid scales   *See* dermal denticles.

plankton   Tiny marine animals and plants that drift along with ocean currents and live near the surface. Plankton is a common food source for filter feeders such as the whale, basking, and megamouth sharks.

Pliocene   A geological period that lasted from 5 to 1.8 million years ago and saw the development of early hominids and the first modern forms of whales. The ancient shark megalodon was found in the oceans at this time.

Port Jackson shark   A harmless, sluggish shark that grows to about 5.5 feet and is found in southern Australia. This shark thrives in shallow water and is oviparous, laying eggs among the rocks.

predator   Any animal who hunts and kills other animals for food.

prey   An animal who is hunted and killed by a predator for food.

pup   A newly born or newly hatched shark, which is a small version of its parents with the same coloration and general dimensions. Shark pups are capable of fending for themselves as soon as they are born.

ram jet ventilation   A term referring to the need of a shark to continuously move forward to keep water circulating through its gills in order to breathe.

ray   A cartilaginous fish and relative of the shark with a flat body and tail.

remoras   Small fish with suckerlike disks that attach to sharks (and other fish and even boats); these fish have a symbiotic relationship with sharks in which they eat food discarded by sharks but also benefit sharks by eating parasites that feed on them.

sand tiger shark   Also known as the gray nurse shark, sand tiger sharks range from gray to brown and are about 10 to 12 feet long. They are fish-eaters who feed at night and have long, sharp teeth in a narrow snout.

scalloped hammerhead   Also known as the kidney-headed shark, the front of the head of this shark is flattened, scalloped, and wide, forming a structure called a cephalofoil. The odd shape of the head makes the shark more hydrodynamic. The head is also full of sensory receptors. Scalloped hammerheads grow to be about 10 to 13 feet long and are found in warm temperate and tropical waters.

school   A group of fish that travels together. Some sharks and rays travel in schools.

scuba   A form of diving with a mask and a tank that provides compressed air or an oxygen mixture. Scuba is an acronym for self-contained underwater breathing apparatus.

serrated   Having a jagged edge. Many sharks have serrated teeth that are well suited for cutting through meat.

SharkPOD   A commercial device that uses electricity to keep sharks away from beaches.

shortfin mako shark   Also known as the bonito shark, the shortfin mako is considered the fastest shark of all and can leap out of the water. Reaching an average length of five to eight feet, this shark has a conical snout and long gill slits, reproduces via aplacental viviparity, and can be aggressive toward humans.

silver tip shark   A large, widespread shark with silvery-white tips on the fins who measures about 10 feet long and lives on coral reefs, offshore islands, and lagoons, eating mostly fish. Silver tips reproduce viviparously.

skates   Cartilaginous fish who are a form of rays and are related to sharks. They usually have a pointed snout.

skin   *See* dermal denticles.

snout   The front part of an animal's face.

spiracle   A special gill slit located just behind the eyes that is found in some sharks, such as tiger and angel sharks; it supplies oxygen directly to the eyes and brain.

squalamine   A shark steroid that is responsible for fighting bacteria and also seems to fight viral infections.

Squatiniformes   An order of sharks with flat bodies, the mouth at the front of the head, and no anal fin. This order includes angel sharks.

stingray   Cartilaginous fish with flat bodies and a long tail with at least one spine who are closely related to sharks.

strandings   A phenomenon in which marine life beaches itself because of disease or faulty navigation. Strandings among whales and dolphins occur more frequently than they do among sharks.

streamlined   Having a contoured shape that minimizes resistance to currents of water (or air). Many sharks have a streamlined shape that allows them to swim swiftly through water.

swim bladder   A gas-filled sac in a bony fish's body that gives the fish buoyancy. Sharks lack a swim bladder. *See also* liver.

symbiosis   A situation in which two dissimilar organisms are closely associated; in some cases the relationship is beneficial to only one organism and harmless to the other (commensalism); in some cases both benefit (mutualism), and in other cases one benefits at the expense of the other (parasitism).

tagging   The practice of attaching a band, collar, or radio device to an animal to monitor the animal's migrations and behavior in the wild.

tapetum lucidum   A mirrorlike reflecting layer within a shark's eye (behind the retina) that amplifies light so that the shark can see well in dim light.

telemetry   A form of electric or electronic communication that relies on transmitters attached to an animal to monitor the animal's behavior and migrations in the wild.

teeth   Sharks may have hundreds or even thousands of teeth at one time, and these teeth are made up of modified placoid scales; teeth are continuously replaced throughout the life of the shark. Teeth are differently shaped from species to species depending on the particular feeding behavior of the shark.

tiger shark   A fierce predator who is about 10 feet long, can be found worldwide in warm seas, and can be very aggressive toward humans.

uterine milk   Nutritive fluids secreted by the shark mother's intestine that help sustain embryos.

vertebrate   An animal with a backbone. Vertebrates evolved during the Cambrian period over 500 million years ago. Vertebrates include the amphibians, reptiles, birds, and mammals. Sharks are vertebrates.

viviparous   A reproductive process in which the animals are born live and not hatched from eggs. Some species of sharks are viviparous.

whale shark   The largest shark and the largest fish, measuring up to 46 feet long and weighing up to 15 tons. This filter feeder eats plankton and small fish.

white tip shark   This gray shark with white tips on its dorsal fin and tail can grow to be about seven feet long; this shark is a sluggish, slender, and potentially dangerous bottom feeder who hunts at night in reefs and in rocks in tropical waters.

wobbegongs   Common, flattened sharks who live on the sea bed. They have an anal fin, five gill slits, two dorsal fins, no fin spines, and powerful jaws. Many wobbegongs are camouflaged so that they blend in with the seabed. They are nocturnal and feed on invertebrates and fish. The largest grow to about 13 feet.

zooplankton   Tiny animals carried by currents that along with plant plankton (or phytoplankton) provide a food source for filter-feeding sharks and other marine life.

Index

S

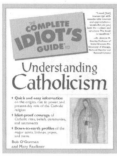

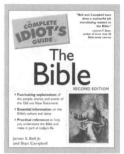

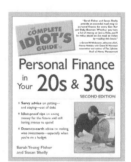

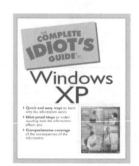